IN THE HANDS *of the* LORD

IN THE HANDS *of the* LORD

THE LIFE OF

DALLIN H. OAKS

RICHARD E. TURLEY JR.

SALT LAKE CITY, UTAH

Photo credits: all photos used by permission. *Deseret News*: pages 126, 222, 226, 314, 329. Brigham Young University: pages 129, 135, 141, 143, 145, 146, 147, 180. The University of Chicago: page 150. Busath Photography: page 163. Intellectual Reserve, Inc.: pages 184, 190, 238, 323, 349, 357, 364. Doug Martin: page 240. White House Photo Office: page 289. All other photos courtesy of the Oaks family.

Visit us at deseretbook.com

Library of Congress Cataloging-in-Publication Data

Names: Turley, Richard E., Jr., 1956– author.
Title: In the hands of the Lord : the life of Dallin H. Oaks / Richard E. Turley Jr.
Description: Salt Lake City, Utah : Deseret Book, [2021] | Includes bibliographical references and index. | Summary: "A biography of Dallin H. Oaks, First Counselor in the First Presidency of The Church of Jesus Christ of Latter-day Saints"—Provided by publisher.
Identifiers: LCCN 2020043651 | ISBN 9781629728766 (hardback)
Subjects: LCSH: Oaks, Dallin H. | Brigham Young University—Presidents—Biography. | Mormon Church—Apostles—Biography. | Law teachers—United States—Biography. | LCGFT: Biographies.
Classification: LCC BX8695.025 T87 2021 | DDC 289.3092 [B]—dc23
LC record available at https://lccn.loc.gov/2020043651

Printed in the United States of America
Lake Book Manufacturing, Inc., Melrose Park, IL

10 9 8 7 6 5 4 3 2 1

CONTENTS

PREFACE

Having known and worked with President Dallin H. Oaks most of my life, I felt honored when he asked me to write his biography. I admired him in my youth, attended Brigham Young University when he was president, saw him as a role model when I went to law school, and began working closely with him eight months after my graduation. In some ways, this biography is as much a product of my close observation as it is a distilling of sources documenting his life.

The sheer abundance of the documentary sources challenged me as a biographer. His life may be as well documented as any Latter-day Saint leader's in history. He was born to educated and literate parents who wrote about him when he was a child. He became a public figure as a radio personality in his youth and has remained in the public eye ever since. The range and depth of published and unpublished sources on his life will test anyone trying to be thorough in studying it.

When aiming at an academic audience, I have sometimes produced writings in which footnotes occupy half as much space as the text. When writing for the general audience to which this book is directed, however, I found such heavy documentation to be impractical for three reasons. First, full documentation would make the book exceed the size readers will buy or even choose to read. Second, most readers would rather have text than notes. Finally, some of the most important sources are not available to the public, making notes less valuable than they would otherwise be.

My initial drafts were heavily documented, and readers can be assured this biography rests on solid research. But to bring the manuscript within the contracted word count and keep the book from putting off readers, we chose to forgo citations to sources they could not access. Yet readers can often guess the source by keeping in mind that many quotations on President Oaks's life up to 1980 come from a personal history he completed that year. That same year, he began keeping a journal in which he continues to write to this day, and many quotations from 1980 on come from it. As one who has read the journals of many General Authorities, from Joseph Smith to the present day, I consider Dallin H. Oaks's to be among the very best. In addition, he has been a prodigious letter writer, and many passages in the text show they come from his correspondence. Finally, I was privileged to interview members of the First Presidency, Quorum of the Twelve, and other leaders for this biography, and when they are quoted without source citation, the quotations generally come from these interviews.

Two final points. Because of how seriously President Oaks takes his calling, he often appears in public to be stern—a point on which family members rib him frequently. In private, he is warm, jovial, caring, and kind, with a winning smile. Few people I have known tell humorous stories with greater skill and relish. I have worked to capture both sides of him in this book. But when it comes to matters of principle, he is the same in public and private. He practices what he preaches.

Richard E. Turley Jr.
May 25, 2020

CHAPTER 1

"FAITH AND ASSURANCE"

Birth and Childhood

"There was no hospital in Provo in 1932, and the Crane Maternity Home was having epidemic difficulties," explained Stella Harris Oaks of the circumstances when her pregnancy reached full term on August 12 that year. "So the decision was made that our first baby would be born at home—in the same room in which I had been born just twenty-six years previously."

Stella's water broke two weeks earlier, meaning this would be a "dry birth," increasing the risk of complications. Yet with characteristic cheerfulness, she faced the long, painful labor bravely. After all, she was attended by four medical professionals: her husband of three years, Dr. Lloyd E. Oaks; his older brother Weston, with whom he practiced medicine; their sister Nettie H. Oaks, a newly graduated nurse; and Dr. Lloyd L. Cullimore, a general practitioner who came to Provo originally under a new federal program to reduce maternal and infant mortality.[1]

"They surrounded me, all in white, and eager to make things as easy for me as possible," Stella recounted. In their eagerness, however, they used "a new, very effective anesthetic . . . so effective that it penetrated and numbed the newly birthing baby, too, so that he did not breathe upon delivery."

Trying to resuscitate the infant boy, the three doctors each "took a turn exercising the tiny body" of the baby, "spatting him, bending him double, and trying every technique known to be effective," Stella remembered. Still, he did not respond. Finally, "Nettie, standing tensely nearby, was suddenly and distinctly prompted to pick up a can of chloroform and spray his upper torso. The sudden freezing cold sensation caused him to gasp for that first precious breath."

Stella saw Nettie's prompting as a "moment of inspiration" that saved the child's life.

Stella had decided the boy's name eighteen days earlier as she sat on a ditch bank in a public park in nearby Springville, Utah. Thousands had gathered for the unveiling of a statue dedicated to pioneer mothers by the Boston sculptor Cyrus Dallin. Hailing originally from Springville, Dallin had gone on to fame as the creator of iconic public sculptures, including the Angel Moroni atop the Salt Lake Temple, the Brigham Young monument at South Temple and Main Street in Salt Lake City, the Paul Revere statue near the Old North Church in Boston, and *Appeal to the Great Spirit* outside the Boston Museum of Fine Arts.[2]

As Stella Oaks watched Cyrus Dallin unveil his memorial to the pioneer women of Springville, topped by a bronze bust modeled after his own mother, she decided then and there to name her first child after the artist—"providing it was a son."[3]

That gave the newborn boy his first name, Dallin. His middle name, Harris, was Stella's maiden name. She was a great-granddaughter of Emer Harris, brother of Martin Harris, one of the Three Witnesses to the Book of Mormon, whose testimony appears in every edition of that volume of scripture. Giving the boy her maiden name would help him remember his mother and the history of his family and church.

"Like my parents, who were both devoted members of The Church of Jesus Christ of Latter-day Saints," Dallin Harris Oaks wrote years later, "all of my ancestors have been members of the Restored Church since shortly after its organization in 1830. Most joined in the 1830s and 1840s, with the last entering the waters of baptism in 1855. All participated in the settlement of Utah in the pioneer period, coming to the state from 1847 through 1862." His ancestral roots were European: three-quarters English, an eighth Danish, and a sixteenth each Swedish and Irish.

Despite this sturdy ancestry, some of the Oaks family members worried about Stella and Lloyd's firstborn son because of the long labor and the oxygen deprivation that occurred when he was born. As Stella later explained, "It had been so long that evidently they were all just worried sick that he would not have his right mentality." She had not worried at all until her sister-in-law Jessie Oaks made a comment.

Suddenly filled with "great worry and concern," Stella looked longingly toward the baby's bassinet for some assurance that little Dallin was okay. His "little hand waved," she recalled, "and I will never forget it because I knew, I mean the Lord helped me know, that it was all right."[4]

Though assured about his mental faculties, Stella strained under the burden of raising the boy, who experienced frequent—sometimes constant—physical ailments. "I remember the tears running down my face as I struggled in weakness to comfort the baby in the night as he screamed with colic," she wrote. Unfortunately, Dallin's condition remained poor over the coming months. "I was nearly broken in health from the long strain of the baby's first year," Stella said. "He had suffered almost daily of earache. It was rare indeed for him to sleep more than twenty minutes, and he always awakened screaming with pain. I did most of my work with him on my hip. I even learned to peel potatoes this way and sweep with one arm."

In a vain effort to cure his chronic sickness, she even had his tonsils taken out when he was fourteen months old.

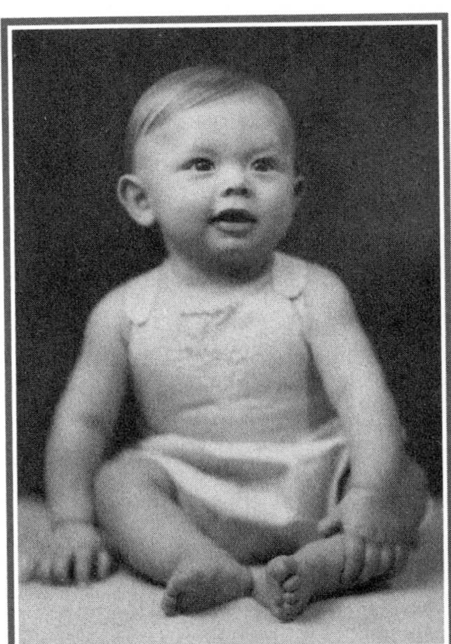

Dallin at eight or nine months old

On top of all that, nine months after Dallin came into the world, he nearly left it again. In a day before children were routinely strapped into vehicles using safety seats or even seat belts, the toddler was riding in the family car. Stella was driving and started through the intersection of First North and Second West Streets in Provo, her vision partially blinded by the brilliant sunlight glaring off the pavement.

The glare kept her from seeing another vehicle enter the intersection. With little time for their drivers to react and brake, the two automobiles collided so violently that Jessie, a passenger in Stella's car, sustained numerous injuries, including cuts on her forehead, wrist, and shoulder. Even worse, the crash catapulted little Dallin from his parents' car like a missile, tossing him headlong onto the concrete street. Miraculously, reported a newspaper writer, the toddler sustained bruises on his head but "did not suffer serious injury."[5]

Stella Harris and Lloyd Edress Oaks

Dallin's parents, Stella and Lloyd, had both grown up on farms, Stella in north central Utah and Lloyd in the eastern part of the state. Stella was the eldest of four children, and Lloyd was the seventh of sixteen. They met at Brigham Young University through Lloyd's brother Weston, whose wife, Jessie, was Stella's cousin. They courted for a necessary five or six years before getting married in June 1929, using their time meanwhile to pursue their educations and, in Stella's case, working to repay loans for that schooling.[6]

Lloyd's college study began with three years at BYU, followed by medical school in Philadelphia. Stella graduated from BYU, taught school, married Lloyd in the Salt Lake Temple, and joined him for his last year of medical school, which was followed by an internship. In the summer of 1931, they moved to Provo, where Lloyd practiced with Weston and another doctor for three years.[7]

Dallin Oaks's hardy, salt-of-the-earth ancestors served in the Church and "did what they were called to do without prominence or public recognition," he wrote. Vocationally, "all were farmers, ranchers, or craftsmen. With the exception of a few pioneer nurses and schoolteachers, there are no professional people in my ancestry," he explained, "until the generation of my parents."

In the spring of 1934, Lloyd left off practicing medicine with his brother and struck out on his own, moving to Twin Falls, Idaho, where he became an eye, ear, nose, and throat specialist, something on which he had begun to focus early in his practice.[8] "My first memories," Dallin recorded, "are of Twin Falls, Idaho, where we moved the summer I was two and where we lived until . . . I was nearly eight."

When Dallin grew old enough, he attended the nearby Washington School. "My first grade report card," he summarized, "showed satisfactory progress in most areas, special recognition in reading, and negative marks beside 'Avoids unnecessary talking' and 'Sings with clear, light tones.'" According to Stella, Dallin adored his first-grade teacher, telling her, "I wish you were smart enough to teach me in second grade too."

Dallin (right) and Merrill in hospital, 1938 or 1939

Dallin's parents were both devout Latter-day Saints, Stella participating actively in the Mutual Improvement Association and Lloyd serving on the stake high council in Twin Falls. Some folks in town had hostile feelings toward the Oakses' church, and a banker counseled Lloyd not to let his membership be known lest it hurt his medical practice. Lloyd did just the opposite, refusing to hide his devotion and church activity. He even established his office next to the old Latter-day Saint meetinghouse downtown. His practice thrived.[9]

Young Dallin visited his father's office frequently—often as a patient. His ear, nose, and respiration problems continued with him in Idaho, where he attended first and second grades. "Twice during my two years of school in Twin Falls," he remembered, "I was out for extended periods, hospitalized with pneumonia." During one of those hospital stays, he shared a room with his brother Merrill, born three and a half years after him and afflicted with similar health problems.[10] The brothers had come down with measles, coughs, and pneumonia near the same time. "They were both very, very ill," Stella recalled, "and our hearts were in our throats for several days," worrying if they would survive. To her great relief, she wrote, they "came through nicely."

Once while Dallin was in the crowded waiting room of his father's medical office, a patient asked him if he was going to grow up to be a doctor like his father and heal people.

"No," he answered. He was going to be "a high priest like my father and bless babies."

Though surprised and mildly embarrassed at Dallin's response, Lloyd was proud of and loved his son, feelings that were mutual.

"I remember also his gentleness and compassion," Dallin wrote. "Once he took me fishing at a lake. He had me take the hook on the end of the line and go far back on the bank. Then, on signal, I would release the hook, and he would cast far out into the lake."

At one point, Dallin ignored his father's caution to keep the point of the hook up, and when Lloyd jerked on the line, the hook drove deeply into the boy's finger.

"I remember," Dallin wrote, "how gently he removed the hook and, instead of berating me for my failure to follow instructions, he begged my forgiveness for putting me in a position where I got hurt."

At another time, father and son went for a walk in Twin Falls that ended up at a sporting goods store. As they looked through the store display window, they saw fishing gear, pocketknives, and other equipment attractive to boys in those days.

"Standing near us and looking longingly into the window was a shabbily dressed boy about my age," Dallin wrote. The Great Depression had hit their town hard, something everyone knew "who had seen the alley tramps walking behind the houses or the cardboard shanties along the river." Lloyd knew that the ragged boy could not afford anything he was viewing.

"My father put his hand on the boy's shoulder and motioned him inside," Dallin recounted. "I watched while he took the boy to a showcase of pocketknives and told him to pick one out." The boy did, and Lloyd paid for it. "I remember that he didn't buy me anything on that occasion," Dallin wrote. But the lesson of kindness his father taught him remained with him throughout his life.

As a good father, Lloyd disciplined his son when needed. Once Dallin disobeyed his mother. Another time, he violated a cultural norm by taking a hat to church and clamping it on his head during services. Yet another time, he "switched a neighbor girl with a willow."

"All three times, my father took me into the closet and explained why I was being punished," Dallin wrote. "'You must be obedient to your mother.' 'We don't put hats on in church.' 'Men don't hit women, and boys don't hit girls.'" Then his father "gravely removed an old leather belt from a pair of slacks in the closet, bent me over, and administered it to my backside a few times.

"It is curious," Dallin recollected, "how vividly I recall this explanation of why I was being punished—for disobedience, for irreverence, and for ungentlemanly conduct—and how I don't remember a thing about how the belt hurt. I think he must have been very stern with his counsel and very gentle with his blow."

Describing the fall of 1939, Stella wrote, "I never remembered being as happy as I was then—three sweet children, a wonderful husband, our new little chapel in which to carry on our church activities, our debts melting away and dreams in the spring of a new home." For Dallin and his family members, life had reached a high point.

Then in October of that year, Lloyd became ill and spent sixteen days in the hospital. Near the same time, Stella came down with a serious case of flu and remained at home, unwilling to let Lloyd see how sick she had grown. At first, doctors concluded that Lloyd had cancer. Soon, however, his brother Weston came to Twin Falls to take him to Salt Lake City. Stella wanted to see Lloyd again before he left. "I called the hospital," she wrote, "and requested they bring him home an hour or so before starting for Salt Lake."

After being helped home, Lloyd lay on the sofa, lovingly but soberly greeting Dallin and his siblings. "I wondered why he seemed so sad and clung to each so fondly," Stella wrote. Three days later, Lloyd phoned her from Salt Lake. He had a new diagnosis—tuberculosis—but told Stella "he was feeling fine and cheerful." By Thanksgiving Day 1939, Weston had gotten him to the Bethesda Tuberculosis Sanitorium in Denver. During the time Lloyd languished there, he and Stella wrote letters to each other, Stella often commenting on the children's progress.

On Christmas Day, Stella, Dallin, and his two siblings, including baby sister Evelyn, celebrated without Lloyd. "I dreaded Christmas so much!" Stella wrote. "But somehow the day passed pleasantly enough." They had a family prayer, and Merrill said he wanted to give it. Stella whispered the words to him, including a phrase "about it being Jesus' birthday."

After the prayer, Merrill commented, "Well, if it is Jesus' birthday, I wish I was up in heaven so I could have a piece of his birthday cake."

"Dallin winked at me and giggled," Stella wrote. But the challenges of life also made the good-natured, laughter-prone Dallin think seriously at a young age. A few days later, Stella wrote Lloyd, "It would astonish you to see Dallin spread the newspaper out and glean the news of the day. He tells me all that is happening. . . . Dallin prays so sweetly for you to get well, and he always adds, 'Bless us to get a home.' He seems to just feel the pulse of any situation."

Dallin, his mother, and other family members had high hopes the Lord would heal Lloyd and bring him home again. They relied on fasting, priesthood blessings, and an unwavering faith. "You shall be healed, Lloyd. I KNOW IT," Stella assured her husband. "You are very precious to the Lord, and He needs you at your post in Zion again. We all need you, darling, and I firmly believe that God is pleased to perform miracles for us when our lives are dedicated to His service. . . . Lloyd, my heart is simply singing for joy, for I know you are going to be healed soon to be a living testimony to those all over who know of your great illness. We have seen Our Father's power so often that we can never doubt that you can receive His blessing."

But it was not to be. Early on the morning of June 10, 1940, with Stella and sister Nettie at his side in the sanatorium, Lloyd Edress Oaks—faithful husband, father, Church member, and doctor—finally succumbed to the disease he had probably contracted while caring for a patient. Lloyd was thirty-seven years old at the time of his death, leaving Stella, age thirty-four, with three small children: Dallin, seven; Merrill, four; and Evelyn, just fifteen months old.

During the previous years in Twin Falls, Dallin recalled, "my parents gave generously to the construction of a new chapel, which was completed in time for his funeral to be the first held in it." Lloyd died on a Monday, and on Wednesday, friends in Twin Falls paid their respects at a funeral there. But Stella chose not to have the burial in

Idaho. Instead, on Friday, after a second funeral in Provo, where they first met, she had him interred there. It was their eleventh wedding anniversary.[11]

In the closing prayer at the Provo funeral, BYU professor Herald R. Clark gave thanks for Lloyd, "our friend and brother," and pleaded with the Lord for Dallin and his siblings. "We are grateful for the children," he said, "and we pray that they may have that very same quality that differentiated Lloyd Oaks from the ordinary man, that he knew how to stand high in his professional career, and yet humble himself as a child before Thee, and that he worked that peace and love and good will and righteousness might prevail on the earth."

Dallin was staying at the farm home of Stella's parents when he first got news of his father's death. It crushed him.

"Grandma Harris and I were alone when she told me that my father was dead," Dallin wrote. "I ran into the bedroom at their old farm home and knelt down and began to pray that it wasn't true. When I had been there just a few moments, Grandpa came in weeping. He knelt down beside me and put his arms around me and promised that he would be a father to me. . . .

"Although I cried many tears over the death of my father, then and later," Dallin reflected, "I never recall blaming the Lord or feeling bitter that he had been taken. I attribute this to the faith and assurance given me by my mother and grandparents, whose attitudes reinforced the sweetness of my memories and turned the potential energy of resentment into joyful anticipation of being reunited with him one day."

Decades after that expression, Dallin talked publicly about the lesson he learned from his father's death: "Faith, no matter how strong it is, cannot produce a result contrary to the will of him whose power it is. The exercise of faith in the Lord Jesus Christ is always subject to the order of heaven, to the goodness and will and wisdom and timing of the Lord."[12]

Stella now found herself with a choice. She and her children could either live with her aging parents indefinitely, or she could strike out on her own to acquire the skills to support her family by herself. She chose the latter, leaving Dallin and his siblings with her parents in Utah a few months later when she left to seek a master's degree at Columbia University in New York.

The death of their father and departure of their mother left the children without both birth parents. But they were not abandoned. "Our maternal grandparents, S. A. and Chasty Harris," Dallin remembered, "took us to their hearts and were our parents for the two turbulent years that followed."

These were not easy times for mother or children. For Stella, "the loneliness resulting from this abrupt separation from her family so soon after the loss of her husband, and the rigors of graduate study, strained her beyond the breaking point," Dallin remembered. In the spring of 1941, "she suffered a complete nervous breakdown." The affliction "required medical supervision away from her family for many months" as she fought mightily to regain her mental health.[13]

Dallin's loving grandparents did the best they could to care for Dallin and his siblings during this time but could not fully replace Lloyd and Stella.[14] "The two years following my father's death were difficult years for me," Dallin confessed. "I, too, felt the shock of separation, having lost the companionship of both Father and Mother and the security of home in one wrenching summer. I have but few memories of my third- and fourth-grade years, and none of them happy."

The two miles between his grandparents' farm and Payson, where the schools were located, meant he had to ride a bus, which was filled mostly with high school students who hazed and bullied Dallin and other grade schoolers. The high schoolers grabbed the seats on the bus, leaving the younger students to stand. Once the bus reached the high school, Dallin had to walk one more mile to the grade school. "If I was late getting back to the bus after school," Dallin noted, "it was gone, and I had to walk the two miles home."

Dallin's maternal grandparents, Chasty Magdelane Olsen and Silas Albert Harris

Like many communities during this period, Payson felt the impact of World War II. Dallin's fourth-grade teacher was "a harried older man" who "held on in those war years to teach three rows of fifth and two rows of fourth graders." His teaching methods included announcing all the children's arithmetic scores to the class, embarrassing Dallin, who struggled with the subject. "In a 20-problem exercise, I usually had 15 or 16 wrong answers," Dallin recalled. "I knew I was the dumbest boy in the room. I remember one occasion when some classmates threw rocks or snowballs at me and called me stupid."[15]

Reading became his escape—and a way to learn without the strictures of the classroom. "My pleasantest memory in this period was reading," he wrote. "From the tiny Payson Library, I obtained and read several books each week," becoming "a rapid and prodigious reader who knew how to use a library." Those skills would serve him throughout his life.

"In August 1942, Mother being much improved, our little family was ready to function unassisted," Dallin wrote, "and we moved to Vernal, Utah, where Mother obtained a teaching position" at the high school. "There I was blessed with a stable home and family environment with the guidance of my marvelous mother. I was also blessed with a great fifth-grade teacher, Miss Pearl Schaefer, who was mature and loving. Through a wise combination of confidence and challenge, she put me back on the path of learning and gave me many happy memories."[16]

CHAPTER 2

"MY JOY KNEW NO BOUNDS"

Youth through High School

The years 1942 to 1945, when the adult world viewed the sorrow and savagery of World War II," Dallin wrote, "were relatively uneventful for a ten- to thirteen-year-old boy in the isolated towns of Vernal and Payson, each with about two thousand inhabitants." His family spent the school year in Vernal, and when summer came, they joined his maternal grandparents on their Payson farm. But there was one major exception to the ordinariness of that existence. During the summer of 1943, when Dallin was nearly eleven and his family was living in Payson, he witnessed a miracle.

"Even in my youth," he recorded in a personal history, "I knew this was a sacred experience, and I have rarely shared it with anyone outside my immediate family." Yet it affected him deeply. "I know," he testified, that "it has been a significant influence on my faith in the power of the priesthood."

At first, the circumstances *seemed* ordinary enough. "On a hot summer afternoon," Dallin remembered, "I was working with my grandfather, repairing a mowing machine in the barnyard about 150 feet from the house." Dallin glanced up for a moment and saw a very young child, his cousin Sterling Grant Harris, "toddling down the road toward the barn." The road went over an irrigation ditch—a common feature of many Utah farms. "Just as I glanced up," Dallin recalled, Sterling "fell on the road, but I thought nothing more of it since we were busy working and toddlers were always falling down."

Twenty or thirty minutes later, Dallin and his grandfather heard Aunt Ann Harris, Sterling's mother, calling for him. "She came to where we were working to ask if we had seen him," Dallin wrote. "I told her what I had seen, and she went back along the road. Soon the tempo of the search heightened, and my grandfather and I joined the searchers. We noted then for the first time that the irrigation ditch was full of water, and that one of the large planks in the bridge across the ditch was missing."

Knowing time was critical, Dallin and his grandfather split up to double the territory they could cover. "Grandpa sent me running down the ditch in the front of the house about a quarter of a mile to the end of our property with instructions to come back up the other ditch to meet him," Dallin explained. "Running as fast as my legs would carry me, I followed the large concrete ditch to the end of our property without finding anything, cut across the bottom of the orchard, and started back up the smaller dirt-bottom ditch to meet Grandpa."

Just as Dallin and his grandfather met, Grandpa cried out, reached into the ditch, and pulled out Sterling's body. "He was floating facedown," Dallin recalled, "and as Grandpa lifted him out of the ditch, I could see that his face was bloated. He had been floating facedown for 20 or 30 minutes. . . . He was not breathing. There was no sign of a heartbeat. He was dead."

What happened next became etched in Dallin's memory.

"My grandfather held the lifeless child by the heels against his chest," Dallin said. "As the water drained from his mouth, I pressed his little sides as you do for artificial respiration. As I did so my grandfather, sobbing with anguish but with great dignity, gave the lifeless body a blessing of the priesthood." Later, Dallin could not remember the exact words of the blessing but never forgot "the impression that he was blessing or commanding him to live until help could be obtained."

Urged by his grandfather, Dallin ran to the farmhouse, shouting for someone to call a doctor. The farm being two miles from Payson, it took ten or fifteen more minutes before medical help came.

"I remember standing outside the small farm home, filled with wonder at the joyful news that little Sterling had begun to breathe and had recovered his heartbeat," Dallin recorded. "He suffered no after-effects, filling a mission to Australia, marrying a lovely girl, and living an exemplary life as a Latter-day Saint husband and father.

"I am witness," Dallin concluded, "to the miracle of his childhood death and restoration."

Dallin (far right) and family members on Payson farm, about 1945

This was an extraordinary experience, one that gave momentum to Dallin's spiritual growth. Yet, as with many young people growing up in the Church, much of that growth came in fits and starts as he struggled through the challenges of youth and adolescence. Some challenges occurred when, as a fatherless boy, he was separated at times from his mother, who had recovered her mental health enough to finish her degree at Columbia University. She left home during the spring and summer months of 1944, 1945, and 1946 for that purpose, leaving him with relatives.

Not long after his mother left in 1944, Dallin wrote to tell her that dogs had killed a rabbit he was raising. He was learning to be independent and make his own decisions, announcing to her, "I am going out of the rabbit business. Next winter I am going to get a pig and take care of our slop."

Though he had many friends in his early teen years, he acknowledged, "I was not very popular with my classmates, who probably thought me too authoritarian and too studious (because I read a lot and talked a lot in class). Some called me 'Professor Oaks.'"

Reading remained a strength. In one diary entry made during the ninth grade, he recorded that he visited the library, checked out two books, came home, got ready for bed, "and finished a 300-page book in about 2½ hours."

He played the oboe in the school band during the eighth grade. Like many new musicians, he sometimes struggled, but his persistence paid off. By summer that year, he was playing in the Payson Summer Band, receiving fifty cents for each weekly concert and marching in holiday parades in surrounding communities. His mother arranged music lessons for him at BYU, which he reached by bus. He flourished under the teacher's tutelage.

Dallin was active in the Church but still learning what it meant to keep the Sabbath day holy. "Although my Sunday church attendance was very faithful," he wrote, "I apparently had no scruples about hunting on Sunday in this period." Looking back, he concluded, "I suppose that guns and hunting provided the firm masculine identification with father, grandfathers, and uncles that was needed by a fatherless boy."

During the summer of 1946—the summer he turned fourteen—he worked with his grandfather on the Payson farm. "This was a delightful time," he reflected, "and my diary is filled with accounts of interesting things I did, sometimes alone and sometimes with him. I milked the cows, 'moed' and hauled wheat and hay, hauled manure and trash, hoed and cultivated the garden, built fences, tended the animals (calling a veterinarian twice when I was in charge in my grandfather's absence), irrigated, built calf pens and sheds, drove cattle to a nearby community on horseback, worked on ditches, cut thistles, hauled limbs in the orchard, worked on roofing some sheds, and sanded and painted the Ford."

The variety of activities reflected partly the broad duties of farm life and partly Dallin's growing resourcefulness and independence. "Once when Grandpa was away, we had a flat tire," he recalled, "and I changed the tire myself. . . . I caught as many as twelve dozen night crawlers on the lawn at night, and sold them to fishermen the next day. . . . On a couple of occasions when the work was done, Merrill and I slipped down to the neighbors . . . to play 'twenty-one' with the face cards Grandma would not allow in our house."

Like most teenagers, Dallin felt the tension between the teachings of family and church on the one hand and the temptations of youth on the other. "This was," he wrote, "a period when I had not yet worked out a controlling relationship between the things I was taught on Sunday and the things I did on that day or during the week. . . .

"Like most in the Church at this time," he also remembered, "our ward had poor attendance (by present standards), and was subject to embarrassing events like the opening weekend of deer hunt, when we had only six or eight old men and fatherless boys at priesthood meeting." But at church Dallin also met many good men, including bishops and Scout leaders, who served as role models for him.

Dallin as Uintah High School sophomore, age fifteen

In the late spring of 1944, while Dallin's mother was at Columbia, the bishopric in his Vernal Ward approached him about receiving the Aaronic priesthood. "You are not twelve," Dallin recorded their words in a letter to his mother, "but you have graduated from Primary and you're one of the finest boys in the ward, so if you'll be at fast meeting, we'll ordain you."

"So it was," Dallin recorded later, "that I was ordained a deacon three months before my twelfth birthday."

Priesthood service provided structure and leadership opportunities that helped him grow spiritually. He attended his priesthood, Sunday School, and sacrament meetings regularly at a time when those meetings took up much of the day. In January 1946, he even wrote in his journal, "Went to church today, and frankly I like church." The next month, he was called as president of his deacons quorum and chose two friends to serve as his counselors.

His father, Lloyd, had been a prominent Boy Scout leader, and Scouting appealed deeply to Dallin, who was fortunate to have a good troop in Vernal. As part of the pioneer centennial celebration in July

1947, a great Scout encampment was held at Fort Douglas on the east bench of the Salt Lake Valley. Dallin worked hard and earned his Eagle Scout award just before attending the encampment. He was a month shy of fifteen years old at the time.

During his ninth and tenth grades at Uintah High School in Vernal, Dallin took seminary. He grew fond of his teachers, men "whose memories are dear," he wrote, "because I felt the combination of their trust and love for me and the gospel."

With school, sports, Church service, seminary, Scouting, music, and summers on the farm, life seemed to be coming together for the young man who had learned the law of the harvest: that seeds sown and nurtured through diligence eventually lead to bountiful rewards. During his school's closing assembly for the year, he wrote with obvious satisfaction, "I was awarded the official 'U' student body award for football, music, debate, and contest play." Spiritually, mentally, physically, and emotionally, he was developing well and seemed destined for success.

One other activity brought him unusual satisfaction: he had managed to combine a money-earning job with a mentally stimulating hobby.

When he was thirteen, he went looking for after-school employment to provide himself with spending money. "I was fascinated by what went on in a radio repair shop near our home in Vernal," he wrote, "and sought a job there with great earnestness." His eagerness exceeded his skills, but that enthusiasm impressed the owner. "I couldn't do anything but sweep the floor," Dallin explained, "but the proprietor . . . consented to pay me ten cents an hour for doing this a few afternoons a week."

Radio was the dominant broadcast technology of the day, a technology with home, government, and military uses that intrigued youth at the time. Dallin had a chance to observe firsthand how the technology worked, and he realized his interest could lead to long-term employment in an exciting industry.

A keen observer, he watched and listened to what went on in the radio shop and decided to supplement his knowledge through his love of reading. "I was fired with the idea that I could study books, learn about electronics, and pass the F.C.C. examination and receive the coveted First Class Radiotelephone Operators License," he wrote. Licensed radio engineers were in short supply, making employment in the field a virtual certainty. "I dreamed of becoming a radioman on a merchant vessel or at some vital communications link above the Arctic Circle," he recalled. "The prospect was irresistible."

Reading had always been his strength, and he began devouring everything he could find on the topic. He bought *Elements of Radio,* a basic text on the subject, and checked out books on radio from the Vernal Public Library. He "read and reread technical material that should have been incomprehensible to a fourteen-year-old boy," he wrote. "I also began to buy radio parts to assemble in my basement workshop, first a crystal set and then more complicated apparatus from army communications gear then cheap and abundant on the surplus market.

"During the winter of 1948," he recounted, "I traveled to Salt Lake City for the four-part F.C.C. examination. I passed three parts, which qualified me for the second-class license. About three months later, I rode to Denver, Colorado, on the bus," accompanied by a friend. There he passed the fourth part of the exam, qualifying him for the first-class license. "My license was dated May 21, 1948, three months before my sixteenth birthday," he wrote. "I was probably one of the youngest license holders in the nation."

Employment quickly followed his certification. "Within weeks," he related, "I had a job at Vernal's newly established 250-watt radio station, KJAM, 1340 on the dial, whose small studios were in the basement of the Vernal Hotel. Although my voice was squeaky, I was promised an opportunity to announce as I gained experience. My joy knew no bounds."

And then something happened to rock his 1948 universe.

By early July, Dallin's mother, Stella, had completed her education enough to qualify for an administrative position in the Provo, Utah, school system. Financially, it was a decided step upward. But it didn't come without cost: it would disrupt her children's increasingly stable lives.

"With heavy heart," Dallin wrote, she "tested her children's reaction to the move.

"About to enter my junior year in high school and just starting a coveted job in a radio station, I had the most to lose by the move," he remembered. He wasn't sure he could compete in school, radio, or athletics in the new, larger town, but he saw the move was inevitable.

Rather than pout in self-pity at their new destination, Dallin did what life had taught him to do when facing challenges: he went to work. He rode ahead of his family to Provo with the moving truck, and after helping unload it, he went searching for employment at a nearby radio station. "When Mother, Merrill, and Evelyn arrived by car a day later," he wrote, "I had a job at KCSU and was optimistic about my future in this new home."

During the years following Lloyd Oaks's death, Dallin still felt his father's influence blessing his life. When Dallin applied to KCSU Radio for a job, he wrote, "My hiring was facilitated by the fact that . . . one of the owners had been a Scout in a troop over which my father was Scoutmaster during his days at BYU. This job, which began at about sixty cents per hour, was to last me through two years of high school and four years of college."

The six years he worked at the station had a big impact on his life. Within six months of his hire, he began working as an announcer. A year after that, by seniority, he became the station's "chief engineer," the person "responsible for all station repairs and renovations and relied on to get the transmitter back on the air when there was technical trouble." That he did all this without any formal schooling on the subject was remarkable.

"I studied the theory in books and learned by doing," he recalled. "I never had any formal class in radio engineering. The experience of announcing forced me to learn to project my voice and to articulate clearly. Introducing recordings, broadcasting sports events, and interviewing persons helped me develop the ability to think and speak clearly under pressure. All these skills were to prove valuable in the future."

Moving to Provo in the summer before his junior year, he had to decide whether to attend Provo High, the large public school in the area, or the private high school attached to Brigham Young University and fondly known as B. Y. High.

"I decided to go to B. Y. High School," he wrote, "because I would feel more at home and more able to compete in a smaller school." The decision quickly proved itself right for him. "I was immediately at home in B. Y. High," he recalled, "starting at right tackle on the football team, playing oboe in the school band, and finding many fine friends," as well as "real challenge and satisfaction in my studies. I was almost immediately happier than I had been in Vernal. The move was a blessing to me."

Trying to balance school with significant professional employment proved difficult but possible with the pattern of hard work that was becoming his lifestyle, and it prepared him for challenging opportunities in future years. The studios of KCSU Radio were south of Provo. Dallin rode a motorbike over the miles between home or school and the station. By January 1949, the job consumed many of his weekend hours.

"I went to work at 3:00 p.m. on a Saturday," he wrote, "worked until I closed the station at midnight, slept on a cot in the small building that housed the transmitter and studios, and worked another eight-hour shift beginning at 7:00 a.m. Sunday."

By the spring of 1949, he was working at times as an announcer, a role that earned more than the hourly seventy cents he got as an engineer. "All this past week," he wrote in his journal on March 27, "I have been a regular announcer with regular shift, at a buck an hour, but I sure worked hard—fifty hours in one week and school to boot!"

His remarkable recall helped him get through school. "I'll do all

Dallin on basketball team, B. Y. High

right," he wrote of a difficult test, "but I never take notes. The Lord just gave me a good memory, I guess." From time to time, school and work conflicted. "Several times," he remembered, "I was called out of class at B. Y. High" to get the radio station's transmitter "back on the air when there was technical trouble."

During his junior year, school sports—particularly basketball—occupied much of his time. Despite his hard work on the court, he felt he was "the worst player on the team." The coaches eventually moved him to the junior varsity squad, where he found satisfaction in competition. He was the high scorer in a victory over a rival school on their own court and called it "the greatest thrill of my lifetime here in Provo."

Despite his rigorous schedule, he managed to find time for other matters of interest. He won a local essay contest that earned him a sightseeing trip flight to Los Angeles in a small plane. He ran for student-body president but lost. At the beginning of his senior year, however, he was elected class president.

His senior year, 1949–50, proved even busier than his junior. Along with increased responsibility at the radio station, sports, music,

Dallin, year of high school graduation, 1950

and drama occupied much of his time. "I played almost every minute of every football game, on offense and defense," he wrote. "I played my oboe in the band. I had the lead role . . . in a children's theatre Chinese production, 'The Land of the Dragon.'" He found success on the track team in both discus and shot put. And, seeing he would not make the basketball team, he opted for broadcasting games in his radio role. "I called the play-by-play for the state tournament," he remembered, and other stations picked up the feed, paying Dallin five dollars a game. Finally, in the days just before graduation, when "warm weather and boredom prevailed over common sense," he confessed, "I was instrumental in planning and executing some sensational pranks."

As his high school years ended, Dallin spoke at graduation and played his oboe in an instrumental trio at the exercises. As he and his class looked forward to summer and college in the fall, none of them anticipated that shattering events in Korea just a few weeks later would plunge their nation into armed conflict. For Dallin, who had joined the National Guard during his last year of high school, it looked as if he might soon be going off to war.

CHAPTER 3

"LIFE WAS COMING INTO FOCUS"

College, Marriage, Children, Military

"The dozens of war stories I had read during and after World War II gave me a fascination with the military," Dallin wrote about the period of his youth. "During my late teens I often considered the possibility of attending West Point. As part of this interest, I visited the National Guard Armory in Provo, liked what I saw, and after discussing this with Mother, enlisted as a private on November 3, 1949." He was just seventeen years of age and a senior in high school.

Though long deceased, his father, Lloyd E. Oaks, also influenced the decision. "Both Mother and I were sentimentally influenced by the fact that this unit of the Utah National Guard, the Headquarters Battery of the 145th Field Artillery Group, was a successor unit to the old 145th Field Artillery to which my father had belonged in his college days," Dallin explained.

Both father and son joined the military thinking to capitalize on skills they had already acquired. Growing up on a farm, Lloyd was an expert horseman in a day when horses pulled field artillery and ammunition caissons. Dallin had long considered radio a ticket to his future, and it influenced his first military assignment. "I was assigned to the communications section as a radio repairman," he recorded. "Our unit had to drill one night each week" and had "a two-week summer camp at Camp Williams, Utah, northwest of Lehi."

Being in the military suited Dallin well. "My enthusiasm was contagious," he wrote, "and over the next two or three years I persuaded ten or fifteen high school and college friends and family, including brother Merrill and cousins Bob Oaks and Kay Wilson, to 'join the Guard.'" Dallin's influence turned out to be long-lasting. After eighteen months in the National Guard, cousin Bob—Robert C. Oaks—went on to graduate with the first class of the U.S. Air Force Academy and later became a four-star general, commander in chief of the U.S. Air Forces in Europe, as well as commander of the Allied Air Forces Central Europe.[1]

Soon the 145th Field Artillery Group to which Dallin belonged was put on alert. Before summer ended, its two battalions were activated and headed to Texas for training. Both ended up serving in Korea. Meanwhile, Dallin's group headquarters battery trained feverishly nights and weekends while awaiting orders.

As a graduate of Brigham Young High School, Dallin had planned to go on to Brigham Young University. "When it came time to register for school in the fall," he wrote, "I fully expected to be on my way to Korea within a few months and wondered if I should even enroll for this, my first quarter at BYU. After prayerful consideration, I decided to register and start school while I waited to be called. In that atmosphere of uncertainty, I began my college work. That same uncertainty and that same decision was to be repeated at the beginning of each of the twelve quarters over the next four years of college."

Wartime considerations made life for the ordinarily busy Dallin even more hectic. "As the Korean War raged," he chronicled, "I continued my part-time military service, work at KCSU, and full-time school, always under tension and uncertainty about when or whether our unit would be called and frequently wondering if I should end the

Dallin (far left) in Fourth of July parade, Provo, about 1953

uncertainty by enlisting as some of my friends had done." As time went on, however, his desire to enlist waned as he moved up in rank and realized he would have to start over if he enlisted.

"When the Korean War began," he explained, "I was a private. I was promoted to corporal on November 1, 1950, the first anniversary of my enlistment." Between then and February 2, 1953, he moved from corporal to sergeant, sergeant first class, and finally master sergeant. "Along the way," he noted, "my assignments changed from radio repairman to Communications Section Chief, to Gun Section Chief firing a 155 m.m. howitzer, . . . and finally, in April 1952, to sergeant major. This was the top noncommissioned officer job in the Field Artillery Group and opened the way for me to be promoted to the top noncommissioned rank of master sergeant."

Dallin had learned radio through self-study, and he decided to acquire part of his army education the same way. He took a correspondence course from the Fort Riley, Kansas, Army General School. "This course included such topics as combat formation (squad and platoon), individual clothing and equipment, individual weapons, administration, signal communication, camouflage and concealment, military sanitation, map reading, physical training, organization of the armed forces, and interior guard duty," he recalled. He received superior ratings—the highest grade—on nearly all the lessons. His overall rating qualified him to be commissioned as a second lieutenant in the National Guard, "but," he explained, "I was ineligible for this commission since 21 was the minimum age and I was only 18 years and 2 months old."

After being commended by the adjutant general of the Utah National Guard for his "earnest enthusiasm" in completing the course quickly "with an exceptional high rating," Dallin applied to take a more difficult course from the Field Artillery School. "This course, the basic one for field artillery officers," he wrote, "contained such subjects as basic artillery gunnery, artillery and motor mechanics, conduct of observed fire, firing battery, and map and aerial photograph reading. I completed this course less than a year later, on October 9, 1951, with an overall rating of excellent." He was just nineteen at the time.

While pursuing his military education, Dallin continued to attend Brigham Young University. Like many students, he began with ideas about what he wanted to do in life, ideas that morphed as he worked his way through school. "I began college with the weak assumption that I would study medicine like my father," he wrote, "but it was soon apparent that this was not for me. The experience of cutting up a frog and dissecting the eye of a beef in an introductory zoology class persuaded me that I had no interest in medicine. In fact, I was not strongly drawn to any field."

Part of the problem was that he was being pulled in several directions at once. "I was seriously distracted by my vulnerability to immediate mobilization in these beginning months of the Korean War," he reflected, "and fully occupied with about thirty hours per week at the radio station." His radio career had blossomed, and he was now chief engineer and senior announcer—roles that allowed him to choose his work hours and made it possible to schedule his day around college classes. He also enjoyed the increased income, which permitted him to retire his motorbike and buy a 1938 Chevrolet coupe.

After deciding he disliked medicine as a career, he thought briefly about other technical fields. But the sciences required expertise in mathematics, an area in which he struggled. He took algebra fall semester as a freshman and got a C+ grade. He then took trigonometry during winter semester and managed just a C-. After that, he dropped the solid geometry course he planned to take during spring term. "I was obviously weak in math," he quipped, "but I knew a trend when I saw one."

Despite working as a radio engineer, he felt that the math "debacle," as he called it, "ruled out radio engineering or other sciences as career choices." Yet he had begun to rule them out anyway. "I thought

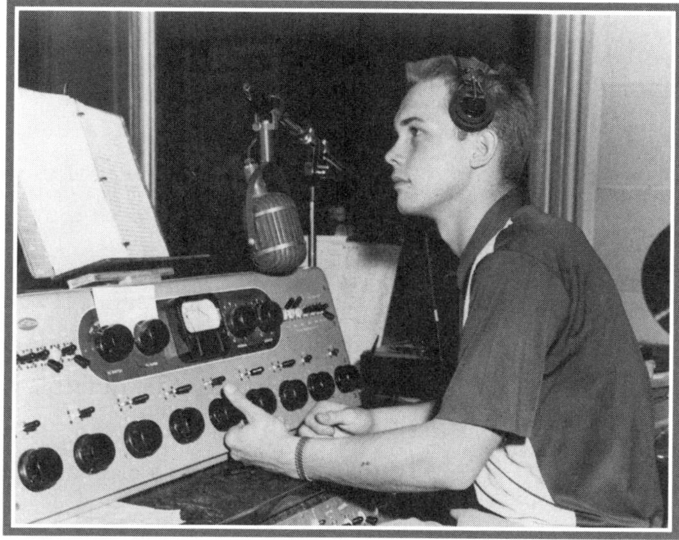

Dallin working in radio studio

Twins June (right) and Jean Dixon

the sciences were too much in the back room," he decided. "I said I wanted to work with people."

There was one particular person in whom Dallin's interest had quickly been growing.

On January 12, 1951, during the middle of his freshman year of college, Dallin went to Payson to broadcast a basketball game between Payson and Spanish Fork High Schools. After the game, Dallin visited with Blanchard Dixon about his son, a friend of Dallin's who had gone to Stanford University on a scholarship. As they chatted, two high school seniors—twins June and Jean Dixon—came up and, as Dallin wrote six years later, "took special pains to say an extended hello to 'Uncle Blanchard,' allowing me to get a good look at two very attractive girls."

The next week, Dallin saw the twins at another basketball game, and on the strength of their prior meeting—brief as it was—he walked up to them and asked, "Would you girls like to stay on to the dance?" Dallin's friend Bruce Preece from Vernal had come to the game with him, and Dallin hoped both young women would respond positively.

"Yes," replied one.

The other, slightly embarrassed, said she had a date.

"On such relatively insignificant details," Dallin wrote, "men's destinies are shaped."

"I took the twin without the date," he explained—after she found a girlfriend to go with Bruce. "I wasn't sure whether I had June or Jean," Dallin admitted, "until the girlfriend said, 'Good night, June,' after the evening's dancing was completed and they were delivered home safely to Spanish Fork.

"Another tiny detail," he acknowledged. "If she had only said 'good night,' I would never have known which twin had been my date, and the uncertainty and embarrassment would have certainly kept me from ever asking one of the Dixon girls out again."

Soon Dallin and June were dating regularly, he a freshman at BYU, and she a senior at Spanish Fork High School. By mid-May, as June prepared to graduate and go on to college, they had stopped dating others.

After high school graduation, June and her sister Jean headed for Zion National Park in southern Utah to work as summer waitresses. Dallin, after finishing his two-week National Guard summer camp, headed the opposite direction with his family, visiting national parks and other sites in Idaho, Wyoming, Montana, and Alberta. "We got home one evening," Dallin wrote, "and I was on my way the following morning for Zions Park" in a green Dodge coupe he had purchased.

After that and other trips Dallin made to see June, he grew tired of the travel and could foresee what it would be like if June went to the University of Utah, as she had planned, while he continued his schooling at BYU. "On finding that I had enthusiastic home support from June's mother," Dallin wrote, "I began to undermine the twins' determination to go to the University of Utah. June was easy to win over, but her loyalty to Jean and Jean's determination for the 'U' was overcome only after they had actually moved to Salt Lake. . . . I won in an eleventh hour 'split decision,' and as I started my sophomore year, June and Jean became freshmen at the 'Y.'"

Dallin turned nineteen on August 12, 1951, just before the school year started. A year earlier, after he turned eighteen, his uncle L. Weston Oaks had ordained him an elder in the Melchizedek Priesthood. As a teenager, Dallin had always been active in the Church, though his radio job sometimes caused him to miss meetings. "During this period, I didn't doubt that the Church was true, and I always paid a full tithing and kept the Word of Wisdom strictly," he wrote, "but I didn't think much about the Church, true or not. The C I received in theology during my freshman year at BYU"—the only C he got except in math—"is perhaps a measure of my indifference during this time," he acknowledged.

"The full-time mission experience is the catalyst that produces a serious religious commitment for many young men," he wrote, "but the Korean War . . . kept me from that experience. I was not quite eighteen when the war started, and with my National Guard unit alerted for possible active service, and with a strict quota system in force (one missionary per ward per year, I think it was) before I turned nineteen, a full-time mission was not a realistic prospect, and I was never called."

"Would I have gone on a mission had it not been for the war?" he later asked himself. "I believe I would." His brother and sister both served missions. "But it is also true," he wrote, "that I was not fervently seeking or planning for a mission. I was preoccupied with other things. The life-giving water had not yet come up from the roots to nourish the branches to bear spiritual fruit. For me, spiritual maturity, fervent testimony, and the desire to serve a mission came later."

In the meantime, his chief preoccupation was June. Before meeting her, he had dated more than a hundred young women—nearly all only once or twice—giving him an opportunity to befriend and evaluate many potential marriage partners. By the summer of 1951, he later reflected, "I was acquainted with enough alternatives to be sure of my choice."

That summer, while June was working at Zion National Park, Dallin labored fifty hours a week and began buying a diamond ring for her. When they started school together at BYU in the fall, he had not finished paying for the ring and so gave her his social club pin instead as a sign of his commitment. "By January 9, 1952," he wrote, "I had completing paying for the ring. On that Wednesday night, I gave June the ring, and we became engaged."

They planned for a June wedding. They both went through the Salt Lake Temple to be endowed on June 4, and Dallin left for his annual two-week National Guard service at Camp Williams soon afterward. On June 24—the day after he returned from camp—they married in the temple. Dallin was still nineteen, and June had reached the same age three months before.

Dallin and June wedding picture

"Meeting June was apparently what I needed to call forth my best efforts in school," Dallin recognized. "In the quarter before we were married, I made the honor roll with a straight-A average, and during my remaining five quarters at BYU I never received anything but an 'A.'"

During the term in which he received his first straight-A report card, he also took an accounting class and liked it. "When I liked accounting," he wrote, "I quickly selected it as my major and never regretted that decision." With that choice and his decision to marry June, his path forward became clearer. "My life was coming into focus," he said, "and I could begin to see where to concentrate my efforts in school."

June's grades also improved following their meeting, and she continued to attend school at BYU after becoming pregnant with their first child. She finished the fall 1952 term of school six months pregnant and with a respectable grade-point average. "That accomplishment," Dallin wrote, "together with keeping house, I considered nothing short of sensational."

Their baby was due on March 24, 1953—June's twentieth birthday and just nine months and three days after their wedding. "We hoped it wouldn't be born early!" Dallin wrote.

As the baby's due date approached, Dallin took his winter term finals while broadcasting a state basketball tournament for small schools from BYU's fieldhouse. The projected birthdate came and went, but the baby did not come with it. Then, on March 28, June and Dallin received word from their doctor that the baby should be taken by Cesarean section. Being young and completely inexperienced in such things, they felt stunned at this unexpected and unfamiliar advice. "Of course, we were terribly shocked," Dallin wrote, "and certain that neither June nor the baby had a chance."

They consulted with Dallin's Uncle Weston, who was a doctor, and others, which took some of the edge off their worry, though June's sister Jean "was almost inconsolable."

Once again, the influence of Dallin's father was present in an important hour, this time in the form of one of his father's medical school associates, Dr. Frederick Hicken, who traveled from Salt Lake to perform the surgery and refused payment for doing so.

In the hospital's guest book, Dallin recorded his feelings in a ditty that also captured the moment of birth:

A harassed young husband am I
A father I'll be by and by,
This baby is late; what a miserable fate,
If he doesn't come soon, I shall die.
I wish I knew what it would be
A she like her or a him like me . . .
The nurse just said "she"
I'm a father. Whoopee!
And that baby was something to see.[2]

At 12:55 p.m. that Monday—just twenty-four minutes after June was wheeled toward the operating room—baby Sharmon Oaks made her entrance into the world and more fully into the lives of her parents, June and Dallin. Consistent with tradition at the time, Dallin ran out of the hospital in a rainstorm to buy gifts to present to his National Guard buddies when he announced his daughter's birth at the drill he was to attend that evening.

June and Sharmon remained in the hospital until Saturday, when Dallin took them to Spanish Fork to stay briefly and then eventually home to the basement apartment that had been his and June's residence since the previous fall. Now the family looked for larger quarters, and on May 1, 1953, they moved into a more pleasant ground-floor apartment. Two days later, Dallin blessed the baby and formally named her in a ceremony at church. June's father and the local bishopric stood in the circle for the ordinance, which was the first baby blessing in the new Provo Eighth Ward chapel.[3]

Dallin was still just twenty, but with his twenty-first birthday approaching, he looked forward finally to receiving his military commission. As soon as he reached age twenty-one, he applied, passed the officer board, and, on September 4, 1953, received his commission as a second lieutenant in the Utah National Guard. "My first assignment," he recorded, "was assistant intelligence officer in the 145th Field Artillery Group, which was, of course, a less significant responsibility than the sergeant major position I had relinquished on being commissioned."

During the summer, Dallin and June both worked to support their growing family. "We tried saving our money again," Dallin wrote, "but this time it was more difficult, with the added expense of feeding Sharmon to [add to] our informal budget. The fall and winter came and went in what was by now a conventional situation. June was pregnant, and I was busy in school and work."

Although Dallin was, by this time in his life, accustomed to a hectic schedule, being a husband and father meant that something now had to give, and he figured out what it was. "During the summer of 1953," he wrote, "I became very fed up with announcing. I left KCSU, except for occasional tasks, and took a job at $1.00 an hour as a bookkeeper for Yellow Cab and Transfer, the Aero Mayflower moving agent and Yellow Cab licensee for Provo. This work, while not so lucrative (I made $1.20 at KCSU), was much more enjoyable, and gave me a chance to see the practical end of accounting."

Near midday on March 6, 1954, June gave birth again by Cesarean section to a baby girl, whom her parents named Cheri Lyn. The doctor who performed the operation "found that June's uterus had not healed properly following the last operation," Dallin wrote. "Only a thin membrane had healed over the incision," and "if June had started into labor, this membrane would have broken, taking her life and the baby's. However, both June and Cheri Lyn came out of the operation in fine style, and we counted our blessings."

On March 28, Dallin blessed their new daughter in a fast-meeting circle that again included June's father. Dallin's mother hosted them to a fine dinner afterward, and at 3:00 that afternoon, Dallin left for what he described as "my first taste of active army life."

By then, he had completed his accounting degree at BYU and registered to enter the Field Artillery School at Fort Sill, Oklahoma, to attend a seventeen-week basic Field Artillery Officer's School. June and the children went to stay with her parents in Spanish Fork, and Dallin bunked in the bachelor officers' quarters on base. His diverse class of seventy-eight officers ranged from National Guard officers and regular marines fresh from Korea to students just graduating from ROTC programs.

"I enjoyed the studies and activities and the companionship of a handful of Marine and National Guard officers with whom I associated closely," he wrote, "but I was very lonesome for June and our two babies, Sharmon and Cheri." Dallin and his associates attended classes from 7:00 a.m. to 4:30 p.m. on weekdays and spent two or three hours studying at night. "That left quite a bit of extra time for me," Dallin said, being accustomed to using every spare minute. "To pass this time in what I considered to be a relatively harmless fashion (compared with the alternatives), I played poker with a group of my closest friends.

"The game was primarily social," he wrote, and he essentially broke even during his time in camp. But something important had begun to awaken within him. "I enjoyed the game and the sociability," he observed, "but recognized that this gambling was not appropriate. I resolved on leaving Fort Sill that I would never play again for money, and I never have."

He noted significantly, "At Fort Sill, I attended the branch faithfully and received great spiritual food from the lesson material and the associations." He taught a Gospel Doctrine class to some one hundred

Church members and read James E. Talmage's *Jesus the Christ*, the first Church book he had read for reasons other than a school assignment. His calling as Gospel Doctrine teacher helped him grow spiritually, and, he wrote, "through viewing the contrast between LDS and non-LDS associates, [I] had a chance to evaluate the fruits of gospel living."

He also continued to grow intellectually. His university class graduated in June 1954 while he was at Fort Sill, and he learned by mail that he finished in the top three percent of the class and had been admitted to the Phi Kappa Phi National Honorary Scholastic Fraternity. When he finished his course at the Field Artillery School on July 20, he learned that he ranked number one in his class of seventy-eight officers. "All of my close friends were in the top 10," he noted, adding by way of explanation, "We did our work before we played cards."

That had become his practice and eventually became his motto: "Work first, play later."[4] It was a habit that would serve him well in the next stage of his life.

About the time he married June, and on the advice of her banker father, Dallin decided to attend law school following his BYU graduation. He later managed to get a few minutes of advice from BYU's president, Ernest L. Wilkinson, who had a successful legal career before going into education. President Wilkinson told him the best law schools in the East (Dallin's geographic preference) were Harvard, Chicago, and Michigan, and so Dallin applied to each for entrance and a scholarship.

In February 1954, he took the required law school entrance exam and scored high. Then, on March 27, the day before leaving for Field Artillery School, he learned he had won a scholarship for three years of tuition and fees to the University of Chicago. Driving west from Fort Sill in 115-degree heat in July 1954, he knew where he and his family were headed next. Soon they would leave Provo for a city one hundred times larger, a sprawling metropolis that was the largest city in Illinois and the second largest in the United States.

CHAPTER 4

"THE CAPABILITIES TO BE A LEADER"

Law School in Chicago

On Monday, September 13, 1954, Dallin and his small family left for Chicago in the 1953 Pontiac they bought from June's father earlier in the year. "We had fixed up the back seat with blankets and a baby bed mattress," Dallin wrote, "and the children rode there and behaved like little angels the whole trip." It was good they did because Dallin and June had plenty of other things to worry about.

They were moving to a new world, and to make it livable, they had decided to bring with them the furniture they already owned, as well as a sofa and two leather chairs belonging to Dallin's mother "and all of the bottled fruit we dared to carry," Dallin remembered. To get everything to Chicago, they rented "a huge trailer"—which when filled probably weighed over three thousand pounds—and tried pulling it behind their car.

"Pulling the heavy . . . trailer over the mountains was quite a strain on the Pontiac and our nerves," Dallin wrote. "Once we stalled but to our surprise started right off again. We stayed in motels and lived mostly off the huge lunch the loving grandmothers had provided." The trip took four days. Finally, on Thursday at 4:45 p.m., they drove into South Chicago.

"The apartment for which I had arranged with the university by mail was spacious but required some work to make it livable," Dallin wrote. "After buying a small automatic washer, a nice double bed, linoleum floor coverings, and a refrigerator (used), we began to be quite comfortable. Our immediate neighbors were students like ourselves and very pleasant."

Away from their extended family and the friends of their youth, they found an anchor for their lives in Church service. "Our church was located only a block south," Dallin recalled. "We both plunged into church activities. I taught the elders quorum and the fifteen- to eighteen-year-olds in Sunday School, as well as serving as a ward teacher," which is what they called home teachers—later ministers—in those days. "June taught the twelve-year-olds in Mutual."

Dallin also found a National Guard armory within a mile of their home. He applied for service there, though it took until December 31 for his papers to be processed and for him to be appointed second lieutenant in Battery B of the 208th Field Artillery Battalion of the Illinois National Guard. As in Utah, National Guard service meant drilling an evening each week and attending two-week camps in the summer.

Church and National Guard service were in addition to what brought him to Illinois, which was law school. "There were 130 in the first-year class at the University of Chicago," he wrote. "I started my study of law with real enthusiasm, but with the humble notion that I would have to work like the dickens to get B's and C's. I worked like the dickens, and was I ever scared!"

Law school is a rite of passage—a competitive, rough-and-tumble initiation that launches those who succeed and survive it into a potentially prestigious and lucrative career. The first year of law school, wrote one professor, "is a time of exhilaration, high expectations, ideals, and

Dallin as a first-year law student

dreams," but "also a time of frustration, stress, conflict, boredom, alienation, depression, and despair."[1]

Dallin worked hard—something to which he was accustomed—but not all the work came easily to him. Writing, a key skill for lawyers, proved especially difficult. "We had a program of legal writing and research supervised by tutors (one tutor to about twenty students)," he wrote. "The writing came particularly difficult for me as I had a hard time grasping exactly what was wanted in the first few papers." He tried to compensate by working harder. "I worked frightfully hard on those papers," he recalled.

Law school is a marathon and not a sprint, and Dallin learned early to set a strong and steady pace. "My typical day consisted of rising at 7:45 and spending from 8:30 to 12:30 in classes, less one hour free sometime in the early morning," he wrote. "By 1:30 p.m., I was back in the law library to study until 11:00 p.m. I usually studied another hour at home." On Tuesday evenings, he studied at home so he could care for the children while June went to Mutual to fulfill her calling. Wednesday evenings he had National Guard drill, and Saturday evenings he typically took off, though he went out with June only four times that school year.

"She was wonderfully supportive," he recalled.

His parents' influence—so strong in his early life—continued with him in law school, encouraging him to obey the Sabbath as never before. During high school and college, when he worked for a radio station, "I routinely worked on the Sabbath," he said. "When I left for law school—a huge new challenge in my life—my mother reminded me that in medical school in Philadelphia my father never studied on Sunday. He felt that he could do more in six days with the help of the Lord than he could do in seven days without it. . . .

"That powerful parental example," Dallin wrote, "communicated at just the right time, prompted me to do the same. Study was my work, and the Lord had commanded us to labor for six days and rest on the seventh. I followed my father's example and my mother's gentle teaching, and I was also blessed for it."[2]

But that didn't make the study of law easy. Dallin took typical classes for first-year law students: contracts, torts, elements of law, jurisdiction, criminal law, property, and agency. "We had our first exams in December," he wrote. "I felt miserable about them all, but satisfied that in Jurisdiction, at least, I had done my best."

Relieved to be through his first finals, Dallin drove his family to West Virginia to spend Christmas with June's brother. The vacation did them all good, but the question of Dallin's school performance still hung over them. Had he made the right choice of careers? In the competitive atmosphere of law school, much depends upon grades. In law school, as in all marathons, those who lead the race at the end win the prizes, which in this case likely meant the best and most plentiful job offers. Those who fall behind at the beginning may never catch up.

"Soon after returning," Dallin wrote, "I received my grades. I had an '85' in Jurisdictions (80–100 is A), the highest in the class, and was able to tell from the other grades that I was to be at least moderately successful in law school. The real pressure was off."[3]

In most American law schools, the highest honor bestowed on first-year students is appointment to the law review. The academic journals of most disciplines in the United States are edited by university professors or other seasoned professionals. The big exception is legal journals. Every major law school publishes a law review, which is edited almost entirely by the school's top students. Appointment to the law review makes students attractive to potential employers but also adds a heavy burden to schedules already weighed down with hard classes.[4]

"Following the report of our winter quarter grades," Dallin wrote, "four of us in the first-year class were elected to the law review. Ordinarily this is done after completion of the whole year, but we had averages sufficiently high that they felt justified in our election. I was very pleased."

As the weeks of school wore on, however, the pressure for grades renewed itself, though in a different way. "With spring tests, the pressure came back," Dallin recorded. "I did very well (all of my first-year final grades were A's), and it became evident to me that with sustained effort I had a chance at the top spot in the class. This was a different kind of pressure than that which existed in the fall (the fear of not succeeding), but very real nonetheless."

When school finally let out in June 1955, Dallin began doing some basic law review work, learning to check footnotes and proofread. He had always been good at library research, and these new skills helped prepare him for an academic life. But he also began recognizing the toll that law review work could take on his grades once school began again. In fact, a classmate and neighbor who did well his first year turned down election to the review, reasoning he didn't have time for it with everything else he was doing.

If Dallin knew how to do anything, however, it was work, and the summer season that brought leisure for some of his classmates just meant more work for him and June. She took the children by train to Utah, where her parents took care of them as she attended BYU, furthering her education by taking classes ranging from American history to modern dance. Dallin, meanwhile, worked on law review, spent two days working on a Church welfare farm in Wisconsin, and for two weeks in July attended National Guard camp in Minnesota.

"I have never worked harder than I worked at camp," he wrote about his experiences that year and the next at Camp Riley. "I had much to learn about being an officer, and had particular trouble delegating authority and work. However, I seemed to be well liked by the men and got along fine with the officers." His battalion's executive officer told him he was "the finest young officer he had ever met," Dallin recorded with satisfaction, "a compliment which was well appreciated."

Dallin was getting used to such compliments. Before he left for camp, he got word that he was to receive the Joseph Henry Beale Prize, the only honor of its kind given to first-year students. Each year, the

Dallin (front row) and other Illinois National Guard battalion officers, about 1956

faculty awarded the prize to the first-year law student "whose work in the tutorial program was judged by the faculty to be most worthy of special recognition." The prize carried a modest cash award of twenty-five dollars. "Apparently the value lay in the honor," Dallin mused, "not the financial reward."

When he returned from camp, he learned of another honor. "I was pleased to find," he wrote, "that I had ended the year #1 in my class." For someone who wondered if he would even survive in law school, this news brought great satisfaction. The dean of students told him he had earned the highest grade-point average in many years at the school. His hard work had paid off.

The distinguished dean of the law school, Edward H. Levi—who would go on to become president of the University of Chicago and United States Attorney General—paid Dallin yet another honor by inviting him to lunch. "He questioned me at length," Dallin wrote, "on my favorite subjects, instructors, what I thought was wrong with the school, etc., and we had a very nice visit." The dean seemed genuinely interested in this remarkable young Latter-day Saint who had managed to excel above all the other students while living his religion.

Dallin took the opportunity to bear witness of his faith. Dean Levi "listened with interest and quizzed me repeatedly on our Word of Wisdom," Dallin wrote. "I felt as if I had made an influential friend." And indeed he had. Edward Levi would remain a friend and mentor for decades to come.

After a month-long vacation with June and their girls, Dallin was back at the law school preparing to start his second year of classes. On top of the regular schoolwork, law review members were expected to write a "comment," or article on some legal topic, for publication in the journal, and Dallin's summertime work on his article put him well ahead of his peers. "As an accounting major with a natural taste for tax law," he wrote, "I completed the comment in record time."

As the top student in his second-year class, however, he did not expect what happened next. The third-year law student assigned as his editor ripped into his article with a vengeance. This was yet another opportunity for learning. Having the editor "tear my work apart in terms of substance and manner of expression was disquieting," Dallin wrote, "but as we rewrote the comment together, I could see how it was being improved, and I learned a great deal from that experience."

By November 1955, Dallin had finished his article, and it soon appeared in the *University of Chicago Law Review,* one of the nation's most prestigious law journals.[5] "I was the first of the second-year students to complete a comment," Dallin wrote, "and had reason to feel optimistic about my progress."

But what followed almost devastated him. "All of my optimism was to be dashed in my next law review experience," he recalled twenty-five years later, "which still stands as one of the few really decisive failures I have experienced in my professional life."

He received an assignment to write a comment on a court of appeals decision about using coerced confessions. "There were hundreds and hundreds of cases of this nature," Dallin wrote, "and I must have read all of them several times." Dallin wrote up his commentary and took it to his faculty adviser, a brilliant but meticulous man who sent Dallin back to the drawing board each time. "I wrote at least a dozen drafts," Dallin recalled, and took them to the professor for his blessing. "In every case, [I] was frustrated by a long list of insights I had missed or additional work I should do.

"The winter wore on," Dallin recounted, "and my smugness about the first comment gave way to feelings of despair and inadequacy. What it boiled down to," he finally concluded, "is that I simply could not please" the professor. "I had the good fortune and the misfortune of having my work reviewed by the faculty perfectionist, who could hardly bear to publish his own work, much less approve the work of another."

After a quarter century, he looked back on that struggle with the perspective of time. "From this experience," he reflected, "I learned a great deal about high standards, analysis, writing and rewriting, and, especially, humility. The comment was never completed. I still have the last drafts I did, and they still pain me to handle them. The latest draft was probably of sufficient quality to be published in most law reviews, perhaps even the *University of Chicago Law Review,* but I am convinced that what I learned by not publishing that comment was probably more valuable to me than what I would have learned by publishing it."

Despite the cloud this cast over his second year of law school, there was plenty of sunshine to compensate. He finished his second year with "an uninterrupted succession of 'A' grades" and was still number one in his class.

In many law schools, distinguished students who don't make the law review instead compete in moot court competition, a chance to ply their writing and speaking skills in settings that imitate the courtroom. Dallin made the unorthodox decision to participate in both law review and moot court—a decision that might have seemed suicidal to some students given the time commitments required. But work did not scare Dallin. He joined four friends on a moot court team "with the understanding that if other work grew too pressing, I should have the option of withdrawing."

Dallin's team won the autumn competition. In the winter contest, Dallin coauthored the legal brief and joined in arguing the case orally. Given his initial struggle with first-year legal writing, he found fulfillment in how the brief turned out. "I don't mind saying that I was simply delighted and smug with the quality of the brief," he acknowledged. "It won the prize for the best brief in the second-year competition."

Years in radio helped develop Dallin's speaking skills, which transitioned nicely into the moot courtroom. "At year's end," Dallin wrote, "I was told confidentially that I had the highest score for oral argument."

Along with all these accomplishments, the most important growth

Dallin experienced during this time was spiritual. "In Chicago during much of law school," he remembered, "I served as elders quorum group leader and in that capacity attended stake leadership meetings and came under the influence of stake president (and lawyer) John K. Edmunds." Dallin found in President Edmunds a role model.

"This remarkable man had a profound influence on my spiritual growth," Dallin wrote. "His example and words, which never failed to inspire and motivate me, had a uniquely powerful influence in helping me set my feet unwaveringly on the gospel path during the often-troubling years of graduate study." President Edmunds taught him, "When you are involved in the work of the Lord, the obstacles before you are never as great as the power behind you."

John K. Edmunds went on to become a regional representative of the Twelve, president of the California Mission (headquartered in Los Angeles), and president of the Salt Lake Temple. He remained close to Dallin and would continue to influence his life.

Dallin's spiritual growth became clear in a letter he wrote halfway through his second year of law school to his brother, Merrill, who was about to depart on a mission. The letter showed Dallin's priorities and echoed the strong influence of their mother.

"You are to be a representative," he wrote to Merrill, "and ponder for a moment whom you will represent. First and foremost, as a bearer of the priesthood you represent our Lord and Savior, Jesus Christ. You are His emissary, His servant, to preach His Gospel. . . . Lastly, you represent your family, the loved ones whose pride in you is felt most keenly at this time; our Mother, whose teachings have been a shield for us all, and whose testimony has been a beacon to guide our footsteps. You will represent her, and all the rest of us, and our prayers will be with you as you do the Lord's work."

For many law school students, the first year is most difficult, and the remaining two years become increasingly easier as they adjust to the rigors imposed by this form of education. But law review students are often an exception to this rule. After a challenging first year, their second year becomes more difficult as they take on the added burden of unpaid law review work. Those who rise to the top of the law review and are chosen as editors for their third year often find that year the busiest and most challenging of all.

In March 1956, as Dallin was nearing the end of his second year of law school, he learned that the law review's board of editors had selected him editor-in-chief for the next year. Their choice surprised him. "I thought my frustrating experience with the second comment would disqualify me," he wrote. "It turned out that quite a few of the dozen or so 'competitors' had not even published one comment by this time, and not one of my class had published two."[6]

But his selection to "the top spot," as he described it, came with a humbling warning. When the editor-in-chief he was replacing trained him in his new duties, he told Dallin that he was chosen to be editor-in-chief because of his leadership skills but wanted him to know "that I should not overestimate my qualifications to the extent of overruling" another more knowledgeable editor "in the areas where he was my superior."

It was a good lesson, and Dallin took it to heart. He would come to be known as one who worked well with others and cultivated a spirit of cooperation among those with whom he labored. As he had said in choosing his major, he wanted to spend his time working with people, and he was finding satisfaction in doing so. Being chosen as editor-in-chief helped him feel he had the capability to be a leader.

The people he enjoyed being with most were his wife and children, and throughout law school, he maintained the steady schedule that allowed him to spend time with them. Being a young husband and father, of course, had its challenges, though June bore the greatest burden of the child-rearing. During the latter half of Dallin's second year of law school, June furthered her education at Chicago's Roosevelt University, leaving the children with babysitters.

June, Dallin, and daughters Cheri and Sharmon

Dallin and June's humble apartment was in a converted army barracks, where an oil-fired space heater provided warmth for the family during the frigid Chicago winters. They filled the heater's tank by hand from oil drums on the street outside.

"When our two daughters were ages two and three," Dallin recounted, "the older one dipped her little cup down into the oil tank on the back of the heater, took a large drink of the clear fuel oil, and then shared it generously with her younger sister. Bad results followed, and June had to rush them to the hospital to have their stomachs pumped. Several weeks later the little girls climbed up into our medicine cabinet and seized a bottle of candy-flavored cough syrup that included some sedative drug. Cooperatively alternating their draws at the bottle, the two finished its contents with predictable results. June grabbed one child under each arm and rushed for the hospital again."

After the second incident, Dallin and June received a visit from a Chicago public health nurse inquiring into their fitness to care for children. As extraordinarily conscientious parents, they were mortified. "In the meantime," however, Dallin wrote, "one of my playful law school classmates was heard to tell a group that Dallin and June Oaks wouldn't drink anything, but their daughters would drink everything."

One of Dallin's favorite activities with his girls was playing "Daddy, Be a Bear." When he came home from school for lunch and dinner each day, they ran up to him and said, "Daddy, be a bear!" He set his books on the table, dropped to all fours on the linoleum floor, and, he explained, "making the most terrible growls, I would crawl around the floor after the children, who fled with screams." He would "chase us around the house," daughter Cheri remembered fondly. "We would squeal and run around."

During his third year of law school, when many prominent firms were courting Dallin actively, one had a professional administer a

Converted army barracks where Oaks family lived in law school

Rorschach inkblot test to potential hires, and Dallin kept seeing bears in the blots. Putting down his pencil, the psychologist probed, "Now, Mr. Oaks, suppose you tell me about your thing about bears."

Dallin told him about "Daddy, Be a Bear," and the man shook his head, jotted something down on a piece of paper, and sent his test subject away.

"I must have passed the test," Dallin concluded, "because the firm raised the proposed starting salary by $1,000 per year when they received his report."

Dallin was attracted to the firm of Kirkland, Fleming, Green, Martin, and Ellis in Chicago. The firm offered him a summer job between his second and third years of law school, which he was able to fit around his National Guard summer camp. He spent most of the summer at the firm on corporate litigation. "Robert H. Bork, a Chicago graduate and promising member of the firm, and I became fast friends," he recounted.

During Dallin's third year of law school, he interviewed with many more firms, and after "looking over the whole field of other possibilities," he elected to remain with Kirkland because a senior partner, Dallin remembered, "assured me that he would push me ahead in the firm as fast as my capabilities would allow, that I could work at whatever (within bounds) I wished, and that he knew I had the capabilities to be a leader of the firm. Being able to see he was doing just that for Robert Bork, and knowing well the impressive list of clients and variety of work Kirkland had, I could not help but give in to his urgings."

In addition to working during the summer at Kirkland and fulfilling his National Guard duties, Dallin had to find time to fulfill his new law review editorial duties. "I spent from 7:00 p.m. to midnight every weeknight and all day Saturday at the *Review* office throughout the summer," he wrote. The law review work was grueling but educational and continued as school started again.

"The administration of the law review during my third year occupied me between thirty and forty hours per week, with schoolwork having to be done in the time remaining," he recorded. His grades slipped, and a classmate without heavy responsibility on the law review squeaked past him for the top grade-point average in the graduating class. But Dallin was right behind him and received the added benefits of juggling what amounted to almost a full-time job on top of schoolwork. "In addition to the great value of editorial work," he wrote, law review leadership "forced you to learn how to do your schoolwork in less time than you would otherwise lavish upon it." The skills required to live with perpetually heavy work burdens were valuable ones that would serve him later in life.

But the heavy burden also pained him at times. "The technique of many law teachers of publicly embarrassing unprepared students usually drove us to exhaustive preparation," Dallin recalled many decades afterward. "I can never forget the day Dean Edward H. Levi called on me in his anti-trust course to state a particular case and explain how it differed from another case. Being poorly prepared that day (because of law review work), I hesitated slightly. Reading the circumstance and wanting to teach a lesson to me and everyone else, he cut me off with, 'Oh, never mind, Mr. Oaks. You have to be good to do that.' Years later I can laugh about that put-down, but the scar tissue inflicted by that experience and the motivation for careful preparation remain."

One reward of Dallin's law review work was that it put him in touch with other great minds. For example, he edited a book review written by Nobel laureate Bertrand Russell, who graciously responded, "Thank you for your letter . . . and for the trouble you have taken in rectifying errors in my article. I accept all of your suggested corrections."

In February 1957, during Dallin's last year of law school, June went home to Utah to deliver their third child. As with the first two children, the third was to be born by Cesarean section, and they wanted the doctor who delivered their second child to deliver this one too.

With two girls already, "I hoped desperately for a boy," Dallin wrote. "The operation was on a Saturday morning," and Dallin waited eagerly in their Chicago apartment for news of the delivery. "I was mopping the floor to keep my nerves calm when the call came," he said. June's father phoned and "was talking calmly" when Dallin suddenly heard his sister, Evelyn, scream, "It's a boy!" Dallin was overjoyed, and they gave the child the first name Lloyd, after Dallin's father, and the middle name Dixon, June's maiden name.

Happy to have another child, especially given June's delicate constitution, Dallin had given up on another hope he entertained. The ultimate goal after graduation for many top law students in America is to clerk for a justice of the United States Supreme Court. These highly coveted positions are extremely competitive, and there was no guarantee that even a student of Dallin's credentials would obtain a spot. Dallin applied for clerkships with Justice John Harlan and Chief Justice Earl Warren. Justice Harlan invited him to Washington for an interview, only to select instead two Harvard men who had postgraduate work experience.

By the time Lloyd was born, Dallin had heard nothing from the Chief Justice. "I had entirely abandoned hope of any success there," Dallin said, "when Dean Levi phoned me during winter quarter finals . . . and announced that I had been chosen by the Chief. Warren had phoned him to inquire whether I was a likely enough possibility to justify asking me down for an interview, and the Dean had sold him such a bill of goods on me that he had told him to tell me I had the job."[7]

CHAPTER 5

"CHARACTER AND ABILITY"

Supreme Court Clerkship

On Thursday, June 6, 1957, Dallin graduated from the University of Chicago Law School with his mother, Stella, in attendance at the ceremonies. With the receipt of his diploma, "my formal schooling was at an end," he observed, though he would never stop learning. During that graduation week, Dallin and June drove Stella around the metropolitan area, and "she announced her thorough contentment with our living in Chicago if that was our desire."

The Saturday after his graduation, the whole family piled into their car and drove 550 miles to Hamilton, Ontario, where Dallin's brother, Merrill, was serving his mission. "We found him entirely happy and efficient in forwarding the Lord's work," Dallin wrote. "He took me out for a morning's tracting (we had three 'cottage meetings'), which we both enjoyed thoroughly." Merrill recalled that they placed three copies of the Book of Mormon as well.

"I am happy to see that going three years to the University of Chicago to get his doctor's degree in law has not weakened my brother, and he is stronger than ever," wrote Merrill in reporting the visit to his mission president. "He did not have the privilege of filling a mission, as the time he turned twenty was during the Korean War, but I feel sure that someday the Lord will require him to fill some type of mission. He has been blessed with so many talents and such a brilliant mind that I know he will always be required to make a return to the Lord in his time, talents, and finances, and he is always humble and willing."

By Tuesday, June 11, Dallin was back in Chicago so he could begin work the next morning at the Kirkland firm. He worked for a month at the firm, and on July 17, after packing for movers who would follow, he and his family left for Washington, DC, arriving in the evening of the following day. Their furniture lagged behind them, and while waiting for it, they stayed with a cousin who served as bishop of the Alexandria Ward into which they were moving. Once the furniture finally arrived, Dallin and his family moved into the apartment they had rented, and on July 25, he began his new life as a law clerk in the United States Supreme Court.

Chief Justice Earl Warren

Chief Justice Earl Warren, his boss, was in Europe at the time, but a man who clerked the year before oriented Dallin and two fellow clerks on their duties. All told, Dallin enjoyed meeting and working with top graduates from law schools around the country who served the nine justices of the Supreme Court.

The outgoing clerk explained that the law clerks' duty "before the court sits, and to a lesser extent after the court is in session, is to prepare memoranda on the petitions for certiorari and appeal jurisdiction statements." In other words, the clerks were the initial gatekeepers in recommending which cases the Supreme Court would hear. That was a heavy responsibility, and not one Dallin relished.

"Gradually," he wrote after some time, "I am beginning to develop a self-confidence in my recommendations, but I suppose I won't be entirely sure of myself until the Chief has read the first few of my memos without commenting on their judgment or completeness." As he came to understand, however, Justice Warren was not one to offer much feedback—good or bad—making it difficult for the clerks to gauge how well they were performing.

While struggling to learn constitutional law and how it applied in the cases he was reviewing, Dallin also had to worry about passing the Illinois state bar examination. "A thorn in my side this August 1957," he wrote at the time, "is the forthcoming bar exam I will take September 4, 5, 6 in Chicago." Before he left for Washington, he had begun taking a bar exam preparation course that he had to abandon for his clerkship. "Unable to continue with the course in Chicago," he worried, "I am having to get by with the outlines, and that is definitely the hard way." His preparations cut into family time, and in a letter to loved ones in Utah, he complained about "the irritation of having to study each evening for the bar." At the same time, he felt a growing gratitude toward his law school professors and what they taught him that he could now apply.

When Sunday, September 1, rolled around, a new worry beset him.

"I was stricken with flu," Dallin wrote in his journal, and "feared I might miss the bar exam." By the next evening, however, he had recovered enough to board a plane to Chicago, where he stayed with some friends and chatted with others. Among those he saw was Monroe G. McKay, a BYU graduate who followed him at the law school and went on to become a U.S. Court of Appeals judge. "The bar exam was technical," Dallin wrote after taking it. "My performance was good in spots & abysmal in others. My success will depend on how they grade the highs (how high) & lows (how low)."

Unsure of the outcome, Dallin flew back to Washington, where he finally had the opportunity to meet his new boss. "Had thirty-five-minute visit with Chief Justice Warren today," Dallin recorded, "and found him a warmer person than I had been led to believe." They talked politics—a common theme in Washington—and more personal matters. "He inquired after my family," Dallin wrote. "I told him that I was the sole lawyer in a medical family. He expressed his joy that his son had started law school."

The Chief also had some words of counsel for his new clerk. "He expressed strong disapproval of court personnel (law clerks or judges) who later write of the intimacies of the court," Dallin noted. "In his feeling, this was 'destructive' of the free exchange of ideas among court members and of public confidence in the court."

Dallin soon got to know the other justices a bit too. "Met Justice Harlan in the hall today, and he surprised me by calling me by name," Dallin wrote of the justice who interviewed him months earlier but did not hire him. "I last met and talked with him in our interview last November."

On September 21, Chief Justice Warren finally called his three clerks together for a formal orientation. He reiterated some of the instruction he had given Dallin in private but added clarifications. "Chief sees no harm in clerks publishing details concerning procedures used on court while they were there" or "personal details on the justice,"

Dallin as U.S. Supreme Court law clerk, 1957–58

Dallin wrote. "It is only the use of the confidential information which would reflect unfavorably on the court or serve to discredit any individual that he sees as evil."

Later in the meeting, the Chief Justice outlined the procedures he hoped his law clerks would follow. The clerk who prepares a memo for a case, he said, will also help draft the justice's final opinion for publication. The Chief and clerk would work together on it. "Chief will write memo" laying out his thoughts on the case, Dallin recorded. The "clerk will then write a draft, & then the clerk & Chief will go into conference to hammer out opinion."

During the meeting, the Chief provided a little feedback to Dallin and his fellow clerks on the work they had done up to that point. The "memos so far," Dallin jotted in his journal, "are 'first-rate,' neither too long nor too short."

It was the kind of feedback they craved. Two weeks later, Dallin got more good feedback. On October 5, he wrote, "Letter arrived today notifying me that I had passed the bar exam." The news was a great relief and allowed him to concentrate more fully on his court work.

The work Dallin and the other clerks did reviewing petitions to the court occupied most of their first three months of service. "Later, when the court heard arguments," Dallin wrote, "we prepared memos on the cases being argued and then helped with the opinions being prepared in cases that had been decided. Along the way, we saw the court and its members in the most intimate way."

The pages of Dallin's journals demonstrate that he worked hard while at the court and sometimes disagreed with the Chief Justice on his decisions about cases. But he clearly respected him as well. On October 7, 1957, the Supreme Court's term began. "I saw the court in session for the first time," Dallin wrote. "The Chief is impressive as the presiding officer."

In the hardworking atmosphere of the court, lunches became a time for Dallin and his fellow clerks both to relax and learn. "Every few weeks," Dallin reported, "the law clerks invited a famous guest to have lunch and informal discussion with us in a reserved room at the Supreme Court." This gave them a chance to meet many of the best-known political figures of the day, including future United States President John F. Kennedy. On October 10, 1957, the clerks hosted Dean Acheson, who served as Secretary of State under U.S. President Harry Truman. "I was overwhelmed with him," Dallin wrote in his journal. "He is undoubtedly the most brilliant all-around individual I have ever met. He talked fluently and persuasively on a range of topics from law clerks . . . to diplomacy."

On October 25, Dallin and the Chief Justice's other two clerks were leaving the office when they ran into William P. Rogers, who had just been appointed by U.S. President Dwight Eisenhower as the country's new attorney general. He had come "to pay his respects to the Chief," Dallin wrote. "The Chief introduced the three of us as 'the fellows who make the wheels go 'round.'"

Now that he had passed the bar exam, Dallin flew to Chicago so he could be sworn in as a lawyer in Illinois. The next morning, a judge swore him in and invited him to lunch with prominent friends. The invitation demonstrated that because of his important position in Washington, key members of the Illinois bar already held Dallin in high esteem despite his being its newest member. Later that day, Dallin dropped by his law firm to say hello before boarding a plane back to his family.

On November 6, Chief Justice Warren offered Dallin unsolicited counsel on his future and what the judge saw as the great possibilities for a young man of his "character and ability." The next night, the Chief rode home with his clerks. "We had a good visit," Dallin wrote. "He always calls us by our first names, and that is an informality which exists in few offices." They, in turn, addressed him as "Chief."

Young graduates who enter the working world often jump to conclusions about their work environments and colleagues, and Dallin initially formed some harsh conclusions about the court and its members. As time wore on and he better understood the court's complexities, however, his opinion swung the opposite direction. "My attitude toward the institution has changed," he acknowledged. Over time, his feelings moderated, as he came to see things in balance. "The Chief isn't much on splitting hairs with a fine legal distinction," Dallin confided to his journal in mid-November, "but he's long on good old common sense."

The workload for Dallin and the other clerks, heavy from the beginning, grew heavier over time. "We are all working most every evening now," he told his journal on November 18. The harder he worked, the more certain he became of his abilities. He also learned to cooperate with other justices' clerks. "I am profoundly impressed with the role for good which a law clerk can have," he wrote. When another justice's clerks followed Dallin's suggestion in editing an opinion, Dallin exclaimed, "I had no idea that my suggestions would have such an impact on the opinion."

Finally, after months of hard work, Christmastime came, and

Dallin was able to devote extended time to his family. "Christmas at home," he wrote succinctly on December 25. Then for the four days that followed he summarized, "June and I on a second honeymoon in New York."

When work started up after the holidays, Dallin became busier than ever. On January 8, 1958, he wrote that he had grown so busy he was rarely able to visit the courtroom and hear cases argued. A notable exception occurred five days later, however, when June came to the court, and the two listened together through the argument of two cases. Afterward, they completed their date by having "bean soup at U.S. Senate cafeteria," he wrote.

Although Dallin's legal career would eventually squeeze out his military prospects, he joined the U.S. Army Congressional Command and Operations Group while in Washington. "Our drills consist of listening to top generals give speeches on the military," he wrote to family in Utah. At the first meeting he attended, the initial speaker was a four-star general, and others in attendance included two major generals, a brigadier general, a half dozen U.S. senators, and numerous congressional representatives. "It was very interesting," Dallin concluded of the classified briefing.

By the middle of his year with the court, Dallin wrote, "I was quite confident in my work and among my fellow clerks. That confidence was hard won, since I had received no evaluations from the Chief Justice, and hardly any from my fellow clerks." Dallin remembered that the outgoing law clerk who first oriented them described the Chief as "an aloof man who seldom criticizes or praises—one almost never knows whether his work is satisfactory or how it might be improved."

Understandably, Dallin was pleased when, on February 3—after five months of work—he finally glimpsed how highly his boss regarded him. "The Chief called me in today," he wrote, "and offered me the chief clerk's job next year if I would stay. He emphasized that he wanted me to do what was best for me, and he wouldn't pressure me. He even offered to talk to the Attorney General, Mr. Rogers, about placing me over in the Department of Justice if I wished to do that rather than stay with him. He said he only offered to do that for one other clerk, Earl Pollock (now with the Solicitor General).

"I had no idea the Chief so regarded me," Dallin wrote, surprised.

On Sunday, February 10, Dallin began serving as chairman of his ward's genealogy committee. His other Church activity while at the court included teaching a youth Sunday School class and the elders quorum, besides serving as ward teaching supervisor for a third of the ward. The latter responsibility was "a big job," he wrote, "since my area included many transients in Ft. Belvoir, Virginia."

On February 14, he finally responded to Justice Warren on his offer to have Dallin serve as chief clerk the next year. "Today I told the Chief we wouldn't be wanting to spend another year in Washington," Dallin wrote. "He was nice about it." The Chief asked what Dallin and June's plans were, and Dallin replied—quite presciently as it turned out—that they planned to live in Chicago for a few years and then probably go "back to Provo and public life."

One of the clerks' duties was to draft opinions for the justices to issue in their own names. On February 27, Justice Warren called Dallin into his office and complimented him on a draft he had prepared. "You've gotten down exactly what I wanted to say and everything I wanted to say," the Chief Justice said. "I like it."

The two men went over the draft sentence by sentence, with Dallin listening carefully to understand the Chief's criticism and suggest alternative language if he did not come up with some of his own. "This exercise in careful listening, understanding of reactions to written work, and framing of responses," Dallin reflected, "cultivated skills I would have ample occasion to use in later professional life."

On March 12, the dean of the University of Pennsylvania law school, a prestigious Ivy League institution, phoned to explore whether

United States Supreme Court, 1957–58

Dallin wanted to become an assistant professor at the school. “I said thanks,” Dallin recorded, “but I’d like to practice a while yet.”

On April 18, the Chief Justice called Dallin in again to review another opinion he had drafted. “It’s a bang-up job,” the justice told his clerk. “I’ve read through the whole thing and think you have not wasted a word. When you have given such careful thought to something, I see no point in tinkering with any of the language. I think we’ll just go with this as it is.”

The Chief circulated the opinion among his fellow justices, and the other clerks praised it. “This was probably the most important opinion on which I worked for the Chief Justice,” Dallin wrote, “and it was nice to have him so pleased about it.”

Dallin’s alma mater, the University of Chicago, announced the construction of a new law school building, and Dean Levi wanted the highest judge in the land to play a role. “At Edward Levi’s request,” Dallin wrote, “I invited the Chief Justice to preside at the cornerstone ceremonies. He agreed.” As the Chief prepared for the occasion, he handed Dallin a draft of his speech and asked him to review it within the hour. Dallin saw ways to improve it and sought more time, which the Chief granted. Later, he told Dallin, "Your suggestions and alterations helped that speech a lot."

On May 28, Dallin flew to Chicago and joined the Chief for the ceremonies. "I had breakfast and lunch with him and accompanied him as he visited friends in the Loop that morning," Dallin wrote. "It was a fine opportunity to get acquainted with him on a more personal basis." The speech went well, and after dinner that evening, Dean Levi invited "the honored guests plus the faculty and me," Dallin wrote, "over to his house for cocktails."

"When the Chief declined a drink, saying he seldom drank after dinner (only before)," Dallin explained, "I told Dean Levi in the presence of the Chief Justice 'that I had the Chief living the Word of Wisdom.' This claim seemed to delight them both."

Despite the demands of his clerkship, Dallin found time to spend with his family while working in Washington. "I enjoyed walks in the woods with Sharmon and Cheri, now 3½ and 4½," he wrote.

"I remember a lot of walks in the woods," Cheri remembered of her childhood. "That's a great memory." June remained a supportive wife and excellent mother. She also supplemented the family income by babysitting for the ward bishop's wife, who worked outside her home.

Like many a father, Dallin found joy in seeing his children grow and progress. "On February 11, 1958, when I came home from work," he recorded, "Lloyd took eight steps toward me, giggling cutely as he did. He had taken his first three steps earlier that day. He was then 11½ months old."

One Saturday in March when Dallin was working at the court, June drove into Washington with their three children to pick up her husband. The family arrived just as the Chief Justice stepped in to talk

June with the children, 1957

to his clerks. "This was the first time the Chief had met our children," Dallin wrote.

"Lloyd walked over and held his arms out to be picked up," Dallin smiled. "The Chief held him for about ten minutes. Lloyd pulled his glasses off several times. The Chief said, 'Don't worry, I've had my glasses thrown in a corner dozens of times.'" He told them stories about his own grandchildren. "Lloyd grinned appropriately," Dallin noted, "and the girls were sweet. I was very proud."

After the Supreme Court's term ended on June 30, Dallin sat down to calculate how often he had agreed with the liberal judge he served. "I calculated that I had agreed with the Chief Justice 59 percent of the time on the votes he cast on cases argued before the court," he wrote. Dallin agreed just 54 percent with the court as a whole during that same period. All in all, he surmised, "I suppose that makes me a bit more 'liberal' than I'd have wanted to admit."

Dallin also kept a record of what he accomplished during his term of service with the court. Among other things, he wrote almost five hundred memoranda related to petitions for the court to take cases,

Chief Justice Earl Warren with Oaks family members in April 1970, after his retirement

roughly half of those from indigent criminals. The work he drafted for justices occupied sixty-nine pages of the official published reports of Supreme Court cases.

On July 3, 1958, as the Chief Justice prepared to leave Washington after the court term, he said goodbye to Dallin and another clerk. Dallin observed that the Chief's goodbye was stiff and restrained. "I sensed a desire on his part to say something endearing," Dallin wrote, "but it was suppressed by the businesslike front he always maintains. As he shook my hand, though, I could see a genuine affection in his eyes."

The feeling was mutual. "On my part," Dallin wrote in his journal, "I felt a keen loss at leaving him. Though these pages scold him severely in regard to his position on many things, in regard to his not overwhelming quickness of mind, and in regard to what I consider his faulty notion of how a judge should reach decisions, I have developed a profound affection and respect for him. I believe him completely honest, sincere, and utterly without guile. He has wonderfully mature judgment about many matters, and he is the most kind and considerate employer one could ask for. I will miss him."

As the years went by, Dallin attended the annual black-tie dinners that the growing number of the Chief's clerks put on for him in Washington. When the Chief Justice announced his retirement, Dallin wrote to express his long-standing affection.

"I suppose all of your official family (of which I will always be proud to count myself a member) received the news of your retirement with mixed emotions," he said. "Those of us who have observed your work schedule at first hand well know what long hours you have toiled in the service of the court and the country. You have earned a rest. But we cannot be other than sad to see you yield up the office in which you have established yourself as one of a few really great chief justices in our history."

Chief Justice Earl Warren had become a father figure to Dallin in some ways, and the former clerk looked upon him with the kindness he might have bestowed on his own father had he lived to old age.

"Recalling something you said to us at one of the law clerks' dinners some years ago," Dallin wrote openly, "I am convinced that you were determined to resign at the peak of your powers and effectiveness. I believe you have done that. And while I hate to see you leave, I think that is the right and proper course. That is what I would have wanted for you if you had been my father, and I feel the same way about you as one of a small group of men who are in a very real sense my fathers in the law."

CHAPTER 6

"TO EQUIP ME FOR SOME FUTURE JOB"

Law Firm and Church Service

At the request of Chief Justice Earl Warren, Dallin remained in Washington for several more weeks to help orient a new slate of clerks. June, meanwhile, worked at home to pack their belongings for shipment by truck. They and their three children finally left Washington in late July and headed west to vacation before taking up their abode in Illinois.

As they drove west, daughters Sharmon, age five, and Cheri, four, were, as Dallin described it, "in reasonably good spirits." But Lloyd, a year and a half old, was "sick with earache, vomiting, and screaming," Dallin remembered. "It was a long night as we alternated driving and trying to sleep."

In Illinois, distant relatives kindly put them up for the night. The next day, they drove across the Dakotas and met June's parents at the east entrance to Yellowstone National Park. "We and the children enjoyed the sights of the park, and then a few weeks in Utah with loved ones," Dallin wrote. On September 15, 1958, Dallin and June attended the temple sealing of Dallin's brother, Merrill, to Josephine Ann Christensen.

Not long after that, they returned to the Chicago area and spent time looking for a house that met the needs of their growing family. "We wanted to be in the western suburbs where housing costs were more reasonable, and along a commuter rail line where I could get to work without driving," Dallin wrote. They eventually located a home they could rent that fulfilled their immediate needs.

"Our rented home was situated on a huge lawn in a grove of oak trees, walking distance from a grade school where Sharmon would begin kindergarten that fall," Dallin recalled. "The open spaces, trees, and lawn were a needed antidote for the overdose of pavement we had endured during the preceding four years." June and Dallin were grateful for this home, which aside from being rented had only one real drawback: it was twenty miles from church.

The family settled into their new home and established new routines, which for Dallin included walking from the train in the Loop to his office near the Lake Shore and back again. "My walking three miles a day," Dallin wrote, "has had quite an effect on my weight. I weigh 181, about 9 to 21 pounds less than any time since we've been married." He felt good about growing more fit but observed, "My trousers fit precariously."

The most demanding part of Dallin's routine was his new job at the Kirkland firm, the largest law firm in Chicago at the time. Having worked with the firm twice before—after his second year of law school and following graduation before his Supreme Court clerkship—he already knew many of the people in the ninety-lawyer organization. Unlike his two earlier experiences, however, this time he was, in his own words, "a full-fledged lawyer and a full, though inexperienced, participant in the extensive large corporate litigation and counseling activities of the Kirkland firm."

At first, he worked under the direction of his friend Robert Bork, whom Dallin considered "probably the most prominent and most favored senior associate" in the litigation area of the firm. A year later, however, Dallin became a principal himself, reporting directly to the senior partners who supervised his work. The clients for which Dallin did the most work were Standard Oil of Indiana, Chemetron Corporation, and B. F. Goodrich, though he advised many smaller corporations too.

The prestige of the job and a good office were offset by the extraordinarily hard work required. He labored six days a week downtown, and his Church callings occupied most of his Sundays. "I don't mind his being gone during the week and on Saturdays," June wrote, "but I really dislike it when he is gone all day Sunday."

After Christmas and New Year's Day 1959, when her parents visited, she wrote, "As long as I am on the subject of not seeing Dallin, I guess I may as well tell you of his schedule last week. He has never been more busy. He worked New Year's Eve and didn't arrive home until 11:00 p.m. He worked all day New Year's Day, and till 11:00 again the next night and again all day Saturday. This week I haven't seen much of him. I'm just glad my folks were here to give me something to think about this past while."

By the middle of the month, the workload had lightened somewhat, and Dallin was able to come home earlier. In February, he wrote rather optimistically, "I love my work, so aside from the inconvenience of being gone long hours, I don't mind a bit." But by the end of March, after getting home one night at 11:00, he wrote to family, "The trouble with doing good work is that everyone wants you to work for him, and it's very hard to say no to the three or four top men in the firm for whom I do most all my work. I'll find a way to cut down, though, for I can't and won't go on at this pace for long. I can't afford to because of the effect on June and the children, not to mention myself."

By March 1960, Dallin and June had scrimped, saved, and borrowed enough money to purchase their first home, an attractive two-bedroom English Tudor–style house in Elmhurst, an established suburb fifteen miles west of Chicago on the train line Dallin used to commute.

Oaks family with newest addition, Dallin D., on June's lap, spring 1961

They loved this little home and soon added two more bedrooms upstairs. Close to school and shopping, it was just five miles from church and cut Dallin's commute time in half.

Though expecting their fourth child, June still helped with the painting, redecorating, packing, and moving. On August 12, she gave birth to Dallin Dixon Oaks in a local hospital. His father wrote, "A superbly qualified obstetrician and surgeon, recommended by our good friend, medical school professor Dr. George G. Jackson, told us afterward that all was in order and that we could plan further family," which had been their desire. "Thus," the elder Dallin wrote, "our prayers were answered, and we were relieved from the scare that followed Cheri's birth."

Dallin moved ahead rapidly in his law firm as the senior partners recognized the quality of his work and gave him more and more responsibility. The managing partner of the firm, Howard Ellis, "took a special fatherly interest in me," Dallin wrote. From 1958, when Dallin resumed working with the firm, until 1961, his last year with it, his income more than doubled, allowing the family to upgrade their living quarters, retire debt, and live well, though modestly.

But the heavy responsibility that came with added income meant that Dallin—a prodigious worker—had to labor relentlessly. In 1959, he received a big assignment that by itself over the next two years consumed up to seventy-five percent of his time. It required drafting numerous legal documents, coordinating with law firms in other states, and extensive travel. "Finally," he wrote, it "wore me down."

He hated the weeks away from home and how tedious the work was. "But most of all," he wrote, "I was dissatisfied in the thought that I was spending a significant portion of my professional life on a single case whose importance was no greater than plus or minus a few cents in the annual earnings of a corporation." The thought set him on a course that would eventually lead to an academic career. He wanted to focus not just on big corporations but also on individual people who were sometimes disadvantaged by large institutions.

In June 1959, an Illinois Supreme Court justice phoned Dallin to see if he would be willing to represent an indigent prisoner in his appeal before the court. This justice had taken a personal interest in Dallin and saw him as a young man who would help a poor person without compensation and persuade his firm to approve. Dallin accepted the responsibility "with the greatest pleasure," and everyone he worked with at the firm consented.

Dallin prepared a lengthy and thorough brief, and on March 15, 1960, he and June went to the state capital, Springfield, where Dallin argued the case before the Illinois Supreme Court—his first appellate court argument. Despite his best efforts, the outcome was not satisfying. The justices acknowledged errors in the trial but found the evidence of guilt so overwhelming that they voted unanimously to affirm the conviction. Nevertheless, Dallin recorded, "I was satisfied that I had done my best" for a downtrodden client. The experience was significant as well because opposing counsel was an assistant state's attorney, James R. Thompson, who later taught at Northwestern University law school, became a U.S. attorney, and was eventually elected governor of Illinois.[1]

Three months after arguing the case, Dallin was surprised when that client's brother showed up at his Chicago office. He wanted to compensate Dallin for the legal work he had done. He placed a thousand dollars in bills on the desk, promising to pay the rest in installments over the next few months.

"I pointed out," Dallin wrote, "that the case had been lost and that I had acted without compensation under the appointment of the court." Dallin told the man he owed him nothing. But it was a matter of honor for the young man, and he kept urging Dallin to take the money.

Finally, Dallin told him that if he wanted to do something to discharge his feeling of obligation, he could pay two hundred dollars, which would cover the firm's actual costs in defending his brother and provide a small token payment to the firm.

"At this," Dallin wrote, "he wept." The young man said he and his wife had spent many months saving the one thousand dollars and now could meet some of their own needs, such as buying a washing machine.

"I was very touched by this," Dallin wrote, "and proud that I had been able to give my services, even unsuccessfully, to a family with such integrity and responsibility." The satisfaction Dallin felt from serving in this way "contrasted sharply," he wrote, "with my diminishing sense of satisfaction in pursuing the economic issues in the corporate litigation in which I was involved. I pondered that contrast in the year that followed and was uneasy."

Another contrast with work in the firm was the satisfaction Dallin and June felt in their Church service. June held a series of teaching calls in their local ward, and Dallin also had callings that allowed him to serve others and grow spiritually.

First, he served as a counselor in the Sunday School presidency to George G. Jackson, the medical school professor who recommended their obstetrician. In the Sunday School role, Dallin wrote, "I had my first opportunity to supervise gospel teaching and to conduct large Church meetings. I studied how to conduct with a minimum of words and with a maximum contribution to the spirit and purpose of the meeting." These were skills he would apply throughout his life.

Dallin also served as a counselor in the Chicago Stake genealogy organization, allowing him to further his long-standing interest in family history. But the Church calling with the most impact required him to sacrifice a great deal of time when he seemingly had almost none to give.

"Dallin was asked to go out tracting with the stake missionary president tonight and tomorrow night," June wrote to relatives on June 14, 1960. "He was unable to go tonight but will go tomorrow. I don't suppose it will be long until he will be asked to go on a stake mission. Actually, I would prefer him gone every night on a mission than I would for him to be down at the office. At least he would come home for dinner and spend a few minutes with the children before their bedtime."

In early 1961, Dallin was invited to lunch by a man he admired greatly, Chicago Stake President John K. Edmunds, himself a practicing lawyer. Over lunch, President Edmunds called Dallin to serve a stake mission and to be a counselor in the stake mission presidency. June's earlier premonitions meant he shouldn't have been surprised, but he was. "I told him," Dallin wrote, that "I couldn't have been any more surprised . . . if he had asked me to be the staff physician in a hospital. I told him I'd never turned down a Church job and that I wasn't going to start now, but . . . did he know that he was calling a man to a position of leadership in missionary work who had never been on a mission?"

Yes, President Edmunds answered, both he and the stake mission president were aware of that, and both felt confident he was the person for the job. In extending the call, Dallin wrote, President Edmunds told him the calling "would require forty hours of proselyting per month, plus gospel study and other time—equivalent to at least three to four evenings per week."

Since Dallin's heavy load at the firm already kept him at work three or four evenings a week, the calling required a great exercise of faith. "I couldn't see how I could accept this calling and still keep up with my law practice," Dallin agonized. "Yet I could not say no to a calling that I knew to be from the Lord, especially when that calling came through a servant of the Lord who had wielded such a powerful influence in teaching me righteous principles. Gathering all my faith, I accepted the call."[2]

That evening, he went on his first missionary visit with the stake mission president, who was then his missionary companion. Thereafter for two years, Dallin labored an average of thirty hours a month doing missionary work and spent additional time fulfilling his duties in the mission presidency. "June supported me completely," he wrote. "The full-time mission experience I had missed was at least partly recompensed in this choice experience." Dallin and his companions baptized some ten people from five different families. "We tracted some," he summarized, "but mostly met contacts we had generated through friendship or on referral from Church members."

At the time, Dallin saw these blessings as at least partial fulfillment of a promise in his patriarchal blessing. "It shall be your privilege to preach the gospel at home and abroad," the patriarch had declared. "You shall manifest power and your faith among your companions wherever you go."

Dallin's call as a stake missionary came about the same time his sister, Evelyn, received a call to serve a full-time mission in France. "This short letter must substitute for my presence at your farewell," he wrote to her from Chicago. "I could not be more pleased." Alluding to his own recent call and reports of missionary success in Europe, he added,

"Who among us who has felt the pulse of missionary work these last few years would not welcome your opportunity? Who would not welcome the call to see and feel at first hand the surge of activity and the power of conversion we now read of in Europe! I thrill for you, I commend you, I—yes, I confess, I envy you. Who would not?"

Dallin offered two pieces of advice. "First," he wrote, "go with faith. We often hear that faith can move mountains. It is more important to remember that it can move people. . . .

"Second," he advised, "be not too easily discouraged, and, what seems more important to missionaries in these times, be not flattered by success. . . . In the flush of success and the joy of conversions, ever bear in mind that you convert no one, that it is the Holy Ghost which bears testimony which converts. You can only arrest the attention and inform the mind of your contacts. Their spirits can be touched and their souls can be won only by Him in whose service you labor."

Dallin took this advice himself. He worked hard and humbly, refusing to be discouraged. His stake mission brought with it a wealth of gospel knowledge as he studied the scriptures and learned from the stake mission president, a man of faith. But perhaps the greatest learning came from Dallin's own exercise of faith. Logically speaking, it did not seem possible for him to fulfill his Church calling and perform well at the law firm. But he came to recognize "the unusual—even miraculous—blessings that come to those who serve the Lord."

After just two weeks of missionary service, he testified to his mother, "I am deriving great happiness from this work, and I know the Lord is blessing me to accomplish my legal work with greater efficiency so that I can give my full devotion to His service." By the end of March, he reported to loved ones: "My missionary work continues at [a] fearful pace. . . . My whole day is upside down already, and my primary devotion is . . . to my missionary work, with law being secondary. Yet I'm getting my work done."

"Though I was devoting less time to law firm work," Dallin later reflected, "my advancement in the firm and my success in my work seemed to accelerate rather than decline. On several occasions, I received late-afternoon assignments for night work when I had an evening missionary appointment. After fervent prayer, I went to the firm library and was prompted in where to look to complete my research assignment and with words to write the memo in record time. In two years, I did not have to break one missionary appointment."

Once he thought he would have to skip a missionary appointment when he was assigned to meet with a legal client the same evening. But then the missionary contact phoned to postpone the meeting because of his own conflict. "Feeling the Lord magnify me professionally as I sought to serve Him," Dallin concluded, "solidified my commitment to serve the Lord first, knowing that I could do more professionally in part of my time with His help than in all of my time without it."

In August 1962, when the stake mission president was released, Dallin was called to take his place and was set apart by a conference visitor from Utah, Elder Boyd K. Packer, an assistant to the Quorum of the Twelve. "June wholeheartedly supported me," Dallin wrote. "She could not be more wonderful." Elder Packer set Dallin apart, blessing him and, through him, June and the children. "Interestingly enough," Dallin wrote, "much of his blessing dealt with how much more effective I would be able to use my time in my work so that time would remain to fill my calling." Dallin knew the blessing would "be fulfilled, as I have enjoyed just such blessings ever since accepting this stake mission assignment."

"The calling to a stake mission was the third and decisive influence that separated me from the practice of law," Dallin later concluded. "The satisfaction I derived from the missionary work in the spring and summer of 1961 and its influence in breaking the pattern of my every-weeknight law firm routine prepared me for the offer I was to receive that summer."

Back in November 1960, Dallin wrote to his mother. "I've been pretty restless lately," he admitted, "not content to spend my life quarreling over whether the X company or the Y company keeps the cash. I get more thrill out of helping some poor soul. . . . I enjoy the competition in big practice, but I fail to see how society is the better for my file-searching."

His stock at the law firm "seems to be at an all-time high," he assured her, but he felt "more certain than ever" his days there were numbered. That month Dean Edward H. Levi had inquired about Dallin's interest in a faculty position at the University of Chicago Law School. Dallin had thought of other options, too—including having a private practice in Provo or Salt Lake City while teaching part-time at the University of Utah or BYU. Spending summers with family and in the mountains appealed to him and June. He told his mother there would "be some soul-searching going on around here these next few weeks, and a good deal of praying too." He asked for her thoughts and prayers and welcomed her counsel.

Dallin and June pondered and prayed fervently about the Chicago offer but in the end "could not feel peaceful about it." When they declined the offer, the dean "was very disappointed, but nice about it," Dallin wrote to family. Feeling Dean Levi would not understand their spiritual reasons, Dallin told him he didn't yet feel he had the professional experience to teach. The dean "replied," Dallin wrote, "that I should keep him posted as to my feelings, and he implied strongly that the offer would be open whenever I chose to take it."

At the end of November 1960, not long after that conversation, one of the senior partners of the Kirkland firm invited Dallin to his office for a chat, saying he sensed his young colleague wasn't happy. "I replied frankly that I was not," Dallin recorded, "that I felt I was not getting the kind of experience I needed." Two senior partners soon assured him they would reduce his travel and give the tedious document-searching tasks to someone else. "Then, to sweeten up the proceedings," Dallin wrote, one of the partners "explained the importance of my long-range happiness by saying that he expects that in not too many years this firm will belong to (be run by) me and two others," including his friend Robert Bork, "so that they wish to 'weld us to them with bands of steel.'

"I rather expect," Dallin guessed, that "they plan to use gold instead." He and June talked about this and reported their reaction in a letter to family: "We'll wait and see how we feel about Chicago and the firm after a while." During 1961, other job offers came in, which they declined. Finally, on Thursday, July 27, Dean Levi phoned Dallin and again offered him a professorship. Dallin was hesitant but agreed to talk. They met that afternoon, and what the dean said "gave me much food for thought," Dallin wrote. As he discussed this with June, he wrote, "I'd only gotten halfway through before she said, 'Let's do it, it sounds good to me.' It sounded good to me too."

"I certainly am not sure that I want to be a law professor for life," Dallin wrote to family, "but I would like to try this for additional experience and prestige. I knew that I could leave teaching for practice at any time, and I felt that at this point a year's experience or two years' experience at U of C would leave me a more valuable person than another year with Kirkland."

Over the weekend, Dallin and June fasted and prayed about the decision, and on Monday, July 31, he phoned the dean and accepted the job, beginning October 1. When he broke the news to the senior partners at the firm, "they were stunned" but quickly regrouped and told him to consider his teaching as "a leave of absence" from Kirkland. They agreed to pay him for part-time work at the firm and said they would welcome him back at any time.

Everything fell together so well, Dallin wrote, "that I felt . . . this whole thing was just being prepared for me ready-made . . . to equip me for some future job I must do."

He was right. He just didn't know yet what it would be.

CHAPTER 7

"THE DIVIDENDS OF ACADEMIC LIFE"

First Years of Teaching

After receiving his faculty appointment, Dallin sent a letter to Chief Justice Earl Warren for whom he had clerked years earlier. "Dean Levi told me that he had written to you about my appointment to the faculty," Dallin wrote. "I began my duties October 1, and I am very happy with my new activity. Among my duties this fall quarter is participation in the seminar we give on the work of the United States Supreme Court, where students read the briefs and discuss the cases being argued during the term."

Dallin knew that was something the Chief would appreciate and added words about his mentor's example. "I have often reflected on your counsel about the happiness and satisfaction which comes from public service," he wrote. "I hope that this new position will offer me those same advantages." Dallin's young family was already benefiting from his move to teaching. "June and the children are also enjoying some of the dividends of academic life," he explained to the Chief Justice, "particularly the greater freedom I enjoy to spend time with them."

On Sunday morning, November 5, 1961—slightly more than a

month after he changed jobs—Dallin sat down in their Elmhurst home to type a long-overdue letter to family members elsewhere. "Lloyd is beside me insisting on pushing the carriage of the typewriter when I get to each end of the line," Dallin wrote. "It does not speed things," he noted wittily.

June was expecting another baby. She "feels well, though she tires easily," Dallin reported. "She says to tell you she feels 'fine.' Right now she is dressing Dallin D. here at the dining room table where I am typing. That little fellow is finally starting to walk." Cheri was "growing like a weed" and was now "about four inches taller than Sharmon." Meanwhile, Sharmon was growing in her own way. "This morning she is giving a 2½ [minute] talk which she wrote entirely herself." Clearly family life appealed to the new professor.

June and Dallin wanted a large family at a time when oral contraceptives were becoming available and many people in society began to call for population control. On one occasion, when June had already had a few children and was pregnant with another, a Church member in Illinois asked her if she was "trying to populate the world all by herself." With June's typical forthrightness, she replied, "I can't think of anyone better to do it."[1]

Dallin loved June and their children, and as good as he felt about joining the faculty, he sensed that he had a greater mission in life than being a law professor. Of the several faculty committees on which he now sat, he mentioned only one specifically. "I am chairman," he wrote, "of the faculty committee on legal aid." He would soon serve also as a member of the Committee on Legal Clinics of the Association of American Law Schools. Helping others was ingrained in his being, and he would devote a lot of time during his tenure at the school to aiding the downtrodden.

Dallin also continued to find satisfaction in his missionary calling. "Today we had our monthly stake missionary meeting," he wrote to family on December 10. "Through November we have baptized sixty-six converts in our stake mission. . . . We are very pleased, and yet we feel the pulse of the work now and are convinced that even greater things lie ahead."

He had a sense of calling that seemed to infuse even his law school work. On Sunday afternoon, February 18, 1962, he found himself at home, worn out and sidelined by sickness. "Today I am home in pajamas, bathrobe, and the good warm house-shoes Mother knit for me, enjoying a brief bout of flu," he wrote to family. He recounted the recent and unexpected death of fellow professor Karl Llewellyn, "probably the most famous member of our faculty." Karl's wife had asked Dallin to be a pallbearer at his funeral. "Only last week," Dallin wrote, "I had sat by Karl and Rabbi Weinstein, a local Jewish dignitary, at a dinner, where Karl explained to the Rabbi that I was one of the few young men who had a glimpse of his (Karl's) philosophy of law and that was why he was so pleased that I had been 'called' (his word) to the faculty."

Later, Dean Levi asked Dallin to teach Karl's class until Karl's widow, Soia Mentchikoff—who was a "professorial lecturer" at the school—could take over. Dallin accepted the assignment with his usual gusto. When he taught the last class session, the students, to his surprise, gave him an ovation. Later, a student approached him in the library and tried to express his feelings of appreciation.

"Mr. Oaks," he began, haltingly. "I, uh, uh, well, I won't be taking any more courses from you in law school, that is, well, I uh, well, uh, that's just how my program works out; what I mean is, I've got no ax to grind, and, uh, well, uh, I just want to tell you that I'm impressed! You're really going to be a helluva good teacher someday."

"I thanked him," Dallin wrote, "for I'm sure he meant a compliment, but I've been snickering about this for a week, and Ed Levi laughed out loud when I told him."

Despite Dallin's prestigious position, he did not lose touch with his humble roots. In the same letter, he added a personal note to his mother and her parents, expressing his love and gratitude. "Grandpa," Dallin wrote, "I think of our experiences on the farm so often. It is a priceless heritage to have one's roots in the soil and one's aspirations in the skies. You gave us both of these."

As April 12 approached—the day June was due to enter the hospital and deliver their newest baby—Dallin grew nervous about the operation. "I will telephone each of you as soon as it is over," he wrote to family members. "We will administer to her beforehand, of course, and count also on your united faith and prayers for her. We are so grateful that Mother Dixon is coming to lend her strength—I am particularly grateful, for I would have been so alone." Dallin and June had picked out a name. "The baby will be named TruAnn if she is a girl," he wrote, "and we remain uncertain on a boy's name."

As it turned out, the baby was a girl, and little TruAnn Oaks soon entered their lives and their family.

In the spring of 1962, only six months after Dallin assumed his professorship at the University of Chicago, he found himself propelled into a prominent and difficult role when Dean Edward Levi of the law

The University of Chicago Law School

school became provost of the university. To help fill the vacancy created by Dean Levi's new appointment, Dallin was named associate dean of the law school, with two assistant deans reporting to him. Although Dallin willingly assumed the role, he did not relish it and hoped it would be just a temporary assignment. "Now don't make too much out of this," he wrote family members. "I'm getting out of it as quickly as a successor is appointed." Still, he couldn't help feeling he was being prepared for leadership in this role he had not sought.

Almost immediately, the role placed a heavy burden on him. "I find this position is no joke or façade," he exclaimed to family on May 6. "Edward Levi tells me he expects me to run things (as much as any dean can run a strong faculty, which isn't much)." On May 25, Dallin added, "This associate dean business has been really boiling along this past two weeks. . . . And it's bound to get worse before it gets better.

"Along with all the rest," he reported, "I've been putting in a heavier than average missionary schedule: over fifty hours of proselyting each month for the past three months, in addition to about fifteen or twenty hours of mission administrative time."

Besides that, he spent two days in Washington, DC, where he spoke with Chief Justice Warren and was pressured by the assistant secretary of the treasury to become a special consultant to help prepare U.S. President John F. Kennedy's tax message for Congress. Dallin declined the offer primarily because it would interfere with a commitment he made to his family to vacation in Utah.

He and June took their children to the services at which Church President David O. McKay dedicated their new stake center in Wilmette, Illinois. "We got good seats, by going two hours early," Dallin wrote, adding about President McKay, "I especially wanted the children to see him since I can still remember seeing President Heber J. Grant when he came to Twin Falls when I can't have been more than about five years old."

Being put into the associate dean role at a young age made Dallin a prime candidate for recruitment by other schools. In October, the University of Chicago appointed him acting dean, and some at the law school wanted to make the appointment permanent. "Two members of the faculty have assured me that my colleagues would enthusiastically support me for the job and that the president . . . would probably appoint me," Dallin wrote to his mother on November 1. "I made it clear that I did not feel ready (yet) and would not accept."

In November, the list of responsibilities Dallin had at work and church led him to write, "I have spent the busiest three weeks of my life this month." One task he listed was trying to get U.S. Supreme Court clerkships for his law school's graduates. He took Rex Lee, a third-year student ranking at the top of his class, to meet Chief Justice Warren in Washington. "My purpose, of course, was to try to get him to choose Rex as his law clerk for next year," Dallin wrote. The Chief "was very gracious."

By December 1962, Dallin felt burdened down by the combined weight of his teaching and administrative loads. He wrote to his friend Robert Bork, expressing frustration with the administrative work, which he called "walking on eggs (or working with them)." The next day, he wrote Stewart Grow, a friend at BYU. "As for me," he confided, "I am still uncertain whether I want to stay in teaching." Administrative work "has not increased my short-term enjoyment of academic life," he admitted. Mercifully, the acting dean role eventually came to an end.

"Finally," Dallin wrote with relief, "my ordeal ended." In early January 1963, the university president appointed someone else as the new law school dean. Dallin "immediately wrote a note expressing my appreciation to the faculty for their 'fine cooperation during a trying period now concluded'" and moved back into "my faculty office with a profound sense of relief and gratitude."

Yet because of this experience, over the next few years Dallin was approached by search committees of several schools looking for new deans.[2] "In every case," he wrote, "I declined to have my name considered. I thought I had had enough administration." The year he left the dean's office, he wrote to family after declining one such opportunity. "I am waiting for something," he wrote, "but I didn't feel that it was that." He received offers to be a visiting professor at numerous law schools—including Harvard, Stanford, and Berkeley—and turned those opportunities down too.[3]

Years later, he wrote, "Little did I dream that the distasteful administrative experience of the deanship had given me experiences and insight that would prove invaluable" in a future major assignment. "In this service, as in other ways," he wrote with the clarity of hindsight, "I was being prepared."

On February 3, 1963, about a month after Dallin left the acting dean's role, Elders LeGrand Richards and Howard W. Hunter of the Quorum of the Twelve Apostles were in Chicago to divide the stake in which Dallin was serving as stake mission president. "A few days before the division," Dallin recalled, "I had a strong impression that I would be called as the second counselor in the presidency of the new Chicago South Stake. Ascribing it to self-aggrandizement, I chastised myself for this impression, but it persisted. On the Saturday morning when the interviews were being held in Wilmette, I moped around the house in Elmhurst, puzzled and bruised that I had not been invited to participate."

Work had long been the medicine he took to reduce the aches and pains of life, and so around 10:00 a.m.—to salve his bruised feelings—he told June he was going to the university. He went into the garage to get into his car when he was unexpectedly called back into the house to take a phone call. The call was from someone at the stake center, inviting him to come in for an interview with the Apostles. Just as he had been prompted, they called him to be second counselor in the presidency of a new stake being split off from the old one.

Always good at keeping confidences, Dallin phoned June later in the day to explain that they couldn't keep a scheduled appointment they had made at a local car dealership. "When Dallin called," June wrote in a family letter, "I questioned him, but he would tell me nothing. I thought that something was going on, but I couldn't quite tell what. When he came home, he continued acting a little strange and yet happy.

"Well," June wrote, "Sunday morning the presidency was announced for the new Chicago South Stake, and I was pleased to know that Dallin had been chosen second counselor.

"In the afternoon session, the new stake presidencies and their wives were asked to speak. I just about died," June told family members. "I don't even get up to bear my testimony very often as I can't control my emotions, but I grit my teeth and did my best, but it wasn't without visual signs of emotion. Dallin certainly said some sweet things, and I was and am so very proud to be his wife."

Elder Howard W. Hunter "gave Dallin such a very sweet blessing when he was ordained a high priest and set apart," June said. "We were well-fed spiritually . . . , and there is no better feeling in all the world.

"I think it will be quite an adjustment for Dallin not to be engaged in missionary work," June commented. "It has been such a part of him for the past two years. I know that he will be an asset, however, to the new stake presidency. Apostle Hunter in his setting him apart commented on his being so young for such a responsibility but said that this was a church of young men, that it had been restored by young men."[4]

"I was then 30½ years of age," Dallin later reflected. "I was to serve for seven and a half glorious years in that presidency, and for nine more months in the one that succeeded it."

He dove into his new calling with the same dedication he had given his missionary work. He learned to tie together his academic learning and spiritual interests. Dallin's first book was *The Wall Between Church*

Chicago South Stake President Lysle R. Cahoon, flanked by counselors John Sonnenberg and Dallin H. Oaks

and State, an edited collection of articles published by the University of Chicago Press. It went into a second printing, sold more than seven thousand copies, and enjoyed excellent book reviews and other feedback. "This book was very topical, in view of the then emerging decisions on school prayer," Dallin explained.

"My work on church and state and the current interest in school prayer," Dallin recalled, "led to my writing an article for lay readership, to explain the Supreme Court's school prayer decisions." Dallin's mother expressed concern about his proposed article since a statement attributed to President David O. McKay criticized the Supreme Court's decision on the topic. Dallin explained that this statement "unsettled" him, "more because I could see that whoever wrote it had never read or had any correct advice on the meaning of the decision than because of any fear about the wisdom of taking issue with him. I am confident that on this matter I have done nothing that will jeopardize my good standing or respect for the Brethren."

"By the way," Dallin added, "I talked to my stake president about this, and he just asked me two questions about it: 'Do you really believe what you say?' and 'Does anything you say or anything in President McKay's statement prevent you from sustaining him as a prophet?' When I answered these questions he said, 'Then what're you worrying about?' That's the sort of tolerance you get in the mission field, but not always in Utah."

Henry D. Moyle—a lawyer, counselor in the First Presidency, and fellow graduate of the University of Chicago Law School—visited Chicago soon thereafter, and Dallin gave him a copy of his school prayer manuscript. They had a great conversation, and President Moyle later wrote him a nice letter, though without mentioning the proposed article. Then on August 12, 1963—Dallin's thirty-first birthday—President Moyle wrote Dallin about it. "I have read it very carefully," he wrote, "and appreciate the keen scope of your analysis, and have no doubt the conclusions you reach are correct. I look upon it as a masterful discussion." President Moyle told Dallin he sent a copy to President McKay "because of his great interest in this case."

Dallin treasured President Moyle's letter and grew hopeful the Church would publish the article in the *Improvement Era,* a magazine later replaced by the *Ensign* and *New Era.* But in September, President Moyle passed away. "I admit that when I learned of his death, not having heard from the *Era,*" Dallin wrote to family, "I assumed that my article was a dead duck."

Eight days after President Moyle's death, however, Dallin unexpectedly received a letter from the managing editor of the *Era* announcing that "President McKay has encouraged us to use your article. President Moyle talked to him about it, called me twice on the telephone, and sent me a letter telling me of President McKay's approval."

The article appeared in the December 1963 issue under the title "Antidotes for the School Prayer Cases."[5] Prominent Latter-day Saint law professor Arvo Van Alstyne, then at Stanford University, wrote

Dallin, calling his article "one of the most timely and objective treatments of the subject for popular consumption which I have seen." He complimented Dallin on "countering some of the more extreme misunderstandings of the Supreme Court which have all too often been rife among Church members."

One morning in late 1963, Dallin delayed going into work so he could attend a school event with his son Lloyd. "This morning I visited his class," Dallin wrote to family that day. "When the teacher asked him to introduce me to the class, he said, 'This is Brother Oaks.' I almost choked to keep from laughing."

To Lloyd, his father may have been "Brother Oaks" in public, but to most members of the Chicago South Stake, he was President Oaks. Next to his family responsibilities, Dallin may have felt more satisfaction in his stake responsibilities than in any other facet of his life.

"This service in the stake presidency," he reflected, "was a period of great growth in faith, spirituality, and experience in Church administration . . . with all of its challenges in interviewing, counseling, planning, speaking, and leading. I learned a great deal from my fellow workers and had many choice spiritual and social experiences."

Once, Dallin opposed the stake president's proposal on where a new stake center should be built. In response, the stake president asked that they pray about the matter and discuss it the next week. "Almost perfunctorily," Dallin wrote, "I prayed about the subject, and immediately received a strong impression that I was wrong, that I was standing in the way of the Lord's will, and that I should remove myself from opposition to it. This was one of the most surprising and most vivid revelations I have ever received in my life. Needless to say, I promptly gave my approval to the proposed construction. The wisdom of constructing the stake center at that location was soon evident, even to me. My reasons to the contrary turned out to be shortsighted, and I was soon grateful to have been restrained by the Spirit from relying on them."

In preparing the many talks he had to give, Dallin learned to pray and jot down the thoughts that came to mind. "This happened so many times," he wrote, that "it became commonplace, and I would not begin to prepare a talk until I had this experience to direct me." Once the inspiration did not come before he left for a meeting where he was to speak. "I began my drive, feeling vulnerable, but trusting in the Lord," he wrote. As he approached his destination many miles from his home, the inspiration came: Speak about your experiences in Chicago's criminal courts.

"I was surprised to receive this impression," he recorded, "since I had always avoided building my talks around personal experiences, preferring a less personal doctrinal or practical theme. I had never referred to these experiences in a public meeting, but now I had a strong impression that I could do so, and several examples came to mind."

Trusting in the inspiration, he wove his personal experiences into a gospel-centered talk and mentioned seeing young shoplifters prosecuted. "Afterwards," he wrote, "a mother thanked me tearfully for being the means of answering her prayer. She told me that their teenage boy had been involved in shoplifting and that they had not been able to communicate with him on the wrongfulness of this practice. On learning that I was to be the speaker that Sunday evening, she had prayed fervently that I would say something to help their son with this problem. The boy was in the meeting, and I had spoken directly on that subject. . . . I have no doubt whatever that the Lord had used me as His instrument to answer her prayers. I was grateful I had heard and heeded His prompting."

CHAPTER 8

"MY WORK IS PROGRESSING"

Professor, Prosecutor, Defender

In December 1963, Dallin received an early Christmas present from the University of Chicago. "I received a bit of news last week," he wrote to family on December 13. "The university has appointed me professor of law with indefinite tenure (permanent appointment) effective October 1, 1964. . . . I hadn't expected this since . . . thirty-two is pretty young to be a full professor."

Dallin's responsibilities as a law professor, member of a stake presidency, and family man all helped fulfill a desire he expressed in college when choosing a major and a career. "I wanted to work with people," he had said. He wanted to serve others, and one way he did that professionally was to focus significant time on the legal problems of the poor.

"A major professional interest during the last seven years of my law school work," he later wrote, "was the problem of legal services for the poor. This built on my experience of reviewing indigent criminals' petitions in the Supreme Court, my subsequent interest in post-conviction review, and my experience advising the law school's legal aid clinic. . . . But the most important impetus was my summer 1964 experience in the criminal courts of Cook County."

Professor Dallin H. Oaks, 1964

Beginning Monday, June 1, during part of his summer break from school, he worked in the state's attorney's office doing work he found "incredibly interesting," he wrote. "There is no opportunity for preparation," he recounted. "The clerk calls the case, the defendant and police officers step forward, you confer hurriedly with the police officers to find out what it's all about, perhaps take thirty seconds to read a two-page police report, identify who the witnesses are (they are sometimes difficult to tell from the accused), and announce to the judge, 'The state is ready.'"

He explained that it was no better for the defendant, who was "represented by a lawyer he has retained or by a public defender designated by the court, neither of which has taken much more pains in preparation than you are privileged to take." After describing the various cases in which he had participated, he enthused, "This is proving to be a very enlightening experience."

"My work is progressing," he wrote several weeks later. "I'm now trying criminal cases all by myself, without even having another assistant in the room. I'm having many worthwhile experiences this summer," he wrote, "the most rewarding one professionally since I left Washington."

Dallin drove to Utah in mid-August and enjoyed time with family there and then returned to Chicago with June and the children. In September, June wrote back to family in Utah, chronicling among other things the recent stake conference that kept Dallin busy because of his stake presidency calling. "Dallin gave such a good talk yesterday in conference," she wrote. "I've heard many say that he is the best speaker in the stake. It seems so easy for him, but he does spend many hours in preparation."

Given his schedule at the time, it was remarkable he could spend any time at all on his talks. After stake conference ended, he wrote to family explaining how busy he had been at school. "I have never been so busy at work," he began—a remarkable statement given his past record. But the list of responsibilities he gave proved his point.

"I have initiated my ABA [American Bar Association] work, launched my first-year Legal Research & Writing Program (including breaking in my five teaching assistants), prepared two special lectures (using slides) on legal research, consulted continually with students on our legal aid project and moot court projects, started my daily classes on trust law, started my revision of the casebook on trusts, of which I am to be co-editor, . . . almost completed my habeas corpus article, undertaken a special report to the Illinois Supreme Court on the status of criminal justice in Cook County, due in about sixty days (this grew out of my summer activities), and managed a conference on judicial ethics, for which I am bringing judges from all over the country (seven of them, including from California and New York) to an all-day session at the law school next Thursday," he wrote. "In addition, I have had stake conference and other responsibilities for the last two weeks that took every evening and all day Saturday and Sunday."

Rather than pleading exhaustion, however, Dallin seemed energized by it all. "It's been an invigorating season," he concluded.

Almost as an afterthought, he mentioned later in the letter that the previous Monday, he had been invited to Washington, DC, "to consult with the Department of Health, Education, and Welfare, National Institutes of Health," and "Bureau of Mental Health," because of his experience in providing "legal aid to indigent persons." It was as if he just got stronger and stronger with every challenge he tackled.

Amid the flurry of events, there was one he missed: the Utah funeral for his maternal grandfather, S. A. Harris, who had been like a father to him after his own father's death. "It was not business that kept me from Grandpa's funeral, nor want of funds," Dallin wrote soberly, "for both are available for such things as these." Rather, he and June had prayed about the matter and felt impressed he should not go. Though Dallin felt they made the right decision, he suffered pangs of emotion at not being there. When he read his mother's account of the services, he wept openly, even though he was on a train into Chicago at the time, surrounded by other commuters.

Thoughts of family members, particularly those deceased, continued to flood his mind, and in November 1964, he wrote to his mother, "I've had genealogy on the mind this last little while." Since she was planning to visit Chicago for Christmas—along with Dallin's brother, Merrill, and his wife, Jo—Dallin proposed that he, Merrill, and Mother drive to New York and Pennsylvania together "to do research on Oaks genealogy." He proposed driving at night (while others dozed in sleeping bags in the station wagon) and doing genealogy during the day. "Let me know how you feel," he requested.

Family history had been a longtime passion for him. Later, when June's parents passed through Chicago on a trip east, June and Dallin set up their tape recorder to capture some oral history. "We managed to get both of them to fill a tape with their recollections of their childhood and early married life," Dallin related. "This, when transcribed, will furnish the basis for a wonderful life history of each of them."

On November 9, Dallin was home caring for the children while

June was attending one of the college classes she was taking for her degree. "June is gone to class," Dallin wrote to family, "and I have been enjoying my first evening home since last week. I've read to TruAnn, helped Cheri with 2½ minute talk for Sunday, washed a few dishes with Sharmon, consulted with Lloyd about a project for Saturday, and put Dallin D. to bed early, as he was quite tired.

"During the week," Dallin typed, "I received another invitation to attend another federal conference on the poverty program this Thursday through Saturday in Washington." During that era of the "war on poverty," he worried that trendy approaches to helping the poor were aimed at symptoms, not causes. He confessed he didn't have "much stomach" for such programs. Rather, he was "a strong advocate of the lawyer's responsibility to aid the poor on a voluntary basis, not only by giving of his time to represent them, but also by reforming the laws that work repressively on the poor." He told family, "I think we make a mistake trying to treat the symptoms of the disease (i.e., bankruptcy proceedings free of charge for wage earners who get too deeply in debt). I believe the money ought to be spent for better adult education and social work with these people."

A significant proportion of his work at the law school concerned helping the poor. "I'm being excused from my winter teaching assignment so I can prepare a new Seminar on the Legal Problems of the Poor (with emphasis on law reform—something I am interested in) and so I can get a legal aid clinic going for our students to furnish aid to criminal defendants," he wrote. "This will build on my experience last summer. We already have a legal aid clinic handling about six thousand civil cases per year for poor folks in the neighborhood. I am faculty adviser to this."

Part of what qualified him for this role, he decided, was his own personal experience with the subject. "I told someone the other day," he wrote half in jest, "that I was the logical 'poverty' expert on the faculty because I earned both my degrees in poverty." He knew he had been richly blessed with educational opportunities, but taking advantage of those gifts had required living on the margins economically. "June and I come closer to being experts than most of our friends, but we treasure those days as students," he wrote.

In February, as part of his program to provide student help to indigent criminals, Dallin represented by court appointment an African-American man, Ernest Thompson, who had been convicted of burglary while struggling to provide for his family. When it came time for sentencing, the judge gave Ernest the lightest sentence allowed for a conviction—one to four years behind bars—and Ernest thanked Dallin. "I just want you to know, Mr. Oaks, that I think you gave me a wonderful representation," he said. "This didn't go as I wanted it to, but I know you did everything you could, and I am grateful."

"I felt well repaid for my efforts," Dallin wrote, "and my three student assistants were very pleased also."

In the spring of 1965, Dallin, June, and family moved from their Elmhurst home to a larger one in an old residential neighborhood on

Oaks home at 10750 South Seeley Avenue, Chicago

Chicago's south side, closer to the university. Built in 1926, this new residence better met their growing family's needs. Originally, Dallin planned to hire a moving company, but after considering the cost, he elected to rent a truck instead and hire someone to help him with the heavy lifting. About that time, Ernest Thompson, who was free while awaiting appeal, contacted Dallin to say he had caught up on some family bills and now wanted to pay Dallin for some extra legal work he had done.

"I told him," Dallin wrote family, that "I hated to take any money from him, as I knew he was short . . . , but I would be delighted to consider myself paid if he'd give me a day's work in helping me move. He expressed great pleasure in accepting."

Ernest, a longshoreman by occupation, worked hard, and Dallin later wrote to family that he was of "superb help, frequently rushing to take the heavy end of every article so I wouldn't strain myself."

"You know about being a lawyer, Mr. Oaks," Ernest told him, "but I know about this lifting."

When they finished, both men were famished, and Dallin invited Ernest to supper with his family in their new home. "I told him," Dallin wrote, "that he was our first houseguest, and we were honored."

After dinner, as Ernest was leaving, he said, "Mr. Oaks, I thank you for inviting me to take a meal with your family." Ernest told June "that none of his friends would believe him if he told them that he'd eaten with his white lawyer, at his invitation, so he just wouldn't tell them."

Dallin felt dining with Ernest had been important for him and his family members. "We gain much understanding by such associations," he reflected.

Dallin's efforts to help the poor also had a national dimension. His earlier contacts with federal agencies on the topic were making him a recognized authority in the field. The federal Office of Economic Opportunity invited him to attend a White House conference on law and poverty from June 22 to 24, 1965. Dallin wrote family members about the conference and noted too "that both of my summer clinical training projects have materialized. I'll have thirteen law students working at various locations around the U.S. with public defenders, neighborhood legal aid clinics, etc., . . . and about twenty students working at the law school writing briefs for indigent criminals whom the public defender is assisting with their appeals (and we are assisting them)."

In November 1965, the Office of Economic Opportunity again invited Dallin to Washington for meetings. He went, got to know the head of the legal services program there, liked him, and felt they would work well together. "After the meetings were over," Dallin wrote, "I went up to the Supreme Court for an appointment with Earl Warren. He welcomed me cordially and invited me to lunch with him and his three law clerks. We went to the National Lawyers Club as his guests, where we spent [from] 12:45 until 4:45 sitting at the luncheon table talking. . . . It was a great visit, one of the best times I've had in ages."

Dallin's only regret was being away from June and their children during that time. "When I get home after two weeks like the past ones," he wrote to family elsewhere, "I just soak up the family. I can't bring myself to shoo them away while I write a letter, and I don't believe any of you would want me to."

When Dallin could be home, he often turned the time with their children into teaching moments. One day, drawing on the experience working on his grandparents' farm, he tried to teach his young son Lloyd about the principle of tithing. If a farmer had ten eggs, he would give one as tithing, Dallin instructed. The same would be true if he had ten lambs or ten bushels of peaches.

"In an effort to test his understanding of the principle," Dallin related, "I asked him if he were a farmer, what he would give as tithing?"

Not yet converted to the principle, Lloyd replied, "A very old horse."

In March 1966, Dallin wrote to family that he was applying to the

Office of Economic Opportunity on behalf of the state of Wisconsin "for about $400,000 to fund a legal aid program for the northern third of the state." Dallin liked the idea of having the government pay "the fees of private lawyers chosen by the client, instead of setting up a whole new set of federal 'legal aid' offices. I'm assisting . . . with this application . . . on assignment from the Office of Economic Opportunity."

On top of all his legal work, Dallin continued to serve in the stake presidency, a time-consuming assignment. In late summer of 1966, during an era when local Church members helped build their own meetinghouses, Dallin accepted an assignment to work on their new stake center. "They put me to work on a scaffold about twenty to twenty-five feet high, nailing up ceiling board on the top of the gymnasium," Dallin wrote, and he dutifully complied. He was accustomed to working with his hands, but working above his head at that height was something unusual. "That took getting used to," he realized.

Along with everything else he was doing, Dallin pursued an interest he had in Church history. In 1967, he and Joseph I. Bentley, a law student at Chicago, began research on important but previously unknown legal proceedings involving Joseph Smith and the Church. Earlier, Dallin and Marvin S. Hill—then a PhD candidate at the University of Chicago and later a history professor at BYU—decided to write an article "on the trial of the murderers of the Prophet Joseph Smith." To write his portion, Dallin needed to do research in western Illinois, and he decided in the late summer of 1966 to turn the trip into a family vacation.

As a young man with a family, Dallin tried to save on vacation costs by roughing it. As a youth, he liked to hunt, fish, and camp. "My dad's a man's man," his son Dallin D. later said—a real outdoorsman. But June was not. "We would go on these camping trips," daughter Cheri remembered, "and Dad would take this tarp and run it from the station wagon down to the ground, and we would skinny our

Oaks family, about 1966

sleeping bags under this tarp. That's how we took a number of our first trips." That frugal approach worked fine for a while, but June eventually reached her limit. "I remember Mom put her foot down," Cheri recalled. "She said, 'I will not be sleeping under a tarp!' That's how we got our first tent."

"Last week we bought a seven-man tent and went camping," Dallin wrote family members. "June said this tent is what would persuade her, so I made the investment. I had to visit Springfield and Carthage to do research on my article . . . , so we decided to make a family day of it. We left here Tuesday morning and arrived in Springfield at noon. I worked through the afternoon in the library while June and kids saw Lincoln's tomb, etc.

"That evening we drove to New Salem and camped in a state park," he reported. "The next day we spent three hours touring the restored buildings (log cabins from the 1830s) in New Salem and then drove to Carthage, where I did a few hours research, then on to a state park in Nauvoo, where we stayed that night. . . . The next morning, we drove around Nauvoo some more, then went to Warsaw (old anti-Mormon center), then on to Carthage for about six hours more research."

They had a great time as a family living in the tent, cooking their food on a charcoal stove, and snoozing on sleeping bags over air mattresses that all "wheezed out their air by morning." Dallin happily announced to family, "June is converted to the out-of-doors," which had long been a love of his, passed on to him by his father. "Wonderful what a little canvas will do," he marveled.

Being with the family was delightful, but another highlight was Dallin's discovery in Carthage of "the original records of the trial of the murderers of the Prophet Joseph Smith—never before published." This discovery propelled the Oaks and Hill article into what proved to be a popular and highly acclaimed book, *Carthage Conspiracy: The Trial of the Accused Assassins of Joseph Smith,* which would be published by the University of Illinois Press in 1975 and remains in print to this day.[1]

In a letter home, Dallin brought the Utah family up to date on the Ernest Thompson case. He reminded them that Ernest had been "found inside a tavern at 5 a.m., drunk," when originally arrested. On his appeal of Ernest's conviction, Dallin reported that he began his oral argument before the three appellate judges by referring to the famous novel *Les Misérables.*

"Victor Hugo immortalized the story of the pathetic Frenchman who was sent to the galleys for five years, for burglary, for breaking a window and stealing a loaf of bread," Dallin began. "If the court please, I would like to suggest that my client Ernest Thompson is a sort of twentieth-century Jean Valjean. He is being sent to the penitentiary for almost five years, for burglary, for breaking a window, entering, and drinking a quart of gin."

The judges, however, did not seem moved, and Dallin thought they may have missed his point. But when the prosecutor rose to respond, "one of the judges leaned forward with a twinkle in his eye and said, 'I presume you are Mr. Javert?'" (Dallin reminded his letter's readers that Javert was "the indefatigable and untiring policeman who pursued Valjean.")

Despite Dallin's best efforts, the court affirmed Ernest's conviction. "Ernest took it like a man," Dallin wrote. "I had told him from the start that I thought there was little hope. I go to court tomorrow to ask permission for him to spend Christmas with his family, so he can start serving the sentence Dec. 28th." By taking his appeal and getting him out of jail on bond, however, Dallin had made it possible for Ernest to get a good-paying job, provide for his wife and three children, and show that "his rehabilitation had already begun" and perhaps even finished. "I argued that in view of these facts, he ought to be granted probation and excused from serving any time, but the court disagreed, probably properly. I suspect that he will serve the minimum, probably about a year."

CHAPTER 9

"GOING ALL THE TIME"

Scholar and Administrator

One attraction of leaving the law firm for teaching was the opportunity it gave Dallin for a summer break from the norm, including the opportunity to focus on his scholarship. In May 1967, he wrote family members that he had "agreed at the urging of the Department of Justice and several key federal judges to supervise a study of the operation of the Criminal Justice Act of 1964 in the one hundred federal [district] courts throughout the country. This is the act that provides for payment of counsel fees and expenses for poor people who can't afford to provide their own defense in federal criminal cases."

Besides supervising a team of workers on the project, Dallin personally visited district courts in Arizona, California, New York City, and Wisconsin. He made his visits to Arizona and California into a family outing, driving west along the famous Route 66. On September 25, June reported in a letter to relatives that it was, on the whole, "the most fun and best summer we've ever had."

An aspect of Dallin's sense of humor that his children appreciated was his playful use of unfamiliar words to characterize things they saw. Once during a rest break on a road trip, they encountered a filthy bathroom that disgusted them all. "It looks like the barbarians have been here," Dallin commented wryly, lightening the mood. The children had not known what "barbarian" meant, but they never forgot his use of the term.

Besides being fun for family, the summer of 1967 proved productive, too. Dallin wrote of his study, "You would think I was the attorney general himself the way the judges and U.S. attorneys and clerks put themselves out to fulfill my requests. They apparently consider this study important."

Dallin reported to eight federal judges who were members of the Judicial Conference Committee to implement the Criminal Justice Act. Their chairman, Alfred Murrah—chief judge of the Tenth Circuit Court of Appeals in Denver—told Dallin how highly he regarded Latter-day Saints. "I've never yet had any experience where my religion was not a strong positive factor," Dallin wrote to family, "but I never cease to be impressed with the high regard in which . . . fair-minded men of the world" held members of the Church.

When the summer ended, Dallin gathered data from his team members and over succeeding months wrote the final report of his study. "Dallin is working harder than he ever has in his whole life," June wrote to family on December 18, 1967. "He is beginning to think that he can finish this report on schedule. He had various lawyers and judges to the university yesterday for a meeting, and they were all very complimentary on his work, and all said they didn't know how he had been able to do so much work."

The study, delivered as promised on the last day of the year, was hailed as "a treasury of information and guidance upon which sound statutory amendments, increased appropriations, and improved administration can be built for the future." Another reviewer called it "a model for future scholarly evaluation of procedural changes in the criminal system."

When Dallin gave his final report to the Judicial Conference

Dallin and others meeting with President Lyndon B. Johnson

Committee in January 1968, one of them, a friend of the U.S. president, took the group to the White House. "Yesterday I had an unusual experience," Dallin wrote in a family letter. "I spent thirty-three minutes with Lyndon B. Johnson in the cabinet room in the White House." Dallin's study was published by the Government Printing Office and distributed to all federal judges and U.S. attorneys. He summarized the study in the lead article of the *American Bar Association Journal* March 1968 issue under the title "Improving the Criminal Justice Act."

In a letter to friends and family on April 12, Dallin mentioned this and other professional milestones over the past three years, including publication of two coauthored books: *Cases on the Law of Trusts* and *A Criminal Justice System and the Indigent: A Study of Chicago and Cook County.*

"In the way of personal pleasures," he noted, "the whole family has taken up camping. June was the last one to be convinced. The children were won over by a tent, but it took tent, Coleman lantern, and camp stove before June joined up with any enthusiasm. Through the children's urging, we have all become fishermen. Last summer we enjoyed some outstanding trout fishing times in Utah, especially the two ventures when Lloyd and I *and June* each caught our limit in an hour's time on flies."

In the prior three years, they had also lost friends and loved ones, "including June's father, Charles H. Dixon," Dallin wrote, "who was also my Father and dear friend." As part of the letter, Dallin bore testimony. "At this Easter Season," he wrote, "it is appropriate to restate our faith and testimony that in the great context of eternity, these partings are for but a brief instant—even as many of us are separated by miles and lack of communication while we live on this earth—but that where ties of love endure and faith prevails, we will yet be reunited to fulfill the measure of our existence."

As part of his summer in 1968, Dallin accepted a visiting professorship at the University of Michigan for five weeks. He taught trusts and wills Monday through Thursday, then drove back to Chicago to spend weekends with family and fulfill his Church assignments. While teaching in Michigan, he took family members to see sights in the area. He enjoyed his visiting professorship but concluded that "all I see makes me happier with my position at Chicago." He was happy for the present but felt he would not remain at the University of Chicago forever.

During the December 1968 Christmas break, Dallin attended professional meetings in New Orleans and combined them with a family camping vacation. Leaving Christmas evening, they drove through Missouri, Kentucky, Arkansas, and Mississippi en route to Louisiana. After his meetings, they continued on to Florida, then north to Atlanta, Georgia, where they arrived just as the new year 1969 ushered in. There they visited Dallin's sister, Evelyn, and her husband before returning home. All, including June, enjoyed most of this camping trip.

Resuming his labors in January, Dallin wrote that he was "head over heels in work teaching a class for the first time: criminal procedure." He also had "an extraordinary amount of committee work at

Oaks family, spring 1971

this time in school." The new year brought a flurry of new activities and recognitions. He accepted appointments to the editorial boards of *Social Service Review* (a social welfare journal) and *Judicature* (a journal of judicial administration), as well as to the advisory board of the Illinois Bar Association's continuing legal education program.

He also went to Washington for a meeting of the advisory board of the National Council of Scholars. The organization began as a political booster group but was "now attempting to do something nationally to overcome the alienation between academics (faculty and students) and the government," Dallin wrote. He "pressed hard for them to include Black scholars" and others "to broaden the group," which, he wrote with satisfaction, "was being done." Those on the board with him included "Dr. Libby of UCLA (Nobel prize winning physicist), Will Herberg of Drew University, Milt Freedman and I from University of Chicago," and Dr. Henry "Eyring from University of Utah (only Utahn)." This was Dallin's first contact with the Eyring family, whose members would be influential in his life.

Amidst all this busyness, the year 1969 brought with it one of the most challenging periods of Dallin's professional life. Two years earlier, after protesting students occupied the University of Chicago's administration building for several days in 1967, university officials appointed Dallin to draft disciplinary procedures to use if similar protests took place in the future. When another protest occurred later that year, over Memorial Day, Dallin was named to a university disciplinary panel responsible for handling the situation.

The skillful way he helped resolve that volatile matter led to his being named chairman of a similar committee in 1969, when even larger protests erupted. This time, a student occupation of the university administration building lasted over two weeks, and the disciplinary proceedings took two grueling months of work on top of Dallin's normal university teaching load. The national spotlight focused on the prestigious university and how it handled protests like those erupting across the country in that era. The committee Dallin chaired ended up holding 105 hearings to decide charges against more than 150 students. Some were expelled, some suspended for various periods, and some received no discipline.

He later summarized, "We participated in a remarkable public and private contest with forces that threatened to divide and discredit the University of Chicago and cripple its teaching mission." The committee patiently and independently considered the cases, receiving praise even from the student newspaper but unable to please all the disparate voices. The most strident of those voices were also violent. At one point while driving, Dallin narrowly avoided being pinned in by other vehicles and kidnapped by a guerilla brigade that wanted to put him on trial to embarrass the university.

"I was driving several members of the committee from the law school north . . . to a restaurant where lunch had been arranged," he wrote. "As we approached the administration building, I noticed that I was being crowded by a car behind me and a car in front of me. As we pulled opposite the administration building, the car in front stopped, and its occupants leaped out and bore down on my car, along with a number of others who rushed out from the administration building, while the car behind me blocked exit in that direction. Just as I realized that some attempt was being made to confine us, I saw an opening and swerved to the left and around the car in front of us and sped away."

Gratefully, some law students formed themselves into a bailiff group to help impose order during the hearings. "Since I had been subjected to an enormous amount of verbal abuse and to the indignity of having a student run up in the middle of a public hearing and spit in my face," Dallin wrote, "the presence of these sturdy and stable law students was of immense comfort to me."

After more than two weeks, the occupiers left the administration building, but not before doing a quarter million dollars in damage. Noisy protests, however, continued. During one hearing, two to three hundred protestors "gathered just outside the hearing rooms and in the access corridors, completely shutting off all doors," Dallin recorded. They pounded on the doors and windows and shouted obscenities to disrupt the meeting.

Dallin adjourned the meeting, and he and the committee sought an exit down a stairway "with a hundred howling demonstrators surging behind us." After Dallin prevailed in a brief scuffle with a student who tried to block their way, the committee members reached the exit, which protestors had barricaded with a heavy table. "As we reached the exit blocked by the table," Dallin recounted, "my huge bodyguard, Sam Evans, a former professional football player, seized the table, spun it away from the door, and sent the student guards sprawling to the floor. The committee bolted out of the fire exit and scattered in the cool night air. I ran a block, clutching the committee's unique records under my arm."

Protests continued, with the committee eventually completing its work amid controversy fueled by the parents of expelled students. A student ombudsman conducted an independent investigation and ultimately came down on the committee's side. "I would suggest," the ombudsman wrote, "that the Oaks committee had more than sufficient reason for the expulsion decisions it made." The writer concluded, "The students who were involved in a constant attempt to harass the Oaks committee, making circuses out of hearings and following the committee around various locations, cannot truly wonder at any shortness of temper on the part of the committee. One might indeed wonder at its restraints."

"We will hold our last hearing this Wednesday or Thursday," Dallin wrote near the end of the ordeal. "We will conclude the whole effort within the quarter when the disruption occurred, in contrast to some universities that have dragged on for months and months. . . . I believe we will have established that the university can govern itself, without the use of police and civil authority. If so, we will have established a pretty important precedent in these troubled times." Difficult though this service was for Dallin, it gave him great personal satisfaction.

When it ended, he received numerous notes of gratitude from faculty members, including one from a renowned chemist who wrote, "The understanding and fairness you showed to all under the most trying circumstances were an inspiration to me, and I marveled at the standards you maintained. I am proud to be a member of the university you have served so well." Another, from a member of the disciplinary committee, read, "There are many capable men at our university, but I am convinced no one could have done the job as excellently as you did. You are firm and just and so very fair."

Given the challenges of 1969, it is no surprise Dallin requested and welcomed a sabbatical semester in 1970 after eight years of full-time service at the law school. He used the sabbatical to work full-time on two projects.

First, he accepted an offer from the president of the Illinois Constitutional Convention to serve as legal adviser to the convention's committee on the Bill of Rights. This group examined such matters as free speech, criminal procedure, and church and state problems. Dallin described the committee chairman, Elmer Gertz, as "an elderly Chicago lawyer who was a protégé of Clarence Darrow."

On January 19, 1970, Dallin recorded that he traveled to Springfield, the capital of Illinois, "to meet with my Bill of Rights Committee." At 4:00 a.m. on January 21, June—who was pregnant—phoned Dallin at his hotel and told him she was hemorrhaging badly and needed to go to the hospital. "Imagine how I felt being away when she needed me," Dallin wrote. June took their daughter Sharmon and sped to the hospital, about fifteen miles away. She called Dallin and bravely told him not to return until after his meetings, "as there was nothing [he] could do."

When Dallin returned to Chicago, he hurried to her bedside in the hospital. She continued to hemorrhage, and they worried about miscarriage. Finally, a week later, the doctors let Dallin take her home. "Through all this," he wrote, "we still don't know whether the baby is still alive." Later, they learned the baby had died. "That was such a disappointment," June wrote, "after waiting for so many years, but we hope that in the not too far future, we'll be blessed with another child. I just put my maternity clothes away."

Of her husband, she wrote, "Dallin continues to be up to his neck with work. He is enjoying working with the delegates to the Illinois Constitutional Convention. He said his work with the discipline committee last winter has helped him in this work as he learned how to handle groups."

By March 16, June's health had improved, and she wrote that Dallin has "never been busier. He is going all the time. It is good he has such energy and vitality, or he'd never survive. He is getting pretty weary now. This business of going to Springfield for two or three days each week is not easy." In April, Dallin had a week off from his Constitutional Convention work, and June savored having him home for those few days. "It has seemed so nice to have Dallin here this past week," she wrote. "I had forgotten what it was like to have him home each night. He still works harder than he should, but I can't fight that."

By early summer, a family letter reported that Dallin "completed five months of service as legal counsel to the Bill of Rights Committee of the Illinois Constitutional Convention." In that capacity, he assisted in writing the Bill of Rights for the new constitution that Illinois voters later adopted.

Elmer Gertz, committee chair, lauded Dallin as "a devout Mormon" who "had a maturity and self-confidence much beyond his years" yet "laughed heartily over everything and had obvious zest for his work." He marveled that Dallin had "a kind of objectivity that one seldom found. . . . He had a scrupulous regard for what was right. . . . Almost without exception, he was able to deal with the diverse personalities without false steps. There was no political maneuvering on his part, no flattery, nothing unworthy of a self-respecting human being. It was simply diplomatic skill and a desire to establish sufficient territory for successful performance of his duties. I often sat back and admired his virtuoso performances."[1]

Dallin's work on the other matter he pursued during his sabbatical was equally successful. He had chosen to fulfill a long-time interest "in doing an empirical study of the effect of the exclusionary rule on the administration of criminal justice." This rule prevented evidence from being used in court if it was gathered or analyzed in violation of a defendant's constitutional rights. Dallin's research culminated in what was probably his most influential legal article. "Studying the Exclusionary Rule in Search and Seizure," which appeared in the *University of Chicago Law Review* in 1970, became a landmark in the field.[2] It was excerpted in many legal books and articles and cited by numerous courts, including by justices of the United States Supreme Court. One legal scholar noted it was the "second most cited" article to have appeared in that law review in its first seventy-five years, second only to an article written by a sitting Supreme Court justice.[3]

Late one evening in August 1970, Dallin and June drove through a poor part of town to take home a sixty-year-old woman who served with June at church. As June waited in the car, Dallin walked the woman to her door. As he returned to the car afterward, he encountered a sixteen-year-old hoodlum. He "stuck a small automatic into my stomach," Dallin recounted, "and demanded my money." Dallin pulled out his wallet and showed him he had no cash. The young man then told Dallin to have June open the car so he could rob her. Dallin refused. The young man threatened to shoot him, but Dallin again refused. Eventually, the youth ran off. "I know the Lord took care of me," Dallin wrote to family, "and that I enjoyed a fulfillment of the promises made in the temple."[4]

In a family letter that summer, Dallin made a major announcement. "I have accepted a position as the new executive director of the American Bar Foundation, to take office September 1, 1970." The foundation, he explained, "is a research organization funded by the

Dallin in his American Bar Foundation office

American Bar Association. . . . I will continue as a professor of law, teaching about a 1/3 load and taking full part in the activities and life of the law school, but my primary assignment will be as the chief executive officer of this organization. They do the kind of work on a grand scale that I have been doing on a small scale for the past five or six years. . . . All that I do there will reinforce my experience for further teaching or prepare me for other administrative-type or scholarly type jobs if my interest turns in that direction."

When Dallin settled into his new role at the foundation, he found himself with a staff of professionals, some of whom had not proven their worth to the organization. He quickly addressed the problem, including, as he explained it, firing the "least productive professionals when they did not measure up after eight months." One staffer responded by contrasting him with the previous executive director, who "barked all the time, but never bit. You never bark," he said to Dallin, "but you bite like hell."

For Dallin, his experience at the foundation, a transitional leadership and administrative experience, taught him principles he would carry with him the rest of his life. He learned the most important concepts from the foundation's board chairman, Lewis F. Powell, a past president of the American Bar Association who later became a justice of the U.S. Supreme Court. "I had never served on a board or worked under the direction of a board, so this was an entirely new experience," Dallin wrote. "I could not have had a better teacher than Lewis Powell. He was an expert at defining the respective responsibilities of a board and a professional staff. He was also brilliant at analyzing how to present matters to a board to obtain fruitful discussions and clear decisions to guide the staff."[5]

By the early months of 1971, Dallin was settling well into his new role at the foundation but feeling he was being prepared for something even more important. The previous year, he began having premonitions that he would replace Ernest L. Wilkinson as president of Brigham

Young University. At first, "I speculated that this was the position for which I was being prepared," he wrote. "Then I would berate myself for such imaginings, accusing myself of being arrogant and puffed up, and of putting my worth much higher than it was. But my mind would return to it again and again, not by way of envy or ambition but by way of premonition."

The recurring feelings bothered him immensely. "I began to pray to the Lord to take away these thoughts and premonitions, that I not be troubled by them and by what my imagination was making out of them," he wrote. "I said in prayer that I was willing to do whatever I should be asked, but that unless there was some purpose in these inklings, I should like to have them removed. In a short time, they ceased."

They stopped, that is, until March 9, as he and June were driving to a professional conference in Williamsburg, Virginia. On the car radio, they heard that President Wilkinson had announced his retirement from BYU, and immediately, the earlier feelings came rushing back to Dallin. He turned to June and said, "This development may change the course of our lives."[6]

CHAPTER 10

"THE LORD MARKED HIM OUT"

The New BYU President

At 8:30 a.m. on March 10, 1971—after an all-night drive—Dallin and June arrived in Williamsburg, Virginia. Dallin's conference did not begin until the afternoon, and so they checked into their motel and decided to drive to the Yorktown battlefield thirty miles away to sightsee. As they drove out of the parking lot, Dallin realized he had left a map of the battlefield in the room and turned around to retrieve it. As he entered the room, the phone rang, and the caller proved to be Neal A. Maxwell, Commissioner of Church Education. He was calling on behalf of the search committee for a new BYU president, and he arranged for Dallin to meet the group in the office of Elder Marion G. Romney of the Quorum of the Twelve on March 19.

The call confirmed Dallin's premonitions, which he reduced to paper a few months later. "From time to time in the years following my graduation from law school," he wrote, "I remarked to June that I felt the Lord was preparing me for some special service. Often these thoughts and remarks accompanied some accomplishment or event, such as my Supreme Court clerkship, my appointment as acting dean of the law school, or my experience on the disciplinary committee, where it seemed that I was granted responsibilities and realized accomplishments far beyond my natural ability. I often expressed the thought to her that where the Lord was giving me so much, He would surely expect a return, and I hoped I would have the wisdom to recognize the opportunity when the call came, and the courage to accept it."

Dallin traveled to Utah as requested and met with Elder Romney's search committee and with Presidents Harold B. Lee and N. Eldon Tanner of the First Presidency. The interviews seemed to go well. Then on Saturday, March 27, back in Chicago, he was at his law school office when June called to say President Lee was trying to reach him. Dallin returned the call, and President Lee got right to his point. "We would like you to be the president of BYU," he told Dallin. "What do you think of that?"

"I was stunned, speechless, overcome with emotion," Dallin recorded. "When I managed to speak, I blurted out an inappropriate question, something like: 'Are you sure you know what you are doing?'

"Then I said I didn't know whether I could go along with the short hair and no-beard regulations." (BYU's dress code had come up repeatedly in the interviews.) "In view of all this," Dallin suggested, "didn't they want to interview me again?"

"Of course," President Lee replied. "We want you to come again and bring your wife."

By that point in the conversation, Dallin had begun to recover from the shock. "If you feel inspired after this second interview that I am the man," he assured President Lee, "of course I will do it."

The next Friday, April 2, Dallin and June met President Lee and President Tanner in Salt Lake. Their conversation swirled around two issues that remained in Dallin's mind. The first was the dress code, and the second was whether Dallin was being called to the position or merely hired for a job.

Dallin and June in Salt Lake City for interview, April 1971

"On the standards question," Dallin wrote, "I had done some praying and thinking in the meantime; so I was easily converted."

The question of whether he was being called or hired, however, proved more complicated. Dallin had a comfortable new position in Chicago, and if he were merely being offered a job, he would stay put. "I was happy at what I was doing," he wrote, "and didn't want the responsibility, but I would accept a call." He had never turned down a calling and was not about to do so now.

With input from President Lee, President Tanner explained that Dallin was being hired—not "called in the sense that an ecclesiastical officer was called." But the "selection was an inspired choice," he added. Later, Elder Marion D. Hanks of the Seventy, a member of the search committee, told Dallin of "the inspiration the committee had felt."

"I received great comfort from that," Dallin wrote, "and will ever be grateful to him for stiffening my back at this time of weakness about whether I could indeed do the job."

Dallin told the First Presidency and search committee "there was no job in the world I could not do with the Lord's help, and now that I had been assured by them that I was chosen under the inspiration of the Lord, I knew I could measure up." Even with that, Dallin continued to seek his own spiritual confirmation, and in an unusual and sacred experience, he soon heard a divine voice declare, "I have chosen you."

As it turned out, Dallin had not been on the search committee's first list of twenty-five potential candidates. "No one on the selection committee knew him," Neal Maxwell recalled. "But the Lord marked him out."[1] Dallin's mother felt the same way. According to his sister, Evelyn, "Mother always felt he had a very special mission. . . . I think that she thought his presidency at BYU was that special mission."

Dallin himself knew that he owed much of what he had achieved in life and what he had become to his wife, June. Meeting with the BYU Board of Trustees on Tuesday, May 4, 1971, he acknowledged, "I have always had the support of my wife, who is one of the queens of the earth."

Later that Tuesday, thirty-eight-year-old Dallin Harris Oaks attended the regular weekly devotional of Brigham Young University in the George Albert Smith Fieldhouse in Provo, Utah. There he was introduced as the incoming president of the university by Associate Commissioner of Church Education Kenneth Beesley, substituting for Commissioner Maxwell, then overseas, who had left a written message.

"Dallin Oaks," the message read in part, "has achieved significantly in the world without being compromised by it—which has earned him the high esteem of academic colleagues and his associates in the Church."

The fieldhouse erupted in applause as the faculty and students welcomed their new president with a standing ovation.[2] He represented a new generation, having been just a freshman at BYU when Ernest Wilkinson began his service as school president.[3]

Dallin answered the warm welcome with expressions of pride in his alma mater. "I am awed by the spiritual strength and intellectual potential of its student body," he declared. "From personal experience, I know the superior quality of its faculty. All of you who share my feelings will understand why I have accepted the invitation to lead this great university, accepting it eagerly but with feelings of profound humility."[4]

Dallin's appointment as university president came as a surprise at first to many because they had not heard of him. Marilyn Arnold, an English professor at the school who later became his assistant, recalled people saying, "Who's Dallin Oaks?" Then someone pointed out, "Oh, he's Stella Oaks's son." And that, Marilyn recalled, "explained everything, because she was very well-known in Provo. . . . Everybody knew Stella."

On August 1, 1971, Dallin officially started in his new role, one that also meant change for his and June's family. Daughter Sharmon had been admitted as a freshman to BYU before her father was appointed president, and she was pleased at the news. "I was going away to school at BYU, but my family joined me!" she recalled. "It was wonderful to have all the benefits of family life—Mom's meals, family prayer and camaraderie—and still be on campus." Her sister Cheri brought enough high school transfer credits with her to be admitted to BYU midway through the first year. June, the new first lady of the university, soon became an admired member of the campus community, which enjoyed having a family with children in the on-campus president's home.[5]

And then there was the family dog, Gretchen, a Great Dane who moved with them. June described Gretchen to a curious journalist as "just a lovable Chicago house dog."[6] Dallin jovially referred to their pet as "the beast." Over time, Gretchen became a well-known member of the campus family, even appearing in the newspaper from time to time.

The Oaks children had grown up with a prominent father—a distinguished lawyer and professor who served in the leadership of their

June with the family dog, Gretchen

stake. While acknowledging that "Dad's pretty important," daughter Cheri said affectionately that, in their family, "he's always been just Dad."

Dallin's new role at BYU catapulted him to even greater prominence than he'd had before, and the children had to adjust to not only a new place to live but a new way others saw them—as children of the president, a role they sometimes felt overshadowed their individuality. It got "a little old," Cheri said. "You want to be liked for who you are and not who your dad is."

Fourteen-year-old son Lloyd, for example, made a friend, and he was happy when the boy invited him to his house. But when the friend introduced him by saying, "Hey Mom, I'd like you to meet the president's son," Lloyd was crestfallen, telling a reporter who interviewed his family, "I thought he'd introduce me as Lloyd Oaks."

Twelve-year-old Dallin D. told the same reporter, "I don't tell anybody I'm related to him."

The whole family laughed at these responses, and the elder Dallin repeated what an acquaintance told him about how Lloyd responded when asked if he was related to BYU's president. "Well," Lloyd answered artfully, "his grandfather and my great-grandfather were the same man."[7]

After settling into his new role, President Oaks met with the press in late September and addressed the faculty and students. "I'm confident that BYU is on the threshold of very important growth in academic standards and prominence in the country at large and the academic community," he told reporters.[8] He counseled students to "budget your time so as not to neglect your studies. Cultivate balance, so that you can benefit from all that is available at this university. But remember that this is a university, and you are here to gain an education. Do not use other activities, valuable or otherwise, as an excuse to neglect your studies."[9]

The *Chicago Tribune,* interested in the former Chicagoan's new role, captured his vision for BYU. "Oaks said the school's goal is to teach the fundamentals in both secular and spiritual knowledge," it

Inauguration of new BYU President Dallin H. Oaks

reported, "and to bring those teachings 'into harmony with the lives of men and women in order to prepare them for a balanced and full life of service to God and fellow man.'"[10]

Although he began serving on August 1, President Oaks's inauguration was scheduled for November 12, 1971.[11] When that day arrived, a host of dignitaries came to participate in inaugurating the new president. They included the Church's entire First Presidency—Joseph Fielding Smith, Harold B. Lee, and N. Eldon Tanner—as well as members of the Quorum of the Twelve and other General Authorities. A surprise visitor was Ernest L. Wilkinson, who had recently undergone open-heart surgery and was not expected to be there but came to honor his successor. Attending also was President Edward H. Levi of the University of Chicago—Dallin's longtime friend and mentor—who came to deliver the keynote address.[12]

"Today," the student newspaper announced, "the spotlight is on Dallin Harris Oaks, the eighth president of Brigham Young University. When he was named BYU's new president last spring, the plaudits for the young administrator poured in." Lewis F. Powell, recent nominee to the U.S. Supreme Court, said, "Dr. Oaks combines the abilities of being a first-rate scholar and a good administrator. That is a rare combination one does not always find these days."

Professor Philip B. Kurland of the University of Chicago Law School said the entire faculty held him in high esteem—a stature not easy to achieve. The dean of the law school, Phil C. Neal, described Dallin as "unruffled . . . having a fine sense of humor . . . immensely interested in other people's problems." Neal said "his relationship with everybody was just splendid."

The inauguration began at 10:00 a.m. in the George Albert Smith Fieldhouse. Harold B. Lee, First Counselor in the First Presidency, gave Dallin his charge, after which the new university president responded.[13]

After paying tribute to the Wilkinson administration, President Oaks addressed the school's future. "We have passed through a period of extraordinary growth at BYU," he told the audience that crowded into the fieldhouse. "We are now entering a period of maturing, deepening, and refining—upgrading the quality of all our efforts."[14]

"I hope we will remember," he said, "that the most important thing about every member of this university community is that he or she is a son or daughter of God. It is our goal to have all members of this community, in all their dealings with one another and with all mankind, set an example of Christian living for the entire world to see."[15]

The "two primary goals for the future," he announced, were "first to reinforce our drive for excellence as an academic institution and second, to preserve the distinctive spiritual character and standards of BYU." "Our reason for being is to be a university," he said. "But our reason for being a university is to encourage and prepare young men and women to rise to their full spiritual potential as sons and daughters of God. We seek to prepare them to live and serve in the world, but we encourage them not to be of the world."[16]

President Oaks's goal to "preserve the distinctive spiritual character and standards of BYU" required him to promote and defend the very matter with which he had struggled in his decision to accept the appointment as BYU's president: the university's dress and grooming standards. He used his first address to the student body to tackle that issue.

"The first and most important thing to remember about our standards of dress and grooming," he began, "is that they are specified by the Board of Trustees of this university. They are not the requirements of the president, the dean of students, the faculty, or the student body officers." Though the "dress and grooming standards are not the most important standards required of those who attend this university," he acknowledged, "they are among the very most visible as we associate with one another and as we come under the eyes of those who visit this campus. Consequently, these matters have been emphasized, and will be emphasized, to an extent beyond their intrinsic importance. . . .

BYU President Dallin H. Oaks

"Unlike modesty," he declared, "which is an eternal value in the sense of rightness or wrongness in the eyes of God, our rules against beards and long hair are contemporary and pragmatic. They are responsive to conditions and attitudes in our own society at this particular point in time. Historical precedents are worthless in this area. The rules are subject to change, and I would be surprised if they were not changed at some time in the future. But the rules are with us now, and it is therefore important to understand the reasoning behind them." He had paid the price to understand them, and he asked no less of the students. They responded to his address with a standing ovation.[17]

The first stated goal of President Oaks's administration—"to reinforce our drive for excellence as an academic institution"—led to important changes in his first year at the university's helm. On August 1,

1972, the anniversary of his first day of service, the Provo *Herald* newspaper attempted to summarize what he accomplished during that year.

"Dynamic, youthful Dallin H. Oaks has been president of Brigham Young University for one year now," the reporter began, "a year punctuated with many significant changes and developments for the nation's largest church-supported university. . . . With hardly time to get his feet wet, he adopted a new [academic] calendar, made plans for an addition to the library, involved students in fundraising, discontinued one college and reorganized two others, reemphasized the university's no-nonsense policy on dress and behavior, set up programs to tighten and improve the curriculum, and initiated a whole series of moves to delegate authority to deans, department chairmen and faculty, and to clarify lines of operation."[18]

In addition, President Oaks built on the foundation laid by his predecessor and devoted an immense amount of time to launching the university's new law school, which required finding a dean, identifying faculty, locating space for the first classes, acquiring a law library, and planning to construct a new law building. Aiding him in this endeavor was Bruce C. Hafen, a Salt Lake attorney whom President Oaks recruited to assist him.[19]

One of the earliest and most important decisions President Oaks made was to retain his predecessor's two principal deputies: Academic Vice President Robert K. Thomas and Executive Vice President Ben E. Lewis. President Oaks concluded his account of the first year's work with expressions of gratitude to them and others. "I have had a very warm reception from the students, faculty, and administrative and staff employees," he told a reporter, "and wonderful support and cooperation from the Commissioner of Church Education, Neal A. Maxwell, and from the Board of Trustees. I have the deepest feelings of appreciation for all of those whose extraordinary efforts have made this year successful."

He then looked ahead. "This past year we have given priority attention to matters of organization and scheduling," he said. "Next year our attention will concentrate on implementing our new year-round calendar, and on study and necessary revisions of our academic programs and curriculum."[20]

The student newspaper concluded, "President Dallin H. Oaks has produced an average of at least one major change per month at BYU since he came into office."[21]

But he was only getting started, and once again, he led by example. Addressing students on September 5, 1972, at the beginning of his second new school year, he promised to review "all academic offerings at Brigham Young University" and called on students to balance "the physical, the cultural, the spiritual, and the intellectual." Repeating his personal motto, he suggested how they could prioritize. "I offer another simple bit of advice for the pursuit of learning: work first and play later," he said. "Never let your social activities get in the way of the learning for which you have been admitted to this university. . . . Despise the mediocre, the effort that falls short of your best!"[22]

A few months later, a reporter interviewed President Oaks and his family to see how they balanced all the demands on their time. "Dinner is probably the most important family experience we have," the president explained, "because whatever else I'm doing, I try very hard to be home for dinner."

June said, "Being BYU's president hasn't made much difference in Dallin's workday. He has always worked very hard and been very busy. He comes home and works at night after dinner. I'm used to his pace—he wouldn't be where he is now if he hadn't worked like he does."

June also spoke of Dallin's role as a parent. "He is very concerned about being a good father," she said. "Sometimes the children will call him and will say, 'I have to talk to you.' He'll say, all right, we'll talk as soon as I finish this or that. And he'll make sure they have the time they need, too."

"About their father, the children spoke freely," the reporter wrote.

Cheri described her father's sense of humor, the fun the family had together, and the way they joked around and teased each other. "Whenever I have a problem," she said, "I can always go to my father, and he'll always drop what he's doing and help me." TruAnn agreed. "He's so fun, especially when he tells us stories," notably James Whitcomb Riley's "The Bear Story," which he always read with "just the right accent." Dallin D. added that his father had "stories for any subject that might arise at the dinner table, and they're all humorous."[23]

While making his family a priority, Dallin H. Oaks pressed on with his duties as university president. In February 1973, he participated in the dedication of the new Marriott Center at BYU, a facility capable of hosting huge crowds for basketball games and assemblies. The center was reputedly the "largest on any campus in the United States."[24] He went on with his duties despite a painful injury sustained during the 1972 Christmas season when he slipped on ice while attending a *Messiah* concert at the Provo Tabernacle. Students and faculty got used to seeing him, arm in sling, as he continued to work until surgery temporarily sidelined him two months later.[25]

But then he was back, pushing ahead as usual. On May 1, 1973, he gathered with other leaders in a parking lot east of the Wilkinson Center on campus to break ground for the new law school building. With a bitter wind blowing, he climbed onto a front-end loader with Elder Ezra Taft Benson of the Quorum of the Twelve and the new law school dean, Rex E. Lee, one of Dallin's former students and key recruits to BYU. With Dean Lee at the controls, they broke asphalt and then grabbed shovels for a more traditional groundbreaking. When the new dean took a particularly "hefty bite" of soil, Dallin retorted, "Don't stop, Rex, keep going till the building is finished."

President Oaks would do the same. Not yet two years into his presidency and only forty years old, he had already accomplished a great deal. But he had much more to do and would keep on going until his time at the school was up.[26]

CHAPTER 11

"ABSOLUTELY EXTRAORDINARY"

The Nine BYU Years

Constructing buildings, like the new law school, became part of the Oaks administration legacy.[1] As it turned out, President Oaks would be at least partly responsible for completing, envisioning, planning, launching, or funding several dozen buildings and other physical facilities needed to fulfill the university's purposes.[2] He also helped drive building expansion at BYU's Hawaii campus and plan BYU's new center to be built in Jerusalem.[3]

"I have . . . been privileged to direct the concluding phase of the great building program initiated under President Wilkinson," President Oaks acknowledged with satisfaction in a 1980 interview. "With the completion of buildings now announced or under construction, the university will be adequately housed for the first time in its history."[4]

In aiding with all the capital improvements on campus, President Oaks always had his eye on how the facilities would contribute to the overall purpose of the institution, and there was no better example of this than the law school. "With the precision timing and unity of a pair of skilled trapeze artists, President Dallin H. Oaks and the J. Reuben

Clark Law School came together in 1971," reflected a journalist. "The timing could not have been better."

"I don't want this to sound like an overstatement," an ebullient Dean Rex E. Lee observed of his mentor Dallin Oaks's contributions, "but no human being, as president of a university, could have been more helpful during the crucial, formative years of the law school."[5] Former Chief Justice Earl Warren, whom President Oaks had served as a law clerk, passed away in 1974 as the law school was being built. "I have lost a great friend," President Oaks reflected at the time.[6] As a sign of the new school's instant stature, when the structure that housed it was finished, Justice Warren's successor, U.S. Supreme Court Chief Justice Warren E. Burger, came to participate in the school's celebration.[7] Dallin felt a measure of personal pride in the creation of the law school and its record over time.

The law school's rise from a mere idea to a noted institution was a tribute to President Oaks's overall academic leadership as well. "Absolutely extraordinary," declared Academic Vice President Robert K. Thomas when describing President Dallin Oaks's effect on BYU's academic standards. "The high academic standards at this university are to a great degree attributed to President Oaks," Thomas noted. "He set the tone of the university." During the Oaks administration, accreditation reports became overwhelmingly favorable.[8]

President Oaks's voice on academics carried weight because of his own sterling academic background and his continued writing, teaching, and service on national boards and in the community.[9] But he was the first to recognize that the achievements of his administration resulted not just from his leadership but also from the loyal and excellent work of a multitude of fellow leaders, especially Robert K. Thomas and Ben E. Lewis. Their familiarity with the faculty and administrators who reported to them, their knowledge of the university, and their superior administration and counsel to him were the most important contributors to his success as a new president coming from the outside.

President Oaks and other key BYU administrators

He learned to love and rely on each of them, and their working relationship, like that of a Church presidency, was a source of joy to all three of them.

Another contributor to his success was the work of his excellent secretary, Janet Calder, who helped enhance his work in many ways over his years at the university. In addition to recruiting Rex E. Lee, President Oaks also brought aboard two other deans, Jeffrey R. Holland and Merrill J. Bateman, who were recommended by Robert K. Thomas. Besides having a great impact on the school as deans, these three recruits would go on to become the next three presidents of the university.

One way President Oaks enhanced the academic atmosphere was to insist on equal treatment for women faculty and students. "He saw women as capable as men," observed Professor Marilyn Arnold. "He was very, very open that way, and very, very supportive." "Equal pay

Dallin H. Oaks, Rex E. Lee, and Jeffrey R. Holland

and recognition for women" was "among the appeals made by President Dallin H. Oaks to the Brigham Young University faculty Monday in preschool conference," reported the *Deseret News* on August 28, 1973, as the fall semester arrived. "President Oaks told faculty members to 'shape up' if any still treat qualified scholars with disdain or ignore their counsel or accomplishments because they are women."

"We have conducted a thorough review of the compensation paid to women in all parts of the university," President Oaks said, "comparing it to the compensation of men with comparable education and performance. Any needed adjustments are being made no later than September."[10]

The university president also focused on how women in the student body saw themselves and their futures. Many people viewed BYU as a place where women went to find a husband or, as it was sometimes said, to acquire their M.R.S. degrees. As the son of a single mother for whom education became the key to providing for her family and contributing to the community, Dallin Oaks became an advocate for women taking their educations seriously.[11]

He cited Church leaders' statements on women and motherhood, adding, "Our young women's primary orientation toward motherhood is not inconsistent with their diligent pursuit of an education, even their efforts in courses of study that are vocationally related." He pointed out that most women will live well beyond their child-rearing years. "A young woman's education," he urged, "should prepare her for more than the responsibilities of motherhood. It should prepare her for the entire period of her life."

Besides, he said, women may not marry as expected or may find themselves as single mothers. Speaking from his own family's experience, he declared, "A mother who must earn a living for the family in addition to performing the duties of motherhood probably has as great a need for education as any person in the world." Furthermore, "education is more than vocational," he observed. "Education should improve our minds, strengthen our bodies, heighten our cultural awareness, and increase our spirituality. It should prepare us for greater service to the human family. . . .

"In short," he summed up, "we make no distinction between young men and young women in our conviction about the importance of an education and in our commitment to providing that education."[12]

While improving academics at the university, constructing buildings, and performing his myriad other duties as university president, Dallin H. Oaks also sought to be a caring husband and father. In 1975, his wife, June Dixon Oaks, gave birth to their sixth and youngest child, Jenny June. The *Deseret News* reported that she was "the first child born to a BYU presidential family while they were residing in the president's home on campus."[13] Dallin and June introduced their new daughter to students and faculty at a university assembly.

"We have had a few expressions of astonishment from acquaintances who assumed we were a little older than we are," Dallin told

Dallin, June, and baby Jenny at BYU assembly

the audience, "and June even made a few jokes herself. The other evening, she was explaining to friends that we had waited thirteen years for this special addition to our family, hoping all the while that we would have more children. 'If we have to wait another thirteen years for the next one,' she added, 'I wonder if we can get maternity benefits on Medicare?'

"But seriously," he went on, "I assure you that this little girl is the greatest thing that has happened to us in the last four years. I firmly believe that the things of eternal significance, even during the period of our education, are not those the registrar records on the permanent transcript of credits in the university, but those the branch or ward clerk records on the membership records of the Church, including baptisms, marriages in the temple of the Most High, and births of the children of God."[14]

Dallin and June's eldest children, Sharmon and Cheri, graduated from BYU while Dallin was president of the university.[15] Each also married in the Salt Lake Temple—Cheri to Louis Eugen Ringger on September 14, 1973, and Sharmon to Jack Donald Ward two months later, on November 21. Sharmon had three children and Cheri two while their parents were still at BYU. So besides carrying out his responsibilities as a father, Dallin also fulfilled his role as a grandfather while overseeing the university. After Sharmon's convocation, according to her brother Dallin D., their father stepped out on the street wearing his academic robes. "An old guy was walking up the street," the younger Dallin related. "He looked at my father and said, 'So you finally made it did ya?'"

In 1978, a journalist wrote of President Oaks, "Though family time is limited, they feel they get quality time, his wife says." June told the reporter, "His mother used to say about her family, 'I love them with all my heart, but not with all my time.'" Dallin Oaks hardly ever relaxed, the reporter said, except when he was with his family. "June and I try to play tennis together one day a week for an hour or so," President Oaks told him. "It has to be after 10 p.m. That's hard because we're already tired, but it's the only time."

During some of his years as president of BYU, Dallin also served as a regional representative of the Twelve, a calling later replaced by that of Area Authority, now called Area Seventy. In this role, he was assigned to work with stakes in the Salt Lake Valley—a substantial Church responsibility for one as busy as a university president.

Sports at BYU gained national attention during the Oaks administration, and the university president was one of the teams' greatest fans.[16] Balancing growing enthusiasm for the teams with good sportsmanship posed a challenge at times for fans, and President Oaks had the duty of helping students temper their emotions. Before introducing Elder L. Tom Perry of the Quorum of the Twelve at a university devotional, the president spoke to the students. "I was proud of the crowd at last night's game," he told them. "I was proud of the fact there was no booing or hissing." He discouraged fans from booing but didn't want to dampen their enthusiasm. "This is not to say that expressions of surprise and wonderment at calls are not appropriate," he said with a smile. "An involuntary 'oh' might be appropriate, but not a 'boo.'"

When Elder Perry got up, he couldn't resist recounting that at one point during a recent basketball game, he heard President Oaks exclaim, "Oh, oh, oh NO!"[17]

The audience loved the story, and a cartoon soon appeared in the student newspaper showing a referee making a nonsensical call. In the cartoon crowd, fans expressed their disappointment with words other than "boo." President Oaks sat with other fans, and above the crowd in large letters appeared "oh, Oh! OH, NO!" Meanwhile Cosmo—the BYU Cougars mascot—cried, "I'm full of 'wonderment and surprise!'"[18]

But it was no laughing matter when leaders of the Western Athletic Conference in which BYU played announced that they had agreed with the Fiesta Bowl and CBS Television to hold the football bowl game on Christmas Sunday in 1977. With the Cougars likely contenders for the conference championship, the choice forced BYU and its athletes to either violate their standards by playing on the Sabbath or not participate in the championship game.[19]

BYU promptly announced it would not play, and President Oaks criticized conference officials for their money-driven decision. "Because of our beliefs about the sacredness of the Sabbath, our athletic teams have never competed on Sunday, and never will," the president resolved. He expressed regret "that the NCAA [National Collegiate Athletic Association] is increasingly scheduling its competition for championships on Sunday and that it is apparently willing to certify bowl games on Sunday," thereby disqualifying "some teams from competition because they adhere to a religious principle."

Resisting conformity to worldly ideals and to pressure for all universities to be the same became a hallmark of the Oaks administration. In the fall of 1974, United States Vice President Nelson Rockefeller

President Oaks with U.S. President Gerald R. Ford, 1978

visited BYU, substituting for U.S. President Gerald Ford.[20] The vice president read a message from President Ford that commended BYU "for its high standards of scholarship, morality, integrity, and patriotism." He declared, "As the nation's largest privately operated university prepares for its centennial celebration, it perpetuates an exemplary tradition."[21]

These words of praise from the nation's highest government officials, however, did not stop federal bureaucrats from trying to micromanage BYU and force the private school into conforming as though it were a public institution. President Oaks spent a substantial portion of his administration using his legal and leadership skills to resist such pressures. During his term, he helped defend BYU from three major threats posed by federal administrators. Ironically, given President Oaks's emphasis on improving women's education and pay, the first two threats arose over equal treatment of women.[22]

In the spring of 1975, officials from the U.S. Department of Health, Education and Welfare claimed that, among other things, BYU's dress and worthiness standards violated federal education law. President Oaks responded by saying he did not oppose the principles of equality and social justice. But when bureaucrats focus more on those topics than education itself, he said, "educators will find themselves surrendering vital institutional controls to government workers," who may lose sight of the real purpose of universities.[23]

He opposed the idea that private universities which receive "even indirectly, a single dollar of federal money" thereby subject themselves to review and regulation of "every decision, activity, facility, educational policy, or communication of that institution."[24] Doing so eliminated much of the difference between public and private universities and squeezed some schools out of existence.[25] "We, as the largest private university in the nation," President Oaks promised, "will be a leader in the fight to stop this."[26] As president of the American Association of Presidents of Independent Colleges and Universities, President Oaks boldly led the fight against bureaucratic overreaching.[27]

The second and principal legal challenge to the school began not long after the first. In July 1976, a young woman tried to rent an apartment in an off-campus complex approved by BYU to house students. Like BYU dormitories, the complex was divided into separate sections for women and men. When she learned the women's portion was full, she petitioned to stay on the men's side and was denied. Seeing this as sex discrimination, she turned to the government, and the case made its way up to the U.S. Justice Department, which sent FBI agents to investigate.[28]

The Justice Department wrote to BYU and thirty landlords in the area, threatening to sue if the school's divided housing policy didn't change over the next month. One magazine reported: "Brigham Young University officials first learned about the suit from landlords who received the letter before they did. They were shocked. It seemed that

BYU President Oaks with Church President Spencer W. Kimball

big government was trying to butt in and destroy the unique religious orientation of the university."[29]

Once again, President Oaks and his administration—backed by Church leaders who made up the school's Board of Trustees—refused to be run over. "As a church-sponsored institution, Brigham Young University teaches the highest standards of Christian morality and expects its students and faculty to live up to those standards," he wrote to the Justice Department. "The First Amendment guarantees of free exercise of religion protect our right to teach these moral principles and to make them a part of the requirements of enrollment and employment in this educational community."[30]

The matter grew into a nationwide controversy, and eventually BYU and the Justice Department worked out an agreement that allowed the school to maintain its housing standard for students but not non-students—a happy solution.[31] Speaking of President Oaks, H. Hal Visick, General Counsel for BYU, lauded: "He's had quite an impact from a legal standpoint. He's got a reputation all around the country because he has been willing to stand up and be counted."[32]

The third challenge came in 1979 from the Internal Revenue Service (IRS), which demanded that BYU release the names of all the school's contributors, implying that most donors had dramatically over-valued their gifts. "BYU, like other institutions which receive charitable contributions, is not involved in determining the value of the gifts it receives," a BYU spokesperson accurately explained. Seeking to preserve the rights of private institutions, President Oaks resisted the request, observing that the school complied with all lawful demands but that this was an "under-budgeted fishing expedition." He also bristled, "We reject as untrue any implications by the IRS that the majority of donors of property to BYU have claimed exaggerated deductions for their donations."[33]

The two sides battled it out in the U.S. District Court for Utah. Through the school's lawyers, President Oaks submitted a memorandum and affidavit declaring that the request went against federal law and court precedent. He asked that the IRS demand be denied.[34] Ultimately, the court agreed. "The case has importance beyond BYU," Hal Visick noted, "because if the ruling had gone against the university, it would mean that any charity would be subject to disclosure of all the names of its contributors simply on the allegation that a few contributors had failed to describe their donations accurately in their tax returns."[35]

That would not be the end of the school's challenges with over-reaching government officials.[36] "My attitude," President Oaks said on one occasion, "is that the bureaucratic army is never demobilized, that if you settle one battle, they'll simply shift forces to another front."[37] Speaking to other educators from church-related universities and colleges in June 1979, he urged continued resistance to forces that would destroy independent schools and the diversity and freedom they represent. "We are not here to resolve our differences but to preserve them," he told the audience. "The distinctive role of the church-related college is diversity." Yielding to pressure from "a government that is less and less willing to tolerate differences," he said, "our educational sector and ultimately our entire society will be homogenized—drab as mortar and uniform as a military camp."[38]

Speaking of the legal challenges the university faced during this period, Jeffrey R. Holland said: "Dallin Oaks was the best man in the Church to deal with that and was remarkably successful. He was a very strong president, and it's a pivotal chapter in BYU's history."

With all Dallin H. Oaks did to defend the university, and with all the times he appeared in formal settings, he also managed to maintain the friendly demeanor and good humor that had characterized most of his life. When it came time to start construction of the carillon tower that would herald the school's 1976 centennial, he donned black clothing reminiscent of the nineteenth century, complete with stovepipe hat, and participated in breaking ground with a team of Clydesdale horses.[39]

President Oaks breaking ground for carillon tower

President Oaks dressed as BYU mascot, Cosmo

Once, at a game in the Marriott Center, he appeared dressed as the school mascot, Cosmo, wrapped like a mummy, and allowed students to carry him around the gymnasium in a coffin. "To the sound of a spooky creaking noise," the student newspaper reported, "the coffin lid slowly began to open. A mummified Cosmo stepped out, and when unwrapped, and 'beheaded,' who appears but Dallin Oaks, making the 'we're number one' sign with outstretched arms!" A student editor wrote, "President Dallin Oaks is a man of great dignity. But even with this dignity, he avoids the 'stuffed shirt' image." He "has not only earned our respect, but I believe he has proved himself to be 'one of us.'"[40]

When the Ezra Taft Benson Food and Agriculture Institute was established at the school, President Oaks participated in a cow-milking contest with the institute's namesake, who was then President of the Quorum of the Twelve Apostles. President Benson sat on the right side of the Holstein, from which it was used to being milked, and President Oaks on the opposite side. "The contest had only been in progress for a few seconds, however, when it became evident that the cow was the

Milking contest

least enthusiastic participant," a reporter wrote. "With a swift kick, she knocked over not only Pres. Oaks's milking bucket, but also the president himself. He flipped over in a not-too-graceful backwards somersault, as President Benson sat on the other side of the cow chuckling at the scene."[41]

President Oaks gave numerous inspiring speeches and devotional addresses and didn't just talk: he walked the walk.[42] "You belong to a community of workers and doers," he told students, "not to a community of dreamers or ascetics, piously and passively waiting for the millennium."[43] In an annual address to students, he gave the four requisites of success as "be worthy, seek learning, work hard, and help others."[44] "Work first, and play later," he said, citing his own motto. Such self-control, he said, was a "master secret of life."[45]

Dallin H. Oaks practiced what he preached, being a good Samaritan and taking time to serve others even as the busiest man on campus. When a visiting Pennsylvania couple were knocked unconscious in a traffic accident near his university home, President Oaks called an ambulance and went to aid the injured. When the ambulance driver showed up alone, the president drove the ambulance so the driver could attend to the wounded en route to the hospital.[46]

While Dallin Oaks served as president of Brigham Young University, his words spoke loud and his actions even louder. No wonder the student body presented him its Exemplary Manhood Award, given annually to a man "who has achieved success through his own courage and application, and whose life is considered a pattern for the men of BYU to emulate."[47]

CHAPTER 12

"JUDICIAL EXPERIENCE"

Utah Supreme Court Justice

Because of his sterling legal reputation, Dallin H. Oaks's name began appearing on lists of potential United States Supreme Court appointees. In early 1976, he spoke with his mentor and friend Dean Edward H. Levi, then U.S. Attorney General under President Gerald Ford. The attorney general told Dallin he had nearly succeeded in getting him appointed to the Supreme Court, remarking that only one thing stood in the way.

"I thought he was referring to my absence of judicial experience," Dallin recorded. (Later, he learned the president did not want to appoint a Latter-day Saint, fearing opposition from civil rights groups because of perceived concerns about the Church's treatment of Blacks and women.) Levi did say, however, that "the president was extremely impressed with your qualifications."

Dallin told Levi he did not plan to be at BYU "until retirement," that "it would be good for the university if I did not serve longer than two or three more years," and that "I would be very interested in a vacancy in the Court of Appeals if one occurred." The Court of Appeals was just one step down from the Supreme Court in the federal system.

Edward H. Levi

Levi considered that answer "very important," and Dallin guessed he would "hear further from him on that question."

On January 16, 1978, Dallin wrote a confidential letter to Church leaders, suggesting, "It is in the best interests of the university to have a policy of regular turnover in the office of president." The leaders discussed the letter and decided they still wanted Dallin as president for the time being. A year went by, then two, and he continued to serve faithfully in that role.

On January 1, 1980, Dallin welcomed in the New Year by starting a daily journal. "Having been urged by the prophet, President Spencer W. Kimball, to keep a daily journal, I choose this significant date to begin," he jotted. His detailed journal, which he kept from then on, was highly introspective, reflecting not just events but also his feelings. At the same time, he was discreet, taking care not to record information that would violate confidences, privacy, or matters he considered too sacred to put in writing.

Dallin had kept personal records in the past, but not on a consistent, daily basis. He had been working on a personal history of his life up to when he became BYU president, feeling "a strong compulsion to complete this history as soon as possible." He even promised himself that he would write "no more articles or major speeches until it was done." Just the evening before, New Year's Eve, he had completed the final chapter. "I feel relieved!" he wrote. Titled *The First 39 Years,* it became a key source on his life to that point.

A week later, while he was returning by private jet from a Union Pacific board meeting in New York, he received a radio communication via the plane's pilot telling him "to watch for a message at the airport in Salt Lake." When they arrived at 7:00 p.m., a woman at the desk told Dallin, "You should go right to the University Hospital, where the entire family is with your mother." When he got there, he learned his mother had just died after a yearlong battle with cancer. She had been among the most important influences in his life, and now she had quietly passed beyond. Dallin and his family members "had a tender few minutes around her bed," he wrote. After that, "we gathered up Mother's belongings, each of us kissed her cold but peaceful face, and then thanked the nurses and left, weeping." But they rejoiced that their mother's thirty-nine and a half years as a widow were over and that she was again with their father.[1]

Stella H. Oaks had served for many years as director of adult education and public relations in the Provo City Schools. Her many other activities made her one of the most prominent and admired women in Utah and the Intermountain area. She was honored frequently for her leadership and teaching in a variety of community activities, such as her key role in founding the Utah County Child Guidance Clinic, where she was the first president. She was also prominent in political and Church leadership. She was elected twice for three-year terms on the Provo City Council and served for four years as the assistant mayor and, for the summer of 1959, as the acting mayor. She served on the Young Women General Board and for eight years as a BYU stake

Stella H. Oaks (1906–1980)

Relief Society president. President Ezra Taft Benson, Elder Gordon B. Hinckley, and other General Authorities attended her funeral.

Because of Dallin's role as BYU president, he had many opportunities to meet with such Church leaders. They knew of his desire to be replaced but had not acted on it. Meanwhile, he was getting very tired. On January 24, 1980, he was up at 5:30 a.m. to teach his 8:00 trusts class at the law school. With everything else going on, he had not had time to prepare and was meeting the class at 7:30 to make up for a session he would miss the next week. "I'm running almost faster than I am able," he confided to his journal, "and wonder how long I can keep it up. But the Lord sustains me so that I always seem to get along at least O.K."

On February 4, he found himself at home in the evening but was "so exhausted," he wrote, that "I could hardly move." Some late-night tennis on the BYU indoor courts revived him. "I felt better at midnight than at 5:00 p.m.," he noted. One thing weighing him down was word from a friend that he had been nominated as chairman of the Public Broadcasting Service and then opposed by some because of his Church membership. "This information touched off all sorts of painful fantasies where I fought discrimination in one way or another and paid a terrible price for it," he wrote.

Then, on February 5, he got a call from Newton Minow, the incumbent PBS chairman, who told Dallin "he thought it was unacceptable for them to use religion as a disqualifier." He told Dallin he wanted him as his replacement. Dallin hadn't campaigned for the job and didn't really care if he was nominated or not, but he couldn't stand to be disqualified because of his religious beliefs. "I feel like I've been promoted for a job I didn't want and then eliminated on a ground I can't accept," he told Minow.

Two days later, Dallin was in Chicago for a PBS board meeting and learned he had been unanimously elected board chair. Later that evening, a Black member of the board who was not on the nominating committee approached Dallin, offering his support in overcoming any prejudice he might face. "I had my doubts," the man acknowledged, "and I've heard others voice concern about the possible effect of your Church membership on your attitudes toward minorities and women, but I've inquired around, and I'm satisfied."

"Now I have a chance to show that my personal record is *a product* of my church, not an exception to its teachings or attitudes," Dallin exulted. "I have also pondered what this election means for my future." He had been on the board only three years and suddenly found himself chairman with virtually no effort on his part. "June and I think this must have some important role in what is to follow in our lives," he wrote, "because we see the Lord's hand in it."[2]

Over his succeeding five years as board chair, Dallin earned the respect of his peers. "What makes Oaks an effective leader?" an industry publication asked. "It is a combination of 'wit and wisdom' and 'special skill in bringing clarity to otherwise murky issues,' says PBS senior vice president, Peter Downey. . . . 'He has excellent judgment and has a good sense of what role the board should play,' says the Corporation for Public Broadcasting board chairman, Sharon Rockefeller. . . . 'He is gentle and funny, but at the same time possesses a steel-like quality to get things done,' says PBS President Larry Grossman, and he has contributed to a 'sense of comfort' between the stations and PBS, even through difficult times."[3]

By March 25, 1980, Dallin was emotionally ready to be released as BYU president. "I must be being prepared for a change," he wrote at the end of a hard day. "I find myself resentful of having to work as hard and under as much pressure and for as long hours as today (seventeen continuous hours . . . without one break). This is an unusual feeling for me." Three days later, normally patient Dallin found himself reacting too hastily to a problem. "I worry myself," he told his journal. "I am so low on emotional energy I think I am prone to mistakes and abrasive actions. I caught this one and soothed it over, but it shouldn't have happened. I need a rest!"

On May 6, he traveled from Provo to Salt Lake because the First Presidency wanted to see him. When he entered the north boardroom of the Church Administration Building, he was greeted warmly by Presidents Spencer W. Kimball, N. Eldon Tanner, and Marion G. Romney, as well as their secretary Francis M. Gibbons.

"President Tanner, as spokesman," Dallin recorded, "advised me that the Presidency had decided to act on my earlier suggestion of rotation in the office and give me a release this summer, when my successor was chosen. I had an immediate good feeling, and no sense of loss. This must be the Lord's will."

Later that day, Elder Boyd K. Packer of the Twelve told Dallin that when the executive committee of BYU's Board of Trustees discussed rotating university presidents, President Kimball, who had been ailing, became "unusually and suddenly strong and assertive," declaring, "I believe we should act now and release Brother Oaks." Witnessing that, Elder Packer felt strongly "that the Lord had just spoken through His prophet." There would be no waiting for a successor to be appointed.

When Dallin met with the executive committee the day after being told of his release, he wrote in his journal, "I still feel elated and peaceful." After Dallin's release from the BYU presidency was announced, with a successor yet to be named, friends began calling to congratulate him. "A good cheerful spirit prevailed," Dallin wrote, "mirroring my own feelings, but each caller was tentative, worrying how we were feeling and wondering if there was more to this than had been stated publicly."

There wasn't—other than Dallin's feeling that it was time, his earlier recommendation to Church leaders that the position rotate, and President Kimball's sudden prophetic pronouncement.[4] A local newspaper wrote of Dallin, "He simply believes in the principle of rotating the presidency and in 'practicing what he preaches.'"[5]

When asked, "What causes you to 'welcome' the release?" Dallin answered, "Mostly because it is good for the university to have regular turnover in its top leadership. At the personal level, June and I have six children and five grandchildren. They haven't seen a great deal of me during the last nine years. I look forward to having more time with them." He was happy to be freed of thankless administrative tasks, too. "Finally," he reflected, "I have missed having a private life."[6]

Asked what he would miss most, he said the people. "As I conclude my nine years of service as president of Brigham Young University on July 31, 1980," he wrote to faculty, staff, and students, "I do so with a profound sense of gratitude for the extraordinary men and women of BYU. . . . It has been a great honor and blessing to serve as president of Brigham Young University. Whatever I do in the rest of my life, I will always be proud of this place and these people."[7]

He intended, he told them, to "remain in the university community for at least a time."[8] Officially, he had six months of leave to research church and state legal matters, including government regulation of private institutions. He would teach his class at the law school. Besides that, he had much to do as PBS chair and would stay busy while deciding what his next full-time role would be.[9]

When summer graduation came, President Kimball praised Dallin as a "great legal gladiator, a distinguished scholar, and a wonderfully successful university president," one whose "steady hand has guided this university through fierce legal battles, shifting social pressures, student growth, and new construction on campus. He has wanted this university to be the very best," President Kimball said, "and that is what it is."[10]

As Dallin thought about his next professional role, he had plenty of options. He could return to the practice of law—which would be lucrative—or to the professor's life. "I would rather be a teacher than an administrator," he told a reporter.[11]

On September 24, 1980—just a few weeks after concluding his term as BYU president—Dallin noted in his journal, "I have been thinking very seriously about the Utah Supreme Court." When he asked Elder Gordon B. Hinckley's opinion, the Apostle "encouraged me to submit my name," Dallin wrote, and suggested consulting with Marion G. Romney, the First Presidency member who was also a lawyer. "I think you ought to do it," President Romney replied. "President Tanner and I talked about you just the other day, and we think you ought to be on the bench, and on a much higher one than this, but this is a good way to start."

Dallin pondered the matter as he flew to New York later that day. Summarizing his thoughts, he described "a current I can feel sweeping me toward service on the Utah Supreme Court." Earlier that day, he phoned U.S. Senator Orrin Hatch of Utah about the idea, and they spoke for over an hour. Senator Hatch felt the court role would help prepare him for any number of key federal positions. "All of this needs to be prayed over," Dallin wrote.

That evening after reaching New York, Dallin took a cab to where he would be staying. He had "a delightful visit" with his cab driver, who was "a vegetable garden enthusiast" like Dallin. "We compared notes on successes and failures," Dallin wrote. "Heart speaks to heart about simple things like this. I promised to send him recipes for dilly beans and zucchini bread."

Back in Utah on September 26, Dallin went to the temple with June "to seek inspiration on our decision" about the future. "During the session," he wrote in his journal, "I couldn't get my mind off the Utah Supreme Court, try as I might (and I did, continuously). In all of this consciousness of the prospect that I might do this, I did not have one negative thought or apprehension."

After the session, he and June sat in the celestial room of the temple, praying quietly by themselves. "As I finished," Dallin recorded, "this thought flooded my mind, being repeated over and over: 'Go to the court, and I will call you from there.'" June "had confirming thoughts and expressed her willingness to make whatever sacrifices are necessary."

Financially, the sacrifices were substantial. Later, Dallin explained that "the annual salary of a Utah Supreme Court justice at that time was a fraction of what I would receive in any of the other alternatives I was considering." And there was no guarantee he would be accepted if he applied.[12]

But knowing the Lord's will, they did not hesitate. The weekend passed, and on Monday, Dallin filed an application with the Utah Supreme Court clerk to be considered for a current opening in the court. Word spread quickly that he had applied.

On October 5, Dallin met with members of the Church's Special Affairs Committee (Gordon B. Hinckley, David B. Haight, James E. Faust, and Neal A. Maxwell, with Richard P. Lindsay, secretary). He reviewed work done for the group that occupied much of his time since leaving the BYU presidency. The committee members thanked him but offered no further suggestions.

"As we concluded our discussion after twenty-five minutes," Dallin wrote, "I asked if I could have a blessing to help me in my work, which I considered so important and for which I needed so much help from heaven." At Dallin's request, Elder Hinckley pronounced the blessing as the others joined with him in placing hands on Dallin's head. Besides blessing him in the work he was doing for the group, Elder Hinckley promised Dallin that he "would be enlightened by the Holy Ghost" and "go on to other employment that would be satisfying and productive."

"How my heart sang as I arose from this blessing," Dallin rejoiced. "My doubts and apprehensions had been settled, and I felt peaceful and confident in facing the challenges I face in doing this difficult work with so many high expectations."

The promise that Dallin would find "satisfying and productive" employment soon came to pass. On November 21, 1980, Utah Governor Scott M. Matheson appointed him to be a justice of the Utah Supreme Court.[13]

On January 5, 1981, Dallin was sworn in as a justice during a ceremony attended by family members, Utah's governor, and the president of the Utah State Bar. Three days later, Dallin wrote, "I trooped out with the other justices . . . and heard my first arguments. Afterwards we went right into conference and gave our opinions." The matters before the court spanned a wide range of subjects, and, as with all the justices, his past experiences had prepared him better for some cases than others. But that was part of the job's appeal: the opportunity to learn and grow.

Meanwhile, he continued to hear of his name being bandied about for positions in Washington. The new deputy U.S. attorney general, a longtime acquaintance, phoned to offer him the job of associate U.S. attorney general over civil aspects of the justice department. "I quickly

Utah Supreme Court Justice Oaks being sworn in

told him no," Dallin recorded, "because I didn't want another administrative job after ten years of that, and because I was very happy on the court. He then asked whether I wanted them to keep my name on the list for solicitor general, and I said yes, because that was an advocate's and scholar's job, and I would definitely be interested in being considered for that." (The solicitor general of the United States reported to the attorney general and was responsible for arguing cases on behalf of the federal government before the Supreme Court.)

Daughter Cheri remembered her father saying "that all he ever wanted to be was a writer and a scholar." He routinely turned down prestigious offers that required him to do administrative work and instead showed interest in those that would require him to spend time doing research and writing, as his work on the Utah Supreme Court did.

Dallin loved being a scholar and a teacher, and he welcomed the student evaluations for the trusts class he taught at BYU's law school the preceding fall. His ratings had climbed over the years, and these latest were really high, with only one law professor having higher ones. Dallin shared this news with June, who "said she thought this was because they felt sorry for me," he wrote, "but I suppose there is something more to it than that. (She keeps me humble.)"

Over the years, June had teased him about how his sequence of jobs—from big firm lawyer through other roles to now state court judge—had left him with progressively smaller salaries and earning potential. Wasn't it supposed to be the other way around? she chided.

In early March, Dallin traveled to New York and Washington, DC, to talk with supporters—including Utah's federal senators, longtime mentor and U.S. Supreme Court Justice Lewis Powell, and Supreme Court Chief Justice Warren E. Burger—about federal appointments, including as solicitor general. They encouraged him to move ahead, but he needed more than their approval. He wanted the divine confirmation he always sought in making key life decisions.[14]

"This morning," he wrote one Friday, "June and I prayed again for guidance on whether I should call the attorney general and submit my name for solicitor general. Both of us felt the impression that I should not, at least not now. This confirms the reluctance I have felt all week, despite the encouragement and impetus of my trip to Washington. So I will not make that call. We are so grateful that we have the faith and the experience to know that we can be guided by inspiration and to recognize it when it comes."

But then he received phone calls from the deputy attorney general telling him he was on the short list for solicitor general and encouraging him to return to Washington for another interview. Eventually he went, reluctantly, and without a strong feeling that it was the role the Lord wanted him to have. He met with Attorney General William French Smith and his deputy for an hour, responding to questions and offering "insights and philosophy."

"I told them I was happy in what I was doing, but I thought the solicitor general's job was the best lawyer's job in Washington, and I would accept if it was offered," Dallin related in his journal. "They said they had heard many good things about me. I left feeling that I had done all that I could do, and the rest was in the hands of the Lord. I felt that all would be well—peaceful. I can't ask for more than that. I am content."

"As I think about the Washington job," he wrote a few days later, "I find myself hoping I am not chosen, since that would be so complicating," though he would accept the offer as the Lord's will if it came. Ten days later, he still felt the same, adding, "I find myself hoping it will not be offered. I can't bear to think of uprooting and moving away from home and family in Provo."

The next day, the attorney general phoned Dallin to say he had named the new solicitor general: Dallin's former student Rex E. Lee, who had served as United States assistant attorney general and dean of BYU's law school. "I am genuinely thrilled for Rex, who is so well qualified," Dallin wrote, "and immensely relieved for me."

"We want to stay close to you," Attorney General Smith assured Dallin twice. He and the attorney general felt good toward each other because of their long interviews, and if the next call were about a judicial appointment, Dallin's credentials would be strong.

CHAPTER 13

"WHAT WILL BECOME OF ME?"

Considering Federal Service

Relieved at not getting the solicitor general appointment, Dallin reveled in being a judge. "I love it!" he wrote. "I want to be a great judge, like the best whose opinions I have admired." He recognized that the first opinions he wrote in his current role might not be important to others beyond those involved in them. But he hoped they would prepare him for future important cases, and perhaps even for a higher court.

His roles as U.S. Supreme Court law clerk, longtime law professor, and scholar of the courts, as well as his occasional appearances and arguments before judges over the years, prepared him well to serve in his new position. Yet some people in Utah were not aware of his rich background, knowing him only as a university president, and he had to demonstrate his abilities from time to time to prove himself.

Speaking at the Utah State Bar's midwinter meeting in January 1981, he gave a talk that showed he "had a good deal of legal experience in various areas and was not just a university president who had been named to the court because he was prominent." That talk seemed to go over well, and recognition soon came from other quarters too.

Justice Dallin H. Oaks

Later that month, at the tenth-anniversary banquet of the federal defender program held in San Diego, the group hailed him as the "father of the federal defender program" because of his acclaimed 1967 study of the Criminal Justice Act.

The growing body of opinions he wrote for the Utah Supreme Court quickly established his skill as a jurist. By the end of his first year of service on the court, he had written thirty-eight published opinions for the majority, three concurrences, and no dissents. The opinions showed the depth of his intellect and made significant contributions to Utah law. After crafting one such opinion, he told his journal, "I get real satisfaction out of solving an intellectual problem" and "making a sound contribution to the common law in an area where there was no precedent."

At the same time, he was, as always, eager to learn and grow, readily accepting criticism from his colleagues. He modified an opinion after receiving insightful suggestions and recorded, "A thoughtful critic is surely more valuable than a thoughtless complimenter!"

Dallin and fellow justices of the Utah Supreme Court

He quickly developed a good rapport with his fellow justices on the court, including Christine Durham, who was appointed in 1982, served thirty-five years on the court, and became its chief justice. "I was not only the first woman, I was the youngest, I think, appointment to the Utah Supreme Court in history," she recalled, and Dallin Oaks "was really the only member of the court who approached me to answer questions, to fill me in on the culture of the court, to let me know what pitfalls to avoid." She described him as "the most generous, kind colleague," warm and "never condescending" despite his greater age and seniority. She felt he had a "generosity of spirit" that pervaded "so much of his career."

For example, "I became very active and was a founding member of the National Association of Women Judges and eventually became president of that association," she noted. "And Dallin was the only one of my colleagues who joined NAWJ, to be supportive of me, and I thought that was remarkable."

She also observed how well he got along with the other judges. "He had a striking skill for collegiality," she said. "There's a lot of tension when you're trying to decide things as a committee, which is really what happens on an appellate court. And he was always ready with a funny story or a joke that would smooth over whatever tensions might have arisen in the course of substantive discussion."

Justice Oaks's most important contribution, according to Justice Durham, was the role he played in revising the judicial article of the Utah Constitution, establishing the intermediate Court of Appeals and unifying the state court system. He loved serving on the Utah Supreme Court and made many contributions, but the question almost from the beginning was how long he would continue serving in that role.

On June 18, 1981, U.S. Supreme Court Justice Potter Stewart resigned. Although normally a vacancy in the nation's highest court might have thrilled Dallin, "I have no excited, apprehensive, or premonitory feeling about this," he recorded that day. Media hoopla on the vacant position continued the next day. "The phone rang all day about the pending Supreme Court vacancy," Dallin wrote. "As for me," he recorded, "I'm not excited about any of this. I think Reagan will appoint a woman this time." *Time* and *Newsweek* magazines included Dallin's name among some half dozen potential appointees, with *Newsweek* even including his picture. "I am strangely unmoved at all of this," Dallin wrote. "No premonitions."

As circumstances had it, he finished reading Frank W. Fox's *J. Reuben Clark: The Public Years*—the biography of a former First Presidency member who earlier in his career served in important public offices. "It is magnificent!" Dallin wrote of the volume. "I doubt that anyone read it with more of a sense of identification than I, since my own life has paralleled his, though on a smaller scale: a period in the East pursuing professional and public service goals, struggling with conflicts between worldly-intellectual values and spiritual ones, followed by a period in the West, struggling with uncertainty over whether the culmination of one's career is in the East with the nation or in the West with the Church."

Dallin felt himself being tugged both directions. "I feel this uncertainty so keenly at this time!" he wrote. "And I am utterly without impressions on which direction my life will go, except to feel that my next move will be a permanent one, or at least a decisive step to identify the nature of my activity in the final decades of my professional life. I am now in a middle ground: in the *West* with the *nation.*"

The next day, Dallin flew east to deliver a message as PBS chairman. He called on Fred Friendly, the former president of CBS News, who was the designated honoree for a PBS luncheon the next day. "He hailed me as 'Mr. Justice,'" Dallin wrote, "and launched an animated conversation about law, journalism, Earl Warren, Kirkland firm, various mutual acquaintances," and "my prospects for appointment to" the U.S. Supreme Court.

On June 30, Dallin gave his PBS chairman's speech to great acclaim and a standing ovation. Later in the day, he returned calls to Utah and learned from one of his fellow Utah Supreme Court justices "that the court was sending the attorney general a letter in my behalf." Dallin had not expected that. In the months he had served with his

PBS Chairman Dallin H. Oaks speaks at annual meeting, 1983

fellow justices, they had grown together through their service. "I was very touched by this unsolicited and unselfish gesture," he wrote.

Dallin had long predicted that President Ronald Reagan would appoint a woman to fill the U.S. Supreme Court vacancy, and he proved to be right. On July 7, as Dallin was driving to work, he heard a radio network bulletin of President Reagan announcing that he had appointed Sandra Day O'Connor of Arizona to the nation's highest court, the first woman in United States history to occupy such a post. "I watched my reactions carefully," Dallin wrote, "and I am satisfied that this important announcement had no more effect on me than on someone not being considered. I didn't and don't feel a bit surprised or disappointed. My prayers are answered!"

In the wake of that appointment, the deputy attorney general asked Dallin if he would be interested in being appointed to the U.S. Court of Appeals for the District of Columbia. Dallin said he "wasn't sure." He preferred "the common-law jurisdiction of state courts" and had "a strong preference for living in Utah," but he also knew that the D.C. Circuit was "the nation's second highest court"—a recognized stepping-stone to the U.S. Supreme Court. "I told him I would just have to think about that," Dallin wrote, "which he encouraged me to do."

On August 3, the deputy attorney general called again, "asking me," Dallin wrote, "if I would be interested in the vacancy on the D.C. Court of Appeals created by" a recent resignation. "At some times of my life, I suppose I would have quivered with eagerness at such an opportunity, but at this moment I felt an immediate impression that I should say (as I did), 'I feel I just should not be considered for this vacancy.'" Dallin explained that the appointment would further disrupt the Utah Supreme Court, which was "still reeling" from the sudden death of its chief justice in his sleep a month earlier.

Dallin also cited family reasons. His son Dallin D. was "just returning from a mission." In addition, two of his children were scheduled to be married in the Salt Lake Temple, son Lloyd to Natalie

Mietus on August 25, and daughter TruAnn to Acel Rock Boulter on November 20.

The caller said he understood and replied, "I'll take this answer for this vacancy only, but we will be back to you for other vacancies on this court and higher courts." That afternoon, the U.S. attorney general himself phoned Dallin, saying, "We'll be talking to you again."

The following day, Dallin wrote, University of Chicago law professor Antonin Scalia phoned "to inquire whether I would be seeking the C.A.D.C. vacancy, explaining he wanted to seek support for himself from Mormon figures but didn't want to ask any if I were seeking it. I told him I wasn't, and I would be glad to put in a word for him." (Scalia eventually received an appointment to the Court of Appeals for the D.C. Circuit and in 1986 went from there to become a justice of the United States Supreme Court.)

Several weeks later, Dallin confided in his journal how tired he was of answering questions about how he was enjoying his work. He always gave the same kinds of answers, all sincere: "It's very rewarding professionally." "I think I've died and gone to heaven." Or "It's the most rewarding work I have done in many years."

He was even more tired of comments from people about the U.S. Supreme Court, remarks ranging from "Sorry you didn't make it" to "You'll make it next time." But he also gave an answer he felt was closest to the mark: "That job is like being called to be a General Authority. Only a fool would aspire to it, but no one would turn it down."

The pull between the secular and the spiritual realms came into focus in January 1982 as Dallin contemplated the death of a fine man he had known who focused on the things of the earth but had no interest in the Church. "I hope I never lose my sense of eternal perspective!" Dallin wrote. He knew the day would come to leave his present post for another that might be the last professional realm of his life. That much was certain in his mind. But he still did not know what it would be. His future was just not clear, and he asked himself, "What will become of me?"

In May 1982, Dallin traveled to Washington, DC, for legal meetings and had a private lunch with U.S. Supreme Court Chief Justice Warren Burger and his administrative assistant, Dr. Mark W. Cannon, a Latter-day Saint. "The Chief just wants to keep in touch with you," Mark explained later. Dallin said that while he "preferred the menu of the state supreme court to any federal court," he had recently undergone a change of feelings. He told Mark he would "seriously consider" an appointment to the Court of Appeals "if one was offered again."

On June 26, Dallin was back in Washington, this time to attend PBS meetings. "I delivered my annual message at the luncheon," Dallin wrote. "We gave Newton Minow, my predecessor, an award. It was good to see him again. He said, 'We've got to get you on the Supreme Court, and I think it's going to happen.' This is just an example of what friends say to me all the time." Dallin usually replied, "Well, that would be nice, but no one should count on it—certainly not I."

In early July, Chief Justice Burger appointed Dallin to be a state justice representative on a United States Judicial Conference subcommittee—an unprecedented appointment and a sign of how highly he was esteemed nationally. This was just one of many honors that would come to him during his tenure as a state supreme court justice.

On July 15, a friend who had been talking with U.S. Attorney General William French Smith told Dallin that Smith had asked about him and declared, "I don't know whether you know this, but it is common knowledge here that if Chief Justice Burger would resign, Oaks is one of the top candidates to be Chief Justice." Dallin wondered if that could really be true but felt willing to accept such a role if it were God's will. "If not," he said, "I am happy. I do not aspire."

On December 17, a friend passed along a magazine article speculating on who would fill future vacancies on the court. The article named William Webster, the FBI chief; Robert Bork, Dallin's old

Chicago associate; Clifford Wallace, another Latter-day Saint judge and friend; and Dallin Oaks.

At the beginning of the year 1983, Dallin remained uncertain about his future, though he seemed content to remain where he was until he felt strong impressions to move. When offered a legal job with a high salary, he turned it down, "saying," as he described it, "that although I esteemed the organization highly, I wouldn't take any other offer, even for $1 million, because I was enjoying my present work so much, and money wasn't that important to me anyway."

With no clarity yet on what else his future might hold, Dallin continued to think about being a federal judge. He asked a prominent friend to represent him if he got called into a U.S. Senate confirmation hearing. "This seems awfully presumptuous, I thought," Dallin reflected, "(and I supposed he did, also), but I have felt for several months that I should make this preparation. I told him there was a 'possibility' of my being named to the Court of Appeals or the Supreme Court during the Reagan administration." Because of Dallin's talent and experience, he was repeatedly approached by people with job ideas or offers, ranging from university president to state governor.

Though Dallin was often on the road, he enjoyed fulfilling his Church calling as a Sunday School teacher of sixteen-year-olds when he was home. On June 12, 1983, his ward bishop invited him in and called him to be Gospel Doctrine teacher instead. He accepted this calling as he did all others but thought wistfully, "I will miss my sixteen-year-olds."

He also enjoyed his service as PBS chairman. On the morning of June 24, as part of a message he delivered at the organization's annual membership meeting, he recognized children's television host and Presbyterian minister Fred Rogers for his three decades of serving children on the air. Later that day, Dallin received a letter of gratitude from Mr. Rogers. "My sense is that you are a man inspired of God," Fred wrote, "and I just needed to thank you—before I left this

Justice Oaks speaking from the bench

morning—for all the care which you obviously devote to PBS." Dallin recorded a similar feeling about Fred—that he was "a man inspired of God."

The care Dallin gave to PBS reflected how he approached everything important in his life, including his family, his Church callings, and his work on the Utah Supreme Court. During the time he served as a justice, he would write 187 opinions for the court—149 of those for the majority—on topics that included administrative law; constitutional law; contracts and other commercial litigation; corporations and partnerships; criminal law; family law; jurisdiction and procedure; property; state and local government; courts; wills, trusts, and estates; and the legal profession—a veritable smorgasbord, or "menu," as he called it, of legal topics. His knowledge of the law was growing encyclopedic, and the Utah Bar Association would recognize his service by naming him its 1984 Judge of the Year.

To help advance Dallin for nomination as a federal judge, Senator Orrin Hatch asked him for copies of some of his most important opinions. "I have decided to cooperate in this effort," Dallin wrote, "as it seems to me I have an obligation in the nature of a stewardship to see that the credentials and experience I have been blessed to acquire are considered on the merits. Then, if I am not chosen, that is the will of the Lord, and I am at peace with my conscience."

Besides, the reasons he had given for declining a federal judgeship two years earlier had resolved themselves. The Utah Supreme Court had recovered from the sudden death of its chief justice, children Lloyd and TruAnn had married and were on their own, and son Dallin D. had returned from his mission and was engaged to marry Marleen May on November 23 in the Jordan River Utah Temple.

On December 8, 1983—two weeks after his son's wedding—Dallin called on White House staff at Senator Hatch's urging. He also met with Richard Wirthlin, a Latter-day Saint who was the "leading pollster for Reagan"; Fred Fielding, "Counsel to the President"; and Edwin Meese, "Counselor to the President." Dallin let them know how he felt about a U.S. Supreme Court appointment. He said he was "available and qualified, not campaigning but considering it obligatory as a stewardship to put my credentials forward for consideration."

By January 1984, Dallin still felt something was coming in his life. He did not know what it was, and absent other thoughts, he made himself available for a U.S. Supreme Court appointment—if that was the Lord's will. On January 5, he visited with U.S. Senator Jake Garn of Utah, who promised strong support. The senator told Dallin he felt his chances to be appointed were "far better" than the one-in-ten chance Dallin suggested. "I felt very satisfied with this meeting," Dallin recorded in his journal.

Six days later, after describing Utah Supreme Court activities in his journal, Dallin added a simple note: "Elder Mark E. Petersen died this evening. He was a dear man and will be sorely missed." Elder Petersen was one of the many Church leaders Dallin came to know over the years.

The following week, Dallin had lunch with Henry B. Eyring, the Church Commissioner of Education, who asked him how he would organize the Church's legal services—a topic on which Dallin had, coincidentally, expended considerable thought of late. It wasn't his area of responsibility, Commissioner Eyring said, but President Ezra Taft Benson had asked him about it, and so he in turn inquired of Dallin. Wondering if this question portended a change in his own status, Dallin commented to his journal, "I do not know or care. I only want to do as I am prompted and serve as the Lord sees fit to direct me personally or through His servants."

Despite seeking diligently for answers, Dallin could not get a spiritual confirmation that he should be a federal judge. Yet, as counseled by a political adviser, he worked on a list of people who could help with his appointment or confirmation if the opportunity arose. "It is prudent to be prepared," he acknowledged to his journal, "but I have done all this hard work on the list without any sense of aspiration or excitement. That is hard to believe, but it is true. It is as if I were acting in a dramatic presentation that may or may not have its opening night, and I don't care either way."

Later in the month, he met Senator Garn in his Washington office, and the senator took him to see White House Chief of Staff James Baker. During their visit, Baker said he saw Dallin's name on a list of potential D.C. Circuit Court of Appeals judges, and Dallin seemed uncertain how to react. That night, he wrote in his journal, "I dread having to make a decision whether to leave my present well-loved 'menu' of cases for a poorer menu in a faraway city in a more important court that could be a steppingstone to the U.S. Supreme Court." He hungered for divine direction on the matter. "I hope the Lord will guide me in that decision," he wrote, "if it ever comes."

Finally, after much pondering and prayer, he received the clarity he had been craving, including a clearer understanding of the revelation he received in the temple years earlier before his appointment to the Utah Supreme Court: "Go to the court, and I will call you from there."[1]

On Friday evening, April 6, 1984, Dallin was in Tucson, Arizona, where he and two others sat as moot court judges at the University of Arizona Law School. When the competition ended, the three judges went to a Mexican restaurant for dinner and an awards presentation. During festivities before dinner—"cocktails for others; nachos for me," Dallin wrote—he was called to the phone near the restaurant's cash register. "I went to the cash register," Dallin recalled, "and a mariachi band was whanging away in the background. It was a chaotic scene."

The caller turned out to be President Gordon B. Hinckley of the First Presidency. "I cannot imagine how he found me there," Dallin wondered in his journal, especially since (as he learned from the law school's dean) the school's switchboard was closed. In any case, President Hinckley asked Dallin to call him when he got back to his hotel. Dallin was accustomed to contact with senior Church leaders and "went on to dinner, without concern, though curious about what could be so serious that he would phone me at this busy time."

After the dinner, as Dallin was being driven back to his hotel, he finally had time to focus on what President Hinckley might want and "wondered if this could be a calling." Though that was possible, he thought, it "was not likely since I had received no inklings or premonitions" of such a thing recently. He knew it was general conference weekend, but—as he wrote two days later—"I was blissfully unaware that this had any significance for my future."

When Dallin got to the hotel, he phoned President Hinckley as requested. After a quick inquiry about worthiness, President Hinckley—in the direct manner for which he was well-known—told Dallin he "was called to be a member of the Council of the Twelve."

"I gasped, 'Oh,'" Dallin recorded in his journal. "It seemed unreal. I heard him say how this would change my life.

"My life," Dallin replied, "is in the hands of the Lord, and my career is in the hands of His servants."

CHAPTER 14

"A DELICATE TRANSITION"

From Justice to Apostle

"Forty-eight hours ago," Dallin Oaks wrote at 10:00 p.m. on Sunday, April 8, 1984, "my world was turned upside down. It will never be the same again." He had prayed long and hard to know what his final occupation in life would be, and now he had his answer. But he had not expected what came. In other major changes in life, he had often had a premonition of what would happen to him. Not this time.

On Friday evening, after President Gordon B. Hinckley called him to be an Apostle of the Lord, Dallin had a hard time sleeping. "I prayed," he wrote. "I tossed and turned. I had chills, especially my feet, which I couldn't get warm. I got up twice and made notes, things to do. I prayed again. And again. I asked how or why I was so unprepared and unwarned for this calling. I found myself wondering if I was hallucinating, if this was really happening."

Why was he away from home at general conference time? "I condemned myself for being in Arizona" on judicial business, he chided, "when I should have known I was to be called. Only on that subject did

I receive a comforting feeling. I felt assurance that my being in Arizona was where I should be—that it was not displeasing to the Lord."

Dallin contemplated the thought and soon understood it. "As I pondered that impression," he wrote, "it occurred to me that my being out of state permitted President Hinckley to give a convenient and proper explanation of my absence, and that my absence would facilitate my transition from state to Church. If I were present and speaking, I would be seen as a General Authority, and might not be able to complete my work as a judge."

When President Hinckley first extended the call by phone, he asked Dallin if he could return to Salt Lake City the next morning to attend the Saturday sessions of general conference. Dallin explained he had to preside over a vital PBS board meeting on Saturday in Chicago. "He said I should go," Dallin recorded, "and complete that assignment. They would present my name and explain that I was out of the state on a prior assignment.

"I then explained a 'problem' with pending [court] cases," Dallin noted, "pointing out that if I began my service immediately, it would cast a shadow over about a hundred pending cases, plus prevent me from completing [my] opinions in about a dozen." It might also cause problems in his PBS work.

"President Hinckley immediately said he saw the problem and thought we should delay my ordaining and commencing service until I had a suitable time to wrap up my judicial work," Dallin wrote. "He asked me to think further on the implications of the announcement and sustaining now with my service to commence several weeks later, and to phone him in the morning at 6:15." Dallin agreed to do so.

President Hinckley said Dallin could tell June about his call, clarifying that "no one else should know." Dallin phoned her, and they spent forty-five minutes, he summarized, "sharing our ignorance, our apprehensions, our wonderment, and our love and determination to serve wholeheartedly and effectively."

During the troubled night that followed, Dallin turned the matter over and over again in his mind, along with other questions that pressed on him. "I got 2½ hours sleep," he wrote.

Though Friday night seemed interminably long, 6:15 a.m. Saturday finally arrived, and as promised, Dallin phoned President Hinckley with his thoughts. Even though Dallin would be returning to Salt Lake Saturday night after his PBS meeting, they agreed he should not show up at conference on Sunday. Better to wait until he could clear the decks of any potential conflicts. "I pledged my wholehearted efforts to clear every obstacle and begin my service as soon as possible," Dallin wrote.

Later that Saturday morning when it came time to sustain Church leaders in general conference, President Hinckley noted the two vacancies in the Twelve occasioned by the deaths of Elders LeGrand Richards and Mark E. Petersen. When he read the names of the two new Apostles—Russell M. Nelson and Dallin H. Oaks—he offered an explanation.

"With reference to Dallin Oaks," he said, "I should like to say that while we nominate and sustain him today, he will not be ordained to the apostleship, nor will he be set apart as a member of the Council of the Twelve, nor will he begin his apostolic service, until after he completes his present judicial commitments, which may require several weeks. He is absent from the city, and necessarily absent from the conference. We excuse him."[1]

The sustaining of Russell M. Nelson as an Apostle that same day pleased Dallin because he knew the famous heart surgeon who would thereafter sit beside him in the Quorum of the Twelve. Eighteen years before their simultaneous calls to the Twelve, then-Professor Oaks had participated in efforts to recruit Dr. Nelson for a position at the University of Chicago medical school. The doctor had decided not to accept the offer, but the interaction allowed the two to get to know each other.[2]

Five years later, in 1971, Dallin became president of BYU, and Russell was called as General President of the Sunday School. They both excelled in their professions and served in stake presidencies and as regional representatives of the Twelve, and they became close friends. "To June and Dallin," Russell wrote in a copy of his autobiography that he gave them in December 1989, "With deepest admiration and gratitude. You are truly special to me. Love, Dantzel and Russell."

Even after taking two days to contemplate his new responsibilities in the Twelve, Dallin struggled to portray the maelstrom of feelings that enveloped him in the hours after his call. "This account does not begin to cover the emotions of that 24-hour period, ending Saturday evening," he explained in his journal. Sunday too, he wrote, "has been like living a dream."

In the Sunday conference session, President Hinckley said of the two new Apostles, "I want to give you my testimony that they were chosen and called by the spirit of prophecy and revelation. There was much of prayer concerning this matter. There was discussion with President Kimball, the prophet of the Lord in our day, and a clear statement from him, for his is the prerogative in these matters. There was a clear and distinct impression, what I choose to call the whisperings of the Holy Spirit, concerning those who should be selected to assume this most important and sacred responsibility."

President Hinckley acknowledged that both were "men of learning and achievement in their respective professions" who had been honored by their peers. "But this is not why they were chosen," he emphasized. "Their service in the Church has been noteworthy," he added, giving examples of that service. "But this is not why they were called," he said again. "They were called," he stressed, "because the Lord wanted them in this office as men who have a witness of his divinity, and whose voices have been and will be raised in testimony of his reality."[3]

Even after this assurance, Dallin remained overwhelmed, numb, as though in shock. "I still feel beside myself," he wrote that evening, "as if I were a player in some drama. The emotional-spiritual impact has not registered." Before bed that night, Dallin penned a prayer in his journal: "May our Heavenly Father bless me to magnify a calling so sacred I can only begin to understand its significance!"

The stress Dallin felt was like that experienced by President Spencer W. Kimball when he was first called to the Twelve decades earlier. Spencer had been surprised—shocked—baffled by the call. He wrote of the sleepless night that followed and how he agonized for days.[4]

Four days after Dallin's call, the new Apostle's numbness began to wear off, only to be replaced by a flurry of "fear and apprehension," he wrote. He bore up under the weight of his new calling as he had borne virtually every challenge of his adult life: by striving mightily. He had long found strength in hard work, and now he began rereading James E. Talmage's *Jesus the Christ* every morning, beginning with the chapters on the Savior's atoning sacrifice. "I have so *far* to go to qualify as a witness of Christ!" Dallin exclaimed. He also began looking up every reference to *apostles* in the scriptures, remarking, "How little I know of that!"

Ten days after receiving his call, Dallin picked up a copy of Spencer W. Kimball's biography and reread what the current Church President had written about his own call to the Twelve. The next day, Dallin wrote to President Kimball. "Yesterday morning, as I sought comfort and understanding to prepare me for my calling," he began, "I read again what you had written about the struggles you experienced in the interval between your calling to the apostleship and your move to Salt Lake City. How well your description fit my circumstance! How comforted I felt to know that a man I love and admire—a spiritual giant—had experienced these same feelings!"

Difficult as this new responsibility was, Dallin fully consecrated himself to fulfilling it. "I feel so unworthy and so unprepared for this sacred calling," he confessed. "Yet I do know that there is nothing I

Dallin ten years before his call to the apostleship with President Spencer W. Kimball

cannot do if I am worthy of the help of our Heavenly Father. My challenge is to be worthy and to be in tune."

He did not doubt President Kimball's revelation in choosing him. "Although this calling came as a complete surprise to me," Dallin wrote, "I have felt not a moment's hesitancy about its divine origin or the fact that it is the answer to my prayers for all my adult life that the Lord would reveal to me in due time how He would have me serve to use the unique experiences with which He has blessed me. I desire to be of use to His servants and to be an instrument in His hands."

The call affected Dallin's family, especially his wife, who had solidly supported him in all his callings, and he concluded his letter, "June joins me in wholehearted devotion to the demands of this service and in this message of love to you and Sister Kimball."

On April 9, 1984, Dallin went to work at the Utah Supreme Court but stayed off the judicial bench to avoid involvement with "cases that could not be decided before my departure from the court," he noted. "I wrote an explanation, which the Chief read from the bench at the beginning of court. After conferring with President Hinckley, who was very understanding and supportive, and with Chief Justice [Gordon] Hall, I wrote a letter of resignation (to the Governor), effective May 2d. I will be ordained at the temple meeting that following Thursday." He explained the transition to his fellow justices, who "were very supportive, and most warm in their congratulations—every one."

The transition from state to Church included making decisions about Dallin's community service activities. President Hinckley did not object to Dallin's remaining on the PBS board. On the other hand, when the *Washington Post*'s Supreme Court correspondent phoned Dallin "to find out if this would take me out of consideration for the U.S. Supreme Court, 'for which your name has often been mentioned,'" Dallin wrote, "I told him it surely would."

Though Dallin's communications with Church headquarters were minimal for one just called as a General Authority, letters of congratulations poured in. "The letters have been arriving all week!" Dallin said. "I haven't read all of them yet, but they are all heart-warming. I was especially touched by the one from Thomas Monson, recalling our first meeting when he reorganized our stake presidency in Chicago, and some things he said to me on that occasion. I remember this clearly, but I hadn't thought he did."

"My feelings this week," Dallin summed up, "have been those of business and preoccupation with a delicate transition, mingled with wonderment and increasing awe at a fast-approaching date when I will commence the fulfillment of responsibilities for which I feel almost totally unprepared." Yet he was not alone. "June gives me great support," he wrote, "and with her love and confidence and with the assurance I feel (and will, I know, feel to an increasing extent as I get more in tune with the Spirit) that my calling is from the Lord, I know I can measure up, in time and with experience and counsel."

Monday, April 16, was Dallin's last day on the bench as a state judge, though he would continue writing opinions for a couple more weeks. "As I took off my robe," he reflected afterward, "I felt the sadness one always feels at concluding a pleasant phase of his life. But I felt no sense of loss or regret. I am living in the future, not the past, and I anticipate my new life with eagerness and optimism."

While in Chicago later that week for a PBS board meeting, Dallin spent time at his son Lloyd's apartment. When Dallin's daughter Sharmon came to pick him up, two of her children, Spencer and Juli, looked at their grandfather over and over again. Finally, Spencer blurted, "I can't believe I am talking to an Apostle!"

"I can't believe it either," Dallin concurred when recounting the incident in his journal.

On Wednesday, May 2—his effective resignation date after finishing his work on pending court cases—Dallin prepared to visit Church headquarters for the first time since his call. He was "full of apprehension about measuring up to the new challenges ahead," he wrote. He had prayer with family members before leaving for his new workplace and "told June and Sharmon that I felt like a little boy, just leaving for his first day at school, full of wonder and concern at the newness of this beginning. Sharmon squeezed my arm in a comforting fashion and said, half seriously, 'Don't worry, Daddy. They'll be nice to you.'"

"They were," Dallin later wrote in relief. "Neal Maxwell and James Faust showed me the meeting rooms in the temple and explained procedures," he recorded. "Boyd Packer called on me as soon as I got to the office . . . and briefed me on things. He said, in a voice choked with emotion, 'I dreamed of you last night. I will tell you sometime. I saw you in a place, and it was very pleasing to me.'"

Dallin attended the monthly General Authority training meeting and a session afterward with the ten of the Twelve who were in town. All present embraced him, and Ezra Taft Benson, President of the Quorum of the Twelve, then took an hour with him, "expressing love and reminiscing."

The next morning, as Dallin entered the fourth floor of the Salt Lake Temple for his ordination, the first person he saw was Elder Bruce R. McConkie, an Apostle he greatly admired. "I greeted him with joy," Elder Oaks later wrote, "and before he spoke a word, I exclaimed out of our concern with his cancer, 'Oh, Elder McConkie, how are you?' He replied not a word, but despite being fully dressed in his temple clothes, he jumped up with both feet and clicked his heels. That was the joyful man I came to know as he mentored me during the remaining year of his life."

At 9:45 that morning, Dallin recorded, "I was ordained an Apostle and set apart as a member of the Council of the Twelve. President Spencer W. Kimball and President Marion G. Romney, both very feeble, sat in chairs in the center of the room with President Gordon B. Hinckley on their left and the Twelve (except Elders Perry in South America and Nelson in China) stood in a circle around me, as I sat on a low stool so as to be within arm's reach of the seated members of the Presidency. President Hinckley was voice."

Before the ordination, following a pattern set in 1835 when Oliver Cowdery spoke to the initial twelve Apostles in the latter days, President Hinckley gave Dallin a charge, to which he responded.[5] Even earlier, Dallin had asked himself the question, "Throughout the remainder of your life, will you be a judge and lawyer who has been called to be an Apostle, or will you be an Apostle who used to be a lawyer and a judge?"

"There is a very large difference between those two," he realized. He was familiar with the law and matters most administrators face: committees, public affairs, personnel, and human relations generally. "I was sure that we all have a tendency to focus our efforts on those things that are familiar and easy—where we feel at home," he wrote. "We are repelled by those things that are unfamiliar and difficult.

"The most important parts of my calling"—in fact "the only parts that are really unique in the service of the Lord," he recognized—"were those parts that I knew nothing about—those parts where I would have to start all over at the beginning. I knew that if I concentrated my time on the things that came naturally and the things that I felt qualified to do, I would never be an Apostle. I would always be a former lawyer and judge. I made up my mind that was not for me. I decided that I would focus my efforts on what I had been called to do, not on what I was qualified to do. I determined that instead of trying to shape my calling to my credentials, I would try to shape myself to my calling."[6]

Francis M. Gibbons, secretary to the First Presidency, reminded him of what President Harold B. Lee said years earlier when Dallin was appointed BYU president. "We are not calling President Oaks because of what he *is,*" President Lee had said, "for others have done more and

Elder Dallin H. Oaks as a newly called member of the Twelve

have greater stature and accomplishments. We are calling him because of what he will become."

As Elder Oaks dug in to learn and fulfill his new role, he had many important, first-time experiences, such as assigning missionaries, sealing a couple, and helping dedicate a temple. Along the way, those senior to him took time to guide him. While traveling with him on assignment, Elder Marvin J. Ashton of the Twelve "gave me much valuable counsel and information and shared many insights about the workings of the Twelve and the Presidency," Elder Oaks wrote on June 3. "Today," he recorded less than two weeks later, "Thomas S. Monson gave me (at my request) over an hour of counsel on the performance of my duties, how the Twelve work and relate, etc. It was very valuable."

Some of his most important insights, however, came by quiet inspiration. When Elder Oaks first assigned missionaries, he did so "prayerfully and with fear and trembling." Afterward, he had "a sweet feeling of lightness (as in care-free) and peace, which I took as a communication that I had made no grievous mistakes," he wrote. On June 9, as he was driving, he felt "several waves of what I can only describe as 'goose bumps' sweep over me," he observed. "Then these words came to my mind: 'This is my work, Dallin my son. Be thou humble and the Lord thy God will lead thee by the hand and give thee answer to thy prayers.'"[7]

"I am grateful for this reassurance and promise," Elder Oaks disclosed in his journal, "which gave me confidence for the morrow."

Elder Oaks's feelings of inadequacy as a new Apostle continued but were partly relieved by an event in the Salt Lake Temple. At a meeting of General Authorities, he was called to bear his testimony, dwelling "on my own feelings of inadequacy," he acknowledged. But when Elder Boyd K. Packer arose to testify, he said something that settled "heavily and impressively on my mind."

Elder Packer explained "that as time passes (and we gain greater experience and maturity in our callings), we are less focused on ourselves—even our inadequacies—and more conscious of the great burden of the kingdom, our responsibility to carry the gospel to the entire world, and the sufferings and needs of all mankind."

"I loved that insight!" the new Apostle wrote. "But it is quite a challenge for a new man to get outside himself and put a shoulder under even a tiny corner of the foundation of the kingdom!"

A few weeks later, Elder Oaks presided at a stake division and spoke "with few notes and relying on the Spirit." The result was gratifying. "This is the harvest of my hours of scripture reading since my call," he wrote with satisfaction. "I am beginning to come up to the pace."

The more competence Elder Oaks gained, however, the more clearly he realized the enormity of the task ahead. On September 13, President Hinckley spoke in the temple meeting of the many challenges the Church faced. "I pray that I can participate and contribute to solving them," Elder Oaks wrote. "I am praying more fervently than at any time in my life, and it is easy to see why."

In his quest to be a special witness of Christ, he particularly enjoyed the guidance of Elder McConkie, who had become known for expounding doctrine during nearly four decades as a General Authority but was battling colon cancer. Elder Oaks had him review a talk he planned to give at the temple dedication in Dallas, Texas. Elder McConkie returned it with only minor corrections. "Then," Elder Oaks wrote, "he enthusiastically and fervently clapped me on the shoulders with his huge hands . . . grinned his big grin and said, 'But the best thing about this talk is that it shows the direction you are taking. It is a genuinely doctrinal talk. It is apostolic!'

"I was so pleased at this comment about my talk," Elder Oaks rejoiced, "as I do wish to understand and expound doctrine, and there is no living Apostle whom I respect more in that sphere than Bruce R. McConkie. I told him I wanted to be one who preaches doctrine. 'If the Lord wanted me to function as a lawyer,' I told him, 'He would have called me to be general counsel. Since He called me to be an Apostle, I am determined to try to be an Apostle.'"

Later, as Elder McConkie lay dying, Elder Packer reflected on what his loss would mean and expressed the importance of having scriptorians among the junior members of the Twelve. "I am so unqualified to carry the banner for such expectations," Elder Oaks told his journal, "yet I feel willing to try, and I feel a certain inevitability about this."

On December 1, 1984, near the end of an eventful year, Dallin and June Oaks sent out a general communication to friends and acquaintances—Church members and others—in the form of a Christmas letter. They described how their family had changed, with five of six children now married and a tenth grandchild on the way. Elder Oaks described how his labors on the Utah Supreme Court had been "the most satisfying law work of my professional career."

He then announced, for the benefit of those who had not yet heard, that he resigned from the court, effective May 2. "This concluded my twenty-seven years in the legal profession as law clerk, lawyer, teacher, judge, and university administrator," he told them with finality. "I loved my profession," he explained, "but, as it turned out, I left it without regret."

He described his new calling and the responsibilities it entailed. "My most important duty," he emphasized, "is to serve as a witness of the life and mission of our Savior, Jesus Christ, that all may learn more of Him and grow in faith and determination to live by His teachings.

"I am satisfied," he affirmed, "that there is no more important work to which I can devote the remainder of my life. I face this new challenge with enthusiasm and humility."

Jesus said, "No man, having put his hand to the plough, and looking back, is fit for the kingdom of God" (Luke 9:62). With the diligence and determination that characterized his entire adult life, Elder Dallin H. Oaks grasped the plow firmly in both hands and did not look back.

CHAPTER 15

"A WITNESS OF THE NAME OF CHRIST"

Testifying of the Savior

Elder Dallin H. Oaks spoke to Brigham Young University students and faculty at a devotional on September 18, 1984. He told them that when he was first called to the Twelve, his feelings "were surprise, fright, gratitude, and resolution, in that order." Now, five months later, he explained, "I have much to learn and millions of miles to travel, but my surprise is over, my fear recedes, my gratitude increases, and my resolution is strong. That is how I feel about my calling."[1]

First among his desires was to be a special witness of the name of Christ, and that meant changing long-engrained habits developed when his life was split between secular work responsibilities and part-time callings in the Church. Now that he was a full-time witness of the Savior, he needed to be more sensitive about how he spoke in secular settings.

For example, after speaking on the topic of church and state to a group of Latter-day Saints who met monthly for dinner, he closed his secular lecture without bearing testimony or concluding in the name of Christ. "It was well enough received by those present," he jotted of his talk, "but I felt awful afterwards, like I had done something wrong." After pondering overnight, "I concluded that I *had* done something wrong," he wrote. "I am not called to give secular lectures to the Saints!" He resolved to conclude all future addresses to Church members "with a spiritual message and a testimony of the Savior," confirming, "That is my calling!"

As Elder Oaks continually sought to do better, he received spiritual comfort that his labors were acceptable. In February 1986, as he was leaving his office "after a hectic day of largely administrative work," he wrote, "I had a choice and utterly unexpected spiritual experience. As I was walking out of a darkened office, I suddenly felt that someone was present in that room. On sudden impulse, I dropped to my knees and offered a short prayer of gratitude for my faith and my calling. I then experienced a wave-like sensation and felt the thought, 'I have heard thy prayers, and thy labors are acceptable unto me.' This was a sweet and comforting experience."

The change that was taking place in his heart became apparent when his Church assignments required him to apply skills developed in his secular past. Previously, he might have reveled in such assignments, but not anymore. In April 1986, he was working on a matter that required his legal expertise, and he marveled in his journal, "I was exhausted tonight. It is hard practicing law on the side. My calling is elsewhere. My joy is now in the scriptures and in the spiritual ministry. I do these other tasks cheerfully on assignment, but my heart is elsewhere."

As he focused more on the spiritual realm, he drew closer to his fellow Apostles. In late 1987, he and Elder Neal A. Maxwell were discussing their work together. "I didn't have a brother," Elder Maxwell said. "You are the closest thing to a brother I have ever had." The kind expression deeply touched Elder Oaks.

In the October 1988 general conference, Elder Oaks delivered a powerful address titled "What Think Ye of Christ?" The title came from

Elder Oaks speaking at October 1988 general conference

a question Jesus asked some Pharisees in Matthew 22:42. "That question," Elder Oaks said, "is as penetrating today as when Jesus used it to confound the Pharisees almost two thousand years ago. Like a sword, sharp and powerful, it uncovers what is hidden, divides truth from error, and goes to the heart of religious belief."

To give the question currency, Elder Oaks cited a few answers modern people give to the question. "Some praise Jesus Christ as the greatest teacher who ever lived, but deny that he is Messiah, Savior, or Redeemer," he said. "Some prominent theologians teach that our secularized world needs 'a new concept of God,' stripped of the supernatural. They believe that not even a suffering God can help to solve the pain and tragedy of modern man."[2]

Elder Oaks quoted a Christian leader who asserted, "Jesus was in every sense a human being, just as we are."[3] By reducing Jesus from deity to man, people effectively denied His role as Savior and Redeemer. "Under the influence of such teachings," Elder Oaks said, "the religion of many is like the creed of the humanists, who declare that 'no deity will save us; we must save ourselves.'"[4]

Elder Oaks suggested that some Latter-day Saints "neglect to teach and testify to some simple, basic truths of paramount importance. This omission permits some members and nonmembers to get wrong ideas about our faith and belief." He asked meaningfully, "What do members of The Church of Jesus Christ of Latter-day Saints think of Christ?"

He answered as a special witness of the Savior. "Jesus Christ is the Only Begotten Son of God the Eternal Father," he declared. "He is our Creator. He is our Teacher. He is our Savior. His atonement paid for the sin of Adam and won victory over death, assuring resurrection and immortality for all men. . . . Jesus Christ is the Savior, whose atoning sacrifice opens the door for us to be cleansed of our personal sins so that we can be readmitted to the presence of God. He is our Redeemer."

After quoting Messianic passages from Isaiah, Elder Oaks turned to the New Testament. "At the beginning of the Savior's ministry," he said, "John the Baptist exclaimed, 'Behold the Lamb of God, which taketh away the sin of the world.' At the end of his ministry, as Jesus blessed the cup and gave it to his disciples, he said, 'For this is my blood of the new testament, which is shed for many for the remission of sins.'[5] . . .

"Although the Bible's explanation of atonement for individual sins should be unmistakable," Elder Oaks said, "that doctrine has been misunderstood by many who have only the Bible to explain it."

He cited latter-day prophets, who declared "that the Book of Mormon contains the fulness of the everlasting gospel in greater clarity than any other scripture. In a day when many are challenging the divinity of Jesus Christ or doubting the reality of his atonement and resurrection," he said, "the message of that second witness, the Book of Mormon, is needed more urgently than ever."[6] Elder Oaks quoted Ezra Taft Benson, then President of the Church, noting that he "has reminded us again and again that the Book of Mormon 'was written for our day' and that it 'is the keystone in our witness of Jesus Christ.'[7]

"I believe," Elder Oaks testified, "that the reason our Heavenly

Father has had his prophet direct us into a more intensive study of the Book of Mormon is that this generation needs its message more than any of its forebears. As President Benson has said, the Book of Mormon 'provides the most complete explanation of the doctrine of the Atonement,' and 'its testimony of the Master is clear, undiluted, and full of power.'"[8]

This, Elder Oaks said, contrasts with "what is called 'liberal theology,'" which "teaches that Jesus Christ is important not because he atoned for our sins, but only because he taught us the way to come to God by perfecting ourselves." He asked, "Could some of us believe that our heavenly parentage and our divine destiny allow us to pass through mortality and attain eternal life solely on our own merits?" He answered, "I believe that some of us, some of the time, say things that can create that impression. We can forget that keeping the commandments, which is necessary, is not sufficient. . . .

"Man unquestionably has impressive powers and can bring to pass great things by tireless efforts and indomitable will," he acknowledged. "But after all our obedience and good works," he testified as a special witness, "we cannot be saved from the effect of our sins without the grace extended by the atonement of Jesus Christ.

"The Book of Mormon puts us right," he affirmed, teaching that "nothing . . . short of an infinite atonement . . . will suffice for the sins of the world," therefore "redemption cometh in and through the Holy Messiah," who "offereth himself a sacrifice for sin, to answer the ends of the law."[9]

"Why is Christ the only way?" he asked. "How was it possible for him to take upon himself the sins of all mankind? Why was it necessary for his blood to be shed? And how can our soiled and sinful selves be cleansed by his blood?" Elder Oaks concluded, "These are mysteries I do not understand. To me, as to President John Taylor, the miracle of the atonement of Jesus Christ is 'incomprehensible and inexplicable.'[10]

But the Holy Ghost has given me a witness of its truthfulness, and I rejoice that I can spend my life in proclaiming it.

"I testify with the ancient and modern prophets that there is no other name and no other way under heaven by which man can be saved except by Jesus Christ."[11]

When he finished, Elder Oaks felt good about his talk, noting in his journal that President Gordon B. Hinckley, First Counselor in the First Presidency, "complimented me twice on a 'marvelous' talk, a compliment unusual for him." But most impressive to Elder Oaks were the feelings of his wife, Sister June Oaks, who generally did not hesitate to tell him if she thought his talks or their delivery missed the mark. "June liked the talk," he wrote, "which meant most of all."

This was just one of many talks he would give to testify of the Savior, His peerless life, and His great atoning sacrifice. In one journal entry, he described reading an uplifting book about the Redeemer and wrote that he felt "inspired to concentrate my own speaking more completely and more intensively on the Atonement of Jesus Christ, the need for a Savior, and all that goes with it."

Decades later, Elder Ronald A. Rasband, who had multiple occasions to speak in the same setting as Elder Oaks, remembered how frequently he quoted Doctrine and Covenants 46:13, which reads, "To some it is given by the Holy Ghost to know that Jesus Christ is the Son of God, and that he was crucified for the sins of the world." Elder Oaks would then say, "That's me. I know that." Next, he would read verse 14: "To others it is given to believe on their words, that they also might have eternal life if they continue faithful." "And then," Elder Rasband said, "he'll invite the congregation or the group he is with to lean on him and lean on his testimony if they're at a time in their life or their testimony that they need a little bolstering."

In one talk, Elder Oaks testified of how Christ's Atonement makes it possible to overcome the otherwise damning effects of sin. "When we have done all that we are able, we can rely on God's promised mercy," he declared. "We have a *Savior,* who has taken upon him not just the sins, but also 'the pains and the sicknesses of his people . . . that he may according to the flesh know how to succor his people according to their infirmities.'[12]

"He is our Savior," Elder Oaks testified, "and when we have done all that we can, he will make up the difference, in his own way and in his own time."[13]

At other times in his ministry, Elder Oaks urged all baptized members of the Church to fulfill their own covenant obligation to witness of the Savior.[14] "Apostles have the calling and ordination to be special witnesses of the name of Christ in all the world," he said, "but the duty to witness and testify of Christ at all times and in all places applies to every member of the Church who has received the testimony of the Holy Ghost."[15]

His role as a special witness of *the name of Christ* in all the world was a frequent topic of Elder Oaks's thoughts and study. He pursued this topic diligently, inviting others to discuss it with him. Among them was Brigham Young University religion professor Joseph Fielding McConkie, son of Elder Bruce R. McConkie, grandson of Church President Joseph Fielding Smith, and great-grandson of Joseph F. Smith, the Church's sixth President. "Professor Joseph McConkie came at my invitation for an hour visit on the scriptural meaning of the *name* of Christ," Elder Oaks recorded. "He said his father was starting to work on this in his last two years. He was thrilled I was taking it up."[16]

In September 1997, Elder Oaks recorded a "strong impression I should write a book titled 'The Name of Jesus Christ.'" A few weeks later, he wrote that he had "started serious work" on the book. "I am beginning by reviewing and classifying all scriptures referring to this." Later, when he brought up the topic at a mission presidents seminar, he "was surprised at the low level of interest," even from some General Authorities. "I will ponder what to do about this," he determined.

He worked intermittently on the book and made good progress. By

April 1998, he had decided to call the book *His Holy Name.* At the end of that month, he was putting the finishing touches on the chapters, at the same time "praying, listening, and working" to be sure the contents were what the Lord wanted him to write. The book was published in October 1998.

"When I was called as an Apostle," he wrote in the preface, "I went to the scriptures for illumination on my responsibilities. I found that I was called to be one of the 'special witnesses of the name of Christ in all the world' (D&C 107:23). A witness of Christ I could understand, but why a witness of the *name of Christ?*

"Sensitized by this unanswered question," he told his readers, "I have been amazed at how often scriptural teachings on very important subjects refer to the name of Jesus Christ rather than to the Savior Himself. There is something important here—something heretofore rarely discussed in our literature.

"This book is the product of more than a decade of prayerful study and pondering on the meaning and significance of scriptural references to the holy name of Jesus Christ. With illumination from the Holy Spirit, it has grown 'line upon line, precept upon precept' (D&C 98:12) but even now it only scratches the surface of a subject that is deep and important." He wrote the book, he said, not as a definitive statement of doctrine, but as "a personal expression that attempts to offer wisdom on the meaning of a frequent and important reference in our scriptures, ancient and modern."[17]

After several chapters of analysis, Elder Oaks reached three conclusions that helped answer his question. One was that "an Apostle is a witness of the priesthood of Jesus Christ" because "the Apostle has a special measure of that authority and the keys to direct its exercise, as authorized, in all the world." In addition, "an Apostle is uniquely commissioned to serve as a witness of the work of the Savior," especially "the great atoning sacrifice of the Lord Jesus Christ and of His plan of salvation, with all of its doctrines, ordinances, commandments, covenants, and blessings." Finally, "an Apostle is the preeminent teacher and testifier of the ultimate purpose of the plan of salvation—for each of the sons and daughters of God to attain his or her divine potential of eternal life, . . . which modern revelation calls the 'fulness' of the Father."[18]

"What think ye of Christ?" Elder Oaks asked again in October general conference 2011, twenty-three years after delivering his first talk with that title. After reviewing teachings of the Savior learned through a lifetime of scripture study, he asked listeners, "Where is our ultimate loyalty? Are we like the Christians in Elder Neal A. Maxwell's memorable description who have moved their residence to Zion but still try to keep a second residence in Babylon?

"There is no middle ground," Elder Oaks avowed. "We are followers of Jesus Christ. Our citizenship is in His Church and His gospel, and we should not use a visa to visit Babylon or act like one of its citizens. We should honor His name, keep His commandments, and 'seek not the things of this world but seek . . . first to build up the kingdom of God, and to establish his righteousness.'[19]

"Jesus Christ *is* the Only Begotten and Beloved Son of God," Elder Oaks testified. "He *is* our Creator. He *is* the Light of the World. He *is* our Savior from sin and death. This is the most important knowledge on earth, and you can know this for yourself, as I know it for myself. The Holy Ghost, who testifies of the Father and the Son and leads us into truth, has revealed these truths to me, and He will reveal them to you. . . . I testify of the truth of these things in the name of Jesus Christ, amen."[20]

CHAPTER 16

"THINGS AS THEY WERE"

Family and Church History

The Book of Mormon declares that "the twelve apostles bear record; and they bear record according to the truth" (1 Nephi 13:24). Standing before Pilate before His crucifixion, Jesus testified, "To this end was I born, and for this cause came I into the world, that I should bear witness unto the truth." When Pilate scoffed, "What is truth?" the Savior did not respond immediately (see John 18:37–38). Nearly two millennia later, however, He answered the question for the Prophet Joseph Smith. "Truth," the Lord declared, "is knowledge of things as they are, and as they were, and as they are to come" (D&C 93:24).

From a young age, Elder Dallin H. Oaks seemed drawn toward a "knowledge of things . . . as they were." History—including family and Church history—naturally interested him. As a boy, he listened attentively to stories about his father.[1] Furthering his interest in personal and family history, he wrote an autobiography in his middle years when the busyness of life might easily have provided an excuse for avoiding the task. Over succeeding decades, he compiled histories of many in his family lines and his wife June's. As a young lawyer and law professor, he coauthored a highly acclaimed book on the trial of the murderers of Joseph Smith and published other works on Church history topics, including coauthoring a meticulously researched law review article that exonerated the Prophet from claims of fraud asserted by critics in his lifetime.[2]

In all this research and writing, he relentlessly pursued the truth. His book on the murders of Joseph and Hyrum Smith, for example, debunked well-accepted but erroneous notions about the killers. A book titled *The Fate of the Persecutors of the Prophet Joseph Smith* had become popular among Latter-day Saints because it claimed the killers died horrible deaths.[3] Its theme appealed to readers' sense of justice but was based on selective evidence, inaccuracies, and exaggeration. Elder Oaks and his coauthor, Marvin S. Hill, demonstrated through pathbreaking research and analysis that the murders were carried out by prominent members of the community—not unusual with mob violence at the time—and that the killers went on to live normal and even reputable lives. True justice would have to await the Final Judgment.

Given Elder Oaks's extraordinary interest in history, it seemed only fitting that shortly after his call and ordination to the apostleship, he received the assignment to serve as one of two Quorum of the Twelve advisers to the Church Historical Department. The advisers typically met monthly with leaders of the department to provide guidance, approve major projects and policy changes, and review publications.

One of his early assignments in that capacity was to find a new staff head for the department. On Friday, December 13, 1985, Elder Oaks recorded that he and Elder Neal A. Maxwell were "working to help fill" the role "with a man who will have the initiative and perspective to use the resources of that department in affirmative efforts to strengthen faith." Two weeks later, during the Christmas vacation period, Elder Oaks was in the office "all day, mostly on the phone and in interviews trying to locate just the right person" to fill the new role and serve with Church Historian Dean L. Larsen, Senior President of the Seventy.

The following Monday, December 30, Elder Oaks was back in the office. In his journal that evening, he wrote of receiving a list of thirteen candidates from one of his former law clerks. "The fourth name on the list, Rick Turley, 'sounded better' to me than the others," Elder Oaks recorded. "I had him over for a bowl of soup at lunch and was surprised to find that he had been a Kimball Scholar and a top *law review man* in law school. Even though he's only been out [of law school] since June 1985, he may be our man. . . . I have about four others who seem suitable for intelligence, loyalty, and interest, all more experienced lawyers than he, but he is likely to be the one, if my feelings prove out."

On Thursday, January 2, 1986, following the New Year's holiday, Elder Oaks was "back to work for a full schedule" and wrote, "I finished my phone search for a new man in Church History, and reported to Elders Packer and Larsen that Rick Turley, recent graduate from BYU Law, was my top recommendation." The next day, he recorded, "Elder Packer interviewed Rick Turley and liked him for the job I have proposed."

The hiring of Richard E. Turley Jr. came at a difficult time for the Church Historical Department. In mid-October 1985, an unknown assailant set pipe bombs that killed Latter-day Saints Steven F. Christensen at his downtown Salt Lake City office and Kathleen Sheets in the driveway of her suburban home. At first, law-enforcement officials assumed the unknown killer was a disgruntled investor in a financial services company for which both Sheets's husband and Christensen had worked. But their theory shifted when a third bomb went off, injuring document dealer Mark W. Hofmann, a young returned missionary who specialized in selling items related to Latter-day Saint and broader American history.[4]

Because Christensen had purchased a famous document from Hofmann—the so-called salamander letter—investigators theorized the murders somehow tied to historical documents, with the Sheets bombing being simply a diversion.[5] The investigation of the case went on for many months and eventually concluded that Hofmann himself was the bomber. The crimes and their aftermath placed a great strain on Church leaders and employees and drew considerable media attention, much of it negative.

Finally, on January 23, 1987, Mark Hofmann entered a downtown Salt Lake City courtroom and, as part of an agreement with prosecutors, pleaded guilty to killing Steve Christensen and Kathy Sheets and committing other crimes growing out of a multiyear forgery spree. As part of the plea deal, Hofmann agreed to answer questions from prosecutors on the charged crimes and related matters. In the subsequent interviews, he admitted to forging many documents related to the history of the Church.[6]

Hofmann's crimes hurt many people, most importantly those he murdered and their family members. In the history community, his forgeries and systematic deception also eroded trust in a world in which trust was key. Well-known bookdealer W. Thomas Taylor wrote, "The very worst thing that could come out of the mess of forgeries and thefts that afflicts our little world these days is that we might . . . behave toward each other with cynicism and mistrust. I do not wish to continue making decisions predicated upon the possible dishonesty of the people I deal with. The strongest case I can make for dealing severely with those few who betray our trust is that it makes it safer to deal with the rest of the world with a measure of faith."[7]

Among Hofmann's many victims were Church leaders who, relying on his representations, purchased documents from him for the Church's historical collections. Elder Oaks had met Hofmann only once very briefly and purchased nothing from him. But following Hofmann's sentencing, Elder Oaks responded on behalf of his fellow leaders. "Ministers of the gospel function best in an atmosphere of trust and love," he said. "In that kind of atmosphere, they fail to detect a few deceivers, but that is the price they pay to increase their effectiveness in counseling, comforting, and blessing hundreds of honest and sincere people they see. It is better for a Church leader to be occasionally disappointed than to be constantly suspicious."[8]

Hofmann's crimes would continue to cast a shadow over Church history for years to come, but by late August of 1989, the atmosphere had improved markedly. At that time, Elder Oaks described his and Elder Packer's regular meeting with Church Historical Department leaders as "mostly routine, because of the good work of Larsen, [John K.] Carmack, and Turley." Elder Oaks would serve as a Church Historical Department adviser from November 1985 to March 2000 and again from February 2005 to February 2010—a total of nearly two decades of service in that capacity. He served roughly five years in that role with Elder Packer, ten with Elder Maxwell, and five with Elder Russell M. Nelson.

During the years Elder Oaks served as one of the Historical Department advisers under First Presidency direction, the department transformed from a besieged entity to a vibrant, proactive institution. It established a purpose statement, improved its security, installed a new library catalog, and developed professional access policies. It also made great strides forward by dramatically enhancing the Church's historic sites program, including a master plan to guide development; conserving the Sacred Grove and nearby structures on the historic Smith family farm in New York; acquiring property for the Priesthood Restoration Site in Susquehanna County, Pennsylvania; restoring the Grandin Building where the Book of Mormon was first published; developing a complex of historic buildings on the Kirtland Flats in Ohio, where the Church was headquartered in its early days; and constructing a trail center at Winter Quarters to commemorate the pioneer crossing of Latter-day Saints to Utah.

Elder Oaks and his fellow advisers had a major impact on the Museum of Church History and Art (later renamed the Church History Museum), focusing staff on the museum's sacred purpose and helping to approve the first and several subsequent international art competitions, a large main-floor exhibit on the Church's history called "A Covenant Restored," and exhibits on numerous other subjects, including a major exhibit on the Relief Society in 1992 and the Salt Lake Temple during its centennial in 1993.

On Friday, February 9, 1990, Elder Oaks wrote that he and Elder Packer "inspected the progress on the permanent exhibit in the Church Museum and were very pleased at the way" the staff "have followed the strategic direction we gave about two years ago." On May 17, he wrote with satisfaction, "I walked through the Church Museum permanent historical exhibit, which opens tonight, and was thrilled and moved to tears. It truly fulfills the Packer/Oaks challenge to display artifacts in a way that will build faith."

During Elder Oaks's tenure in helping guide the Church Historical Department, he had a hand in facilitating, reviewing, and making suggestions about some of the most important Church history publications of the era, including the four-volume *Encyclopedia of Mormonism*; *Victims: The LDS Church and the Mark Hofmann Case*; the *Teachings of Presidents of the Church* series, especially the volume on Joseph Smith; *The Journals of George Q. Cannon* series; and *Massacre at Mountain Meadows.* He also played a role in establishing the magisterial Joseph Smith Papers project and the Church Historian's Press, launching a revolutionary new four-volume history of the Church titled *Saints: The Story of the Church of Jesus Christ in the Latter Days,* and building a new, state-of-the-art Church History Library.

Because of his lifelong love of history, Elder Oaks rejoiced in his assignment as an adviser on Church history matters. In February 2007, for example, he wrote of a ninety-minute meeting he and Elder Nelson had with department leaders Marlin K. Jensen, Richard E. Turley Jr., and Steven L. Olsen. Elder Oaks observed that he and Elder Nelson "enjoyed abundant inspiration in answering many tough questions," and he added, "I enjoy this assignment and these brethren."

A few weeks later, Elder Oaks recorded with satisfaction that the

First Presidency had approved the advisers' proposal to publish an *Ensign* article on the Mountain Meadows Massacre. The presidency resolved, "*We* should tell this terrible story."[9] The next year, after reading the recently published *Massacre at Mountain Meadows*—written by Ronald W. Walker, Richard E. Turley Jr., and Glen M. Leonard—Elder Oaks described the book in his journal as "a devastatingly depressing narrative, brilliantly researched and told." In November, Elder Nelson and Elder Oaks appeared before the First Presidency and supported Church History Department leaders "in their successful effort to get First Presidency approval for three vital steps" needed for advancing the Joseph Smith Papers.

Because Elder Oaks's family lines went back to early figures in Church history—including Emer Harris, a brother of Book of Mormon witness Martin Harris—Elder Oaks's family history and the history of the Church intertwined and were often indistinguishable. During some of the years that Elder Oaks oversaw the Church Historical Department, he also oversaw the Church's family history organization. Because of his personal emphasis over many years on his own family's history, he naturally fit into that role, which he saw as an inspired labor.

Working on his mother's history over the Christmas holiday in 1994, Elder Oaks felt divine aid in his writing. "I felt an unusual degree of inspiration," he wrote, "with thoughts communicated to my mind on how to organize the material, insights sensed, and words given on what to write. More than that, the clock seemed to stand still. Time after time, I would finish a long-drawn-out task and then be astonished to check the clock and find that only thirty or sixty minutes had passed. I was conscious throughout that a miracle was taking place. I counted this as a confirmation that the Lord wants this history done and that He wants me to do my part of it now! By 4:30 I had completed work that I thought would take a week. . . . Amazing!"

Three months later, he set apart his brother, Merrill, as a mission president, and at a dinner afterward that included their sister, Evelyn, Merrill presented them and their spouses with a copy of their mother's history edited by his daughter, Amy J. Oaks Long, "just off the press." "It looks wonderful," Elder Oaks wrote of the compilation. "I am thrilled!"

In February 1997, Elder Oaks recorded in his journal, "June and I worked on assembling histories of our pioneer ancestors." On March 22, he "spent most of the day writing pioneer histories for June's Dixon lines." Two days later, he "edited Oaks pioneer histories." On Easter Sunday that year, Elder Oaks worked "redoing and expanding the Emer and Charles Harris histories, in response to impressions, and found and incorporated much new material." The following month, he wrote a draft on the last of his wife June's lines. "I counted up," he wrote, "and was astonished to find a total of [50] ancestors of June and Dallin (all of them!) who came to Utah in the pioneer period, 1847–69."

He spent part of his July break that year preparing a history called *50 Pioneers* that he and Sister Oaks were excited to finish and distribute to family members. "June and I are convinced that my assembling, synthesizing, and clarifying work will *greatly* facilitate our posterity's and our extended family's acquaintanceship with their pioneer ancestors," Elder Oaks wrote. "That was my goal."

That year 1997 marked the 150th anniversary of the arrival of the first Latter-day Saint pioneer company in the Salt Lake Valley after a journey of more than a thousand miles across the North American continent. With all the commemorative events that year, Elder and Sister Oaks decided to join the leaders of their Bonneville Stake on a handcart trek. "We drove 350 miles to Independence Rock" in Wyoming, Elder Oaks wrote, "and then to the nearby Church Information Center (the old Sun Ranch) by Martin's Cove." He spoke to the group at the mouth of the cove and then, "on impulse," he wrote, "I waded the Sweetwater River" near where rescuers helped carry stranded handcart pioneers in 1856.

On a subsequent day, he and Sister Oaks "met at the monument on the route from the Sweetwater over Rocky Ridge to Rock Creek (13 miles away)," he chronicled. "I spoke to the group (50–60) after we had pushed and pulled four handcarts some two miles to the top, reviewing the principles we should learn from the pioneers." Sister Oaks, who was ill, drove to Rock Creek, while Elder Oaks "walked and helped with a handcart the whole way (about 4½ hours). I could hardly put one foot ahead of another for the last few miles," he recorded.

A few weeks later, he flew to Ontario, California, where he was taken to a San Bernardino County museum display on early settlement of the area that included information on one of his Seely ancestors. The next morning, Elder Oaks wrote, "I joined 2,600 others (including some wagons and handcarts) . . . in a five-mile walk down El Cajon pass." It was a "very sentimental walk for me," he noted, as he remembered ancestors who followed that route while migrating from Utah to the San Bernardino Valley in 1851. The next evening, Elder Oaks spoke at a park pavilion in the mouth of Cajon Pass, "where," he wrote, "I gave a thirty-minute talk on pioneers to about 6,600" people, most of them Latter-day Saints. Among other things, he challenged those in the audience, "You have the dust of the trail. Now you need the water of the destination." That elicited applause from the listeners.

In February 1999, Elder Oaks labored through a busy day that included reading a book manuscript prepared by former Assistant Church Historian Davis Bitton on George Q. Cannon, a prominent Church leader of the late nineteenth and early twentieth centuries.[10] The next month, he finished reviewing the Cannon volume, worked on Sister Oaks's history, and spoke to descendants of Brigham Young at the Lion House.

In 2002, when the rebuilt Nauvoo Temple was dedicated, Elder

Oaks felt particularly close to his ancestors. He wrote that in the first dedicatory session, "I had a very special spiritual experience of knowing that my father (who died in 1940) was there in the session, with my mother (who died in 1980). I had the thought that they had come for my father's brother"—Charles Oaks, father of Elder Robert C. Oaks of the Seventy—"who at that moment was gravely ill at his home in Provo." Elder Oaks did not know it, but Charles had died that morning.

In the final session, Elder Oaks spoke, and he talked about his ancestors. Later, a woman wrote to say she had been watching him during the closing hymn and saw two men dressed in white standing by him, presumably his ancestors. Elder Oaks replied, "I do not know who the two men were that you saw standing beside me, but I have no doubt that they were loved ones from beyond the veil." He wondered if they were his father and uncle, come for Charles.

Besides doing a great deal of work on his own family's history, Elder Oaks helped oversee the Church's family history operations at one of the most dramatic times in its history. In September 2007, for example, he attended a meeting of the Temple and Family History Executive Council in which he heard "continued long briefings on roll-out of FamilySearch." The "scale and direction of this great advance in family history" impressed him, and he declared it "very important."

Finally, on January 19, 2010, Elder Oaks received a letter from the First Presidency releasing him from his roles over the Family History and Church Historical Departments. Elder Oaks expressed mixed feelings of great relief from the heavy responsibility, on the one hand, and loss on the other, especially of his connection to Church history. "My release from Church History Adviser is painful after twenty-four years," he confided to his journal, "but right."

Yet he never lost his interest in the subject matter, and as a senior leader he continued to play an important role in making certain that the history of the Church and of the families of the earth, including his own, received the attention mandated by scripture.

CHAPTER 17

"THINGS AS THEY ARE"

Public Affairs

"The twelve apostles bear record . . . according to the truth" (1 Nephi 13:24), and that truth includes "knowledge of things as they are" (D&C 93:24). For many years, Elder Oaks had responsibilities directly related to the current issues faced by the Church. Those duties included membership on, and later chairmanship of, the Public Affairs Committee. The diverse public affairs work of the Church includes media relations, interfaith relations, and government and community relations throughout the earth. This work drew Elder Oaks into many assignments to speak on the Church's behalf.

As a newly called Apostle in 1984, Elder Oaks attended meetings of the Church's National Advisory Council, a group of knowledgeable people who advised Church leaders on public affairs matters. In addressing the group as its luncheon speaker, Elder Oaks chose a challenging topic. "I spoke about the dilemma of Church Public Communications," he wrote, which was "whether to emphasize *similarities* with the rest of Christianity, minimizing the value of the message, or overemphasize *differences,* minimizing the audience."

The truth was that Church members had to do both: emphasize

the essential doctrines of the restored gospel while at the same time working with other people of faith in areas of common concern. This Elder Oaks has been able to do successfully throughout his years as a General Authority. On one occasion, for example, he flew to Chicago to meet with his former University of Chicago law student James Serritella, counsel for the Catholic Archdiocese there. They spoke about "common interests in law and policy" between the two churches.

Not long after Elder Oaks's call to the apostleship, the Mark Hofmann forgery-bombing case catapulted the Church into the media limelight. Elder Oaks helped respond to the international media interest the case aroused. Experienced with media matters since his days at BYU, he urged public statements to counteract disturbing media conclusions drawn about Church leaders, and he participated in a news conference with journalists.

Several months later, after Hofmann was arrested and formally charged with murder and other crimes, the First Presidency responded to the united urgings of Elders Boyd K. Packer, James E. Faust, Neal A. Maxwell, and Dallin H. Oaks and released a list of documents acquired from the documents dealer. The day before, Elder Oaks wrote, "This is so important to establish openness! I am lighthearted tonight as I contemplate how much air will be cleared by tomorrow's disclosure."

The following year, after Hofmann pleaded guilty and additional facts came to light, Elder Oaks recorded in his journal: "The outcome vindicates the Church in every particular! How blessed we are! The Lord truly looks after His work and His servants. We are buffeted by the world and afflicted with the consequences of our own mistakes, but when the stakes are large and the survival or significant momentum of the work is on the line, we are saved as by a miracle."

On August 7, 1987, Elder Oaks represented Church leaders in delivering an address at a BYU symposium titled "Church History and Recent Forgeries." Elder Oaks concluded, "The symposium achieved its purpose completely, bringing together the principal figures in law enforcement and history and allowing the media and public to have a sense of closure on this episode and a demonstration of the outright rejection of the contents of Hofmann's forgeries."[1]

Subsequent events, however, led Church leaders to feel their role in the Hofmann case had not been accurately portrayed. During the first week of September 1988, Elder Oaks advocated in meetings of the Public Affairs Committee and the Council of the Twelve that the Church support the publishing of a book on the Hofmann case. Previous books, he felt, were damaging. "Many inferences have been drawn against the Church, incorrectly," he wrote, "and we have much favorable evidence that has never been disclosed or used. To avoid a verdict against us by the jury of history in a case where our position has never been heard, we need another book."

Independently, Richard E. Turley Jr., managing director of the Church Historical Department, had reached the same conclusion and suggested the idea to Elder Neal A. Maxwell. When Turley learned that members of the Twelve felt the same way, he readily agreed to write a book on the topic, provided he could have full access to all evidence on Church leaders' involvement in the case and retain full editorial control of the book's contents. They agreed, and, as part of the agreement, Elder Oaks gave Turley his relevant journals and other evidence.

Later, when Elder Oaks read Turley's manuscript, he wrote in his journal: "The facts are there, and his effort will set the record straight for purposes of history. Those who want to believe the worst about the Church and its leaders will do so, but those who want the truth and have ears to hear and hearts to understand will at last have the complete facts on the Church . . . involvement in the Hofmann affair."

He and Elder Packer met with Turley, passing on their comments "without trespassing his author's prerogative," Elder Oaks recorded. Turley remained independent in his authorship, and on Wednesday, November 8, 1989, Elder Oaks wrote a letter to President Gordon B. Hinckley about the book, explaining "our limited prerogatives in reviewing his manuscript." President Hinckley met with Turley, "made a few suggestions (non-directive)," asked some questions, "and stepped back so Rick could submit the manuscript as he saw fit," Elder Oaks recorded. In all, Turley submitted the manuscript to some two dozen readers, in and outside of the Church, for peer review before he published the book, which gained a broad readership.[2]

The Hofmann case was just one of many issues Elder Oaks faced in the years he served on the Public Affairs Committee. Though he always tried to appear cool under pressure, the stress of handling problems at work sometimes became so great that he needed to take a break from his usual workaholic pace. "I feel the strain of successive 15–16 hour days," he wrote on one occasion. Several days later, he realized he was having "one of those rare days when I felt so much unrelenting pressure that I could feel butterflies in my stomach." He recognized the emotion as "an old feeling of tension I had sometimes at BYU," and he opted for the same solution he tried there: "I finished out the day's activities, and then took the evening off for diversion—in this case just reading and relaxing with a TV program."

On balance, over years of interviews for media stories, Elder Oaks generally felt good about the results and credited divine inspiration for successes. Following an interview he and Elder Jeffrey R. Holland of the Twelve had for a major news magazine cover story, Elder Oaks wrote, "We responded like a team and had abundant inspiration for our answers (I learned from them)."

Elder Oaks sometimes sought priesthood blessings before such interviews. "President Packer gave me a powerful blessing for my interview," he wrote in 2007. "With that and my intense preparation and fervent prayers, I was profoundly blessed. I do not think I could have done better." A few weeks later when he had a chance to review a transcript of the interview, he felt profound gratitude. "To me," he confided in his journal, "the content was astonishingly good. I was surely blessed/inspired in my answers."

The Church's eleventh article of faith declares, "We claim the privilege of worshiping Almighty God according to the dictates of our own conscience, and allow all men the same privilege, let them worship how, where, or what they may." Without compromising core beliefs, the Church's leaders promoted strong interfaith ties, especially as many people in the world became less religious than in the past. The leaders felt that working with other people of faith helped not only to promote belief in a Divine Creator and religious liberty generally, but also made possible humanitarian and other good work globally on a scale that might not otherwise be possible.

In 1998, Elder Oaks returned to Chicago to participate in a discussion led by distinguished University of Chicago professor Martin Marty, an ordained Lutheran minister. The discussion included several prominent ministers, professors, and executives. "We discussed how congregations and denominations do and should make an impact on politics and court," Elder Oaks recorded. "I rejoiced in the strength of [Latter-day Saint] theology and governance and grieved at the way some or most of these good people are evolving into political or social welfare organizations, without theological anchors. I tried to be insightful without being insulting, and think I succeeded."

Over the years, Elder Oaks met with people of many religious backgrounds, especially Christians, Jews, and Muslims, promoting religious freedom and cooperation. Over time, he became recognized as someone whose past experience on the Utah Supreme Court and as a law professor and university president informed his work as a religious leader, and people of many faiths looked to him for wisdom on how to practice religion and work cooperatively as religious organizations in an increasingly secular world. In 2015, for example, he participated in a court and clergy conference in California attended by religious leaders, judges, and lawyers. Elder Oaks gave the plenary address. "The audience was very receptive, and the questions that followed were friendly and easily answered," he wrote. "Many expressions of appreciation and admiration. I was truly blessed."

During Elder Oaks's legal career, he had worked for the United States government and the state governments of Illinois and Utah. After becoming an Apostle, he was frequently consulted by other Church leaders on governmental matters, especially if they had legal implications. At times, he welcomed this as a natural extension of his calling and a good use of his past experience. At other times, however, he found political matters distracting and even annoying.

As an Apostle called to preach the gospel throughout the world, he quickly gained a global perspective and appreciated the need for diplomacy in international relations if the Church was to fulfill the commandment to "bear testimony of my name and to send it abroad among all nations, kindreds, tongues, and people" (D&C 112:1).[3] Global diplomacy required befriending all while offending none, if possible. The Church's twelfth article of faith proclaims, "We believe in being subject to kings, presidents, rulers, and magistrates, in obeying, honoring, and sustaining the law," and that meant interacting with leaders of many backgrounds and political persuasions. Elder Oaks, a patriotic American with years of National Guard and Army Reserve experience, sought to establish friendly relations with diplomats and citizens of such countries as China and Russia.

As countries previously closed began opening up to the Church over the years, he rejoiced with other leaders and saw the hand of God at work. In September 1989, as the Church was preparing to send missionaries to Russia for the first time in decades, Elder Oaks hosted "three deputies of the Supreme Soviet, in the United States to pursue ideas to guide their work in considering amendments to the Soviet Constitution." He answered questions from them on Saturday, and on Sunday, he took them to the Tabernacle Choir broadcast. One of the deputies "said the choir was the most impressive thing he has seen in America, and spoke of deep religious feelings on hearing them sing,"

Elder Oaks with Mikhail Gorbachev

Elder Oaks wrote. "In conclusion, touched by the sweet spirit, I invoked the blessings of God upon them in their efforts to assure greater freedom and justice to their people."

Seven years later, after missionary work in Russia was well established, Elder Oaks had words of praise for the man whose efforts helped open up the country. "June and I attended a small dinner for, and I went to the [Salt Lake City] lecture by, Mikhail Gorbachev, who is a *very* impressive man," Elder Oaks wrote. "He received a very warm welcome!"

In March 1991, Elder Oaks chose to use a devotional at Brigham Young University to give a status report on the Church's progress in China, a subject that occupied much of his apostolic ministry over the years. The insights he shared were also prophetic. "When the first [Latter-day Saint] missionaries began their work in Great Britain and Europe," he told the students, "they were often going to the countries of their own ancestry, where the laws and customs were similar to those in the United States. That has been the pattern for more than a century.

In Europe and in the nations of the Americas, our missionaries have been welcomed or at least tolerated.

"In contrast, in the century ahead," he predicted, "we will knock on the doors of nations with whom we do not have ancestral ties. In addition to differences of language and nationality, we will face barriers of culture and some barriers of hostility from wars or resentments against prior colonial or other repression." He offered a personal perspective on the then-current situation in China and how the Lord would fulfill prophecies about the gospel going to all nations.

"We cannot send missionaries to the People's Republic of China, but each year China sends thousands of its choicest sons and daughters to various foreign lands to study," he pointed out. "In those places they quite naturally meet our missionaries, and many of these Chinese students are joining the Church. . . . We encourage our Chinese members to return to China. Their country needs them in China, and the Lord needs them in China. The work in China will go forward . . . in a natural law-abiding way because of those who have received the message of the restored gospel."[4] Over the succeeding decades since that talk, the Church has grown in China just as he foresaw.

At times, Elder Oaks's attention was drawn from his apostolic role of taking the gospel to all nations and diverted to government matters in the Church's backyard. In 1989, he helped to outline "a strategy for explaining the Church position in the imminent reevaluation of the liquor control laws of the state of Utah." Clearly, he had the skills for such work. "But that is not my favored activity or way of fulfilling my calling," he lamented. "More to my liking was the 1½ hours spent with Neal Maxwell's committee on the Church in developing nations. We are seeking ways to simplify Church organization, procedures, publications, and buildings and bureaucracy to make it feasible and affordable to take the gospel to every nation, etc. We feel the flow of revelation and rejoice in what is evolving from these discussions."

On another occasion, while dealing with a property matter in

Hawaii, Elder Oaks confided to his journal, "My legal skills and public policy (and Church communications) skills seem to be most in demand, but I prefer to work in the ecclesiastical areas such as doctrine, testifying, and planning how to proclaim the gospel to the world." Yet he faithfully did what he was assigned, even if it did not appeal to him. "We each put our own offering on the altar," he wrote, "and I am glad to put whatever is asked."

During the fall of 1994, at the urging of its Acting President, Boyd K. Packer, the Quorum of the Twelve discussed the need for a scripture-based proclamation to set forth the Church's doctrinal position on the family. A committee consisting of Elders Faust, Nelson, and Oaks was assigned to prepare a draft. Their work, for which Elder Nelson was the principal draftsman, was completed over the Christmas holidays. After being approved by the Quorum of the Twelve, the draft was submitted to the First Presidency on January 9, 1995, and warmly received.

Over the next several months, the First Presidency took the proposed proclamation under advisement and made needed amendments. Then on September 23, 1995, in the general Relief Society meeting held in the Salt Lake Tabernacle and broadcast throughout the world, Church President Gordon B. Hinckley read "The Family: A Proclamation to the World" publicly for the first time.[5]

During the period that the proclamation was being drafted, Church leaders grew concerned about efforts to legalize same-sex marriage in the state of Hawaii. As that movement gained momentum, a group of Church authorities and Latter-day Saint legal scholars, including Elder Oaks, recommended that the Church oppose the Hawaii efforts. At the same time, Elder Oaks anticipated the effect of that public opposition.

"This would touch off an ugly nationwide debate for the hearts and minds of Americans in which the Church would step into a serious vacuum of leadership," he forecast in his journal. "I feel (and said) that this is the time and that is what the Lord wants us to do, but it is a serious step that can only be taken by a united First Presidency and Twelve."

The proposal to oppose the Hawaii legislation was approved by the First Presidency and the Twelve on January 6, 1995, catapulting the Church into a prominent role in opposing same-sex marriage. The proposed Hawaii law, which would have applied in only one state, was defeated by efforts in which Elder Oaks and other General Authorities participated. However, in a 2015 case from California, the U.S. Supreme Court overturned millennia of marriage law and tradition by ruling that "same-sex couples may exercise the fundamental right to marry in all States" and that no state could "refuse to recognize a lawful same-sex marriage performed in another State on the ground of its same-sex character."[6]

The fallout from that decision embroiled the Church in controversy and raised questions among its members. Amidst all this, Elder Oaks and other General Authorities relied on their legal and ecclesiastical experience in discussing how the Church should react in its teachings and policies. They also labored to protect the religious freedom of churches and the rights of their members to live according to sincerely held beliefs that might run counter to cultural expectations reflected in legal rulings.

Among his many duties as a Church leader, Elder Oaks met with government officials from many nations. In July 1992, for example, U.S. President George Herbert Walker Bush made a courtesy call on leaders at Church headquarters in Salt Lake. "It was an informal and wide-ranging discussion in which all participated," Elder Oaks noted. After the discussion, President Bush "told President [Howard W.] Hunter he had never met a group of men with more comprehensive knowledge of what was going on in all parts of the world."

Elder Oaks shakes hands with President Bush

On matters of government, Church leaders sought to be nonpartisan in their statements and behavior—meeting, for example, with the leaders of both major parties in the United States, the Republicans and the Democrats. In Utah, where Republicans severely outnumbered Democrats, Church leaders worried that the two-party system did not function as well as it should. In early 2001, before the state legislature met, Elder Oaks "hosted lunch for Republican leadership in Utah legislature and gave them needed cautions about not overreaching their Democratic counterparts in the two-party system."

In 2009, Elder Oaks accompanied Church President Thomas S. Monson to Washington, DC, to present five volumes of family history to U.S. President Barack Obama, a Democrat. At noon on Monday, July 20, President Monson and Elder Oaks met with Democratic U.S. Senator Harry Reid, a Latter-day Saint who at the time was serving as Senate Majority Leader. Senator Reid "took us in his car (with his Capitol security) to [the] White House," Elder Oaks recorded.

"President Obama welcomed us warmly in his oval office," Elder

Oaks wrote, "walking us directly to a side table where the five volumes were placed. We stood for our entire visit, which was good since we moved around as needed and concluded by rolling out a large pedigree chart on his desk and taking pictures. President Monson read the cover letter, and then I did most of the talking in describing the history and some major points of interest. President Obama was enthusiastic, reflected on his knowledge of [the] Church from [his] Honolulu days, and said he wanted to review all this with Michelle and his daughters."

Despite the difficulties of doing public affairs work for the Church, like all work well done, it proved a source of satisfaction to Elder Oaks in the long run. "I feel I am very involved in virtually every very important matter where members of the Twelve are engaged," Elder Oaks observed with wonder. Much of that involvement was specifically directed by President Boyd K. Packer when he oversaw the Quorum of the Twelve. "I am often consulted on subjects where I am not formally assigned, and President Packer uses me on most of his important issues," Elder Oaks wrote. "This comes with seniority and experience and is satisfying to me."

CHAPTER 18

"SHE CULTIVATED THE FLOWERS"

June Dixon Oaks

The Apostle Paul famously declared that "neither is the man without the woman, neither the woman without the man, in the Lord" (1 Corinthians 11:11). Elder Dallin H. Oaks's wife, June Dixon Oaks, helped make him who he became. In listing the major turning points in his life, he put at the top his "first date with June." His marriage to her gave his life balance, resolve, and purpose. Suddenly the good student became a great one, the hard worker a tireless laborer, the spiritual novice a true disciple.

"My academic achievement and career successes have been based on the fact that I married someone I loved, who helped me focus my energies," Elder Oaks wrote. "I had a B average when I met June; after we married, I had an A average. . . . She never complained and she made every sacrifice possible for every professional, church, and family goal we pursued."[1] In their marriage, they followed a traditional division of responsibility, he as the breadwinner and she the homemaker. They also considered their marriage a true partnership. "June was a full participant and partner in all the major decisions affecting our lives," he wrote. "Her counsel was precious, and her support for my professional progress and preferences was exemplary."

One great contributor to their success, they felt, was the age at which they married, a result of the Korean War limitation on missionary service. "We married when she was 19 years and 3 months, and I was 19 years and 10 months," he wrote. Dallin was so young that he needed written consent from his mother to get the marriage license. "We were both mature for our ages, but we both had some growing up to do," he saw in retrospect. "It is well that we married young and grew up together, since both of us had dominant personalities. Both of us needed the malleability of our youth to accommodate to another who was equally strong. It is also well that our children came when we were young. Early family responsibilities drew us together in common efforts that unified us and shaped our marriage into a cooperative model."

The fact that both had strong personalities helped their relationship. They respected one another, and neither cowered to the other. "Mom was not an 'Anything you say, Dear' type wife," their daughter Cheri said. "Mother was very equally yoked with Dad," son Lloyd observed. "Despite our disagreements (and we had many at the beginning)," Dallin wrote, "we communicated candidly with one another, worked out differences between ourselves, and then supported one another invariably and faithfully."

They verbally jousted with one another, but with clear boundaries. "They never called each other names, or criticized in public," daughter Sharmon remembered. But they learned how to engage each other to relieve pressure or stress. As their children came along and grew, the youngsters at times mistook the intent of their parents' frank dialogue. "One time," Sharmon recalled, "my sister and I were crying because we had a friend whose parents had just divorced, and when we heard our parents arguing, we were sure the same thing was about to happen."

When the two girls expressed their worry, their parents explained that having "'heated discussions' occasionally . . . didn't mean they didn't love each other," Sharmon said. "They taught us that conflict will occur between husband and wife. The important thing is learning to work things out."

A sense for the tenderness of their private expressions comes through in a letter Dallin wrote to June in 1954 during his seventeen-week course at the Field Artillery School in Fort Sill, Oklahoma. "This separation has certainly served to bring my love for you into sharp focus," he wrote. "I realize now, as you may do also, that I never really appreciated consciously how much a part of me you are. June, you are everything. I am empty without you and our children. My love for you grows more mature and more intense every day."

Despite this underlying warmth, the two were often physically reserved in public. "June," Dallin wrote, "was a very private person when it came to praise or expressions of affection. Even holding hands in public was a rare thing for her to tolerate. 'Someone might think I liked you,' was her frequent joking comment. At the same time, in our own home and with our children, she was as open and expressive and loving as even the most affectionate person (I am one of those) could desire."

Because Dallin and June were so restrained in public, however, people just assumed they were reserved in private, too. Sharmon remembered "bursting into the kitchen and catching them kissing. There was no lack of affection in hugs and kisses in our family," she said, "but it was nice to know they were kissing when nobody else, they thought, was around. It made me feel secure." Yet "when I told my friends" about their affection, she said, "they seemed surprised at this. Then I'd add how they'd often dance together in the living room, too, and how they liked to go with just each other to dinner and movies."

"My dad said that the best thing a father can do for his children is to love their mother," Sharmon wrote. "He loved my mother. I heard him say so many times, embarrassing my mom, 'Kids, isn't your mother

June during her husband's service as BYU president

beautiful? She's so wonderful. I love her so much. She is my best friend and my sweetheart.'"

One thing Dallin loved about June was her straightforward manner. "Mom was very honest," daughter TruAnn remembered, and "said what she thought. Sometimes we felt that she was too honest." June was equally candid with her husband. After Church leaders decided to release Dallin from being president of BYU, she felt unsettled about their future. "I am perfectly at ease with the uncertainty," Dallin wrote at the time. But June was not, "since it interferes with her plans about where we will live and keeps us from getting a permanent home."

One day they were discussing this in front of friends, and Dallin chided June about her feelings, saying, "Just get out and look around and let me know when you have found a home."

"Instantly," he wrote, and "with eyes flashing," she tossed back, "Let me know when you have found a job!"

Her honesty made her the best reviewer of her husband's work, especially his talks. "It is hard for a General Authority to get an objective evaluation of his performance as a speaker," Elder Oaks wrote. "We are left to trust our own feelings. . . . I am glad June is so candid in her reactions to my talks. She is my best and most helpful critic."

In the early days of Dallin's service as a General Authority, June noted the difference between his Church and non-Church talks. "I'm sure the Holy Ghost is present when he talks in a Church service—and it testifies to me the things he is saying are true," she wrote in her journal. But she felt this was missing in "his secular talks." She also felt that at times he tried to intellectualize his Church talks too much. "It seems to me," she recorded in her journal a year after his call, that "he is trying to be so scriptural and doctrinal he has lost some of the 'spirit.' I am yearning for the same feelings I used to feel when he spoke in Chicago" during his Church service there.

He loved it that she would give him "straight-up, candid evaluations of his performance in any setting" and that no matter how incisive the criticisms, they "were always loving and constructive." He trusted her motives. "She wanted me to be better and better, and she helped me more than I can explain," he wrote. Regardless of who else might hear or read what he had to say, she was, as he wrote in his 1982 journal, "my most critical and most valued audience."

As Elder Oaks labored over one of his earliest general conference addresses, he read the draft to June, who told him it was boring. "I redid it to try to make it more interesting," he wrote, "and she said it was a big improvement. She really helped me by this candid and constructive criticism. I can count on *her* to tell me what she really thinks." Later, he wrote, "Life is never dull with June."

Humor peppered her life and language and thus his too, adding spice to their relationship. In 1986, they left on a trip together to South America. "On our flight to New York City," Elder Oaks wrote, a flight attendant "asked June and me if we were newlyweds. Surprised and delighted by this inquiry, we asked why she would ask this. 'You look like you aren't bored with each other,' she responded."

During the same flight, Elder and Sister Oaks "talked of what

Elder and Sister Oaks and their children

would happen if one of us died," Elder Oaks wrote. "June then boldly told me who I should marry if I survived her."

"How come you want to boss that event?" he asked her teasingly.

"If I've got to share you," she replied, "I think I ought to be able to choose who I will share you with."

"Don't you think it ought to be someone I would like?" he argued.

"I'd rather it wasn't," she grinned.

"We both enjoyed a good laugh at that," he wrote at the time. Neither knew they had fewer than a dozen years left together in this life. But they made the most of their togetherness. Summing up their trip, Elder Oaks wrote that it "was especially enjoyable for both of us. June's companionship and lively personality were, as always, a delight to me. She is obviously loved and respected by all as a genuine person who loves people and the gospel, without hypocrisy or guile. She supports me faithfully, but does so without submerging her own identity.

She is good for me and good for my work. She is certainly a foolproof antidote for pomposity."

June's straightforward manner and speech, especially coming from a General Authority's wife, struck many as refreshing. "We were on this trip with Carlos and Colleen Asay," another General Authority and his wife, June wrote in 1987. "We had a good time with them. Brother Asay said I was like a breath of fresh air. I guess I'm so uninhibited I do not fit the mold."

That proved especially important when Elder Oaks was conducting mission presidents seminars, often in far-flung parts of the world where isolation and loneliness were potential issues, particularly for presidents' wives. "I urged her to accompany me on all these assignments," he wrote, "because when she was there the personal associations—an important part of these meetings—always escalated from drab to exciting." Of these occasions, June wrote, "In the mission presidents seminars, Dallin and I just kid and tease each other, and the mission presidents' wives seem to appreciate us just being like them." "She didn't mince words," daughter Cheri remembered. "People loved her because she was 'real.' She was very real."

She was also tough. "June hit herself in the left eye with her tennis racket," Dallin wrote in a 1985 journal entry. "She had eight stitches later, but in the meantime finished her game. She is tough as well as beautiful!" June saw such toughness as necessary for facing life's difficulties, and she strove to build it in her children as well, brooking no wimpiness on their part. "When we would come crying to Mom stating that it hurt when you moved your elbow 'this way,'" son Lloyd remembered, "Mom would state, 'Then don't move it that way.' . . . Mom expected her children to stand on their own two feet. She supported us in what we wanted to do. She did not tolerate self-pity or whining. . . . I've told some army friends that Mom was as stoic as John Wayne, and that she did not raise wimps."

Her desire for her children to be tough and well-behaved, however,

June serving dinner to the family

did not mean June was insensitive. "She often listened to others' problems for extended periods of time," Lloyd noted. President Thomas S. Monson recalled that when Dallin was president of BYU, the two of them went to the locker room after ball games to boost the team members. "Be nice to them," President Monson recalled June counseling, "particularly that boy who missed the important shot. Tell him he will make it next time." President Monson reminisced, "I've never heard anyone more concerned about a team player than the elect lady of Brigham Young University."

Even if June didn't seem sympathetic at times to family members' complaints, "Mom was always sensitive to the needs of her children," said daughter Jenny, her sixth and last child, born when June was forty-two. Like most spiritually wise people, June recognized that service was the key to happiness, especially during times of trial. She did not wallow in self-pity but instead reached out to others in periods of sorrow and taught her children to do so by her example, finding service opportunities everywhere.

"Imagine the surprise of one student who rang the doorbell of the

[BYU] President's Home and within moments found himself in a chair receiving a haircut," her children Sharmon and Dallin D. wrote. "This student, the son of one of June's Chicago friends, had stopped by on another errand. Noticing his hair was in direct and conspicuous violation of BYU's dress and grooming standards, June good-naturedly coaxed him into an immediate and free haircut in the kitchen of the President's Home."[2]

"What is your greatest achievement?" June was once asked. "Our children," she replied.[3] "Motherhood," Elder Oaks agreed, "was June's priority and preoccupation. She was the best friend of her daughters and the best teacher of her sons. She taught her children to love God, to seek education, and to make music." Though both he and she played a role in raising their children, "hers was the dominant force."

"Mom was all her daughters' best friend," daughter Cheri recalled. "We could discuss anything with her. We loved to be with her. She made any activity more fun. Mom was always so proud of your accomplishments. I gave a vocal recital one year, and when I looked into her eyes, she had tears. It made me feel so loved."

"Mom's first priority in everything was her children," Jenny agreed. "I always knew that Mom would rather be home with me than traveling around the world, meeting dignitaries, or even attending a wonderful party. . . . My favorite place in the house to be was always wherever Mom was. She was always busily engaged in a good cause, and she lit up the entire room with her warm personality and love."

Because June loved her children so much, she was "definitely a 'Mother Bear,'" Jenny remarked. "She was intensely protective of her little cubs, and woe be to anyone who hurt her little ones in any way. . . . Mom wasn't afraid of anyone or anything." Once, when the family lived at BYU, an unstable man threatened to harm one of the Oaks daughters. When police offered temporary protection for the family, President Oaks declined, "explaining that, in this case, his daughter probably didn't need the protection, but the man might need it if he tried anything while June was around."[4]

"Mom had such a huge capacity to love," said Jenny. "Mom loved everyone, especially her family. She yearned to nurture all those in need. She was quick to tell people she loved them, and was constantly demonstrating her love through her actions."

After Dallin was called to be an Apostle, June accepted a call in her ward to teach the Valiant Bs (she called them "the violent bees"). A few years later, she was assigned "a large, unruly class of thirteen-year-olds in Sunday School," her husband recounted. "These teenagers, especially the boys, posed a difficult challenge that June finally overcame with love and persistence." One of the boys' mothers wrote, "My oldest boy was one of her 'very interesting' Sunday School boys. That is when I learned to love June so much. She taught him, at the time a very difficult young man, so much about the gospel and about the Lord. . . . He said, 'She loved me. I know she did.'"

"My words are inadequate to the privilege of trying to describe June as a wife and companion," Elder Oaks wrote. "For forty-six years she loved and served me and her family, magnifying us all and making a home that everyone loved to visit. Whatever I can represent with my own words and the words of others will be inadequate to describe her magnificence." Speaking to his brethren of the Twelve in 1996, he said that June had been a "full partner and major contributor to all that has been done in my life since our marriage."

June supported Dallin, and he in turn supported her in her life decisions. "As soon as I had finished my education," he told BYU students, "June resumed hers, and the completion of her bachelor's degree was an important family project during most of our years in Chicago. She had supported me magnificently during my education, and I felt it an obligation and privilege to give support and cooperation in the completion of hers." June completed her education but did not seek full-time employment outside the home.

"June was rarely employed after our marriage," Elder Oaks wrote, "but she had a few paid jobs and enjoyed the experience and boost of earning some 'mad money' (as she sometimes called it) to spend as she liked." For the most part, she focused on being a homemaker, in both the figurative and literal senses of that title. "In all of our homes," he recalled, "June was the leading fixer and handyman."

Once, when they were remodeling their dining room and kitchen, June grew "tired of waiting for electrical and plumbing work in the kitchen, so did it herself," he noted in his journal. "Mother was constantly fixing things and upgrading things about the house," son Lloyd wrote. "She stated she could not wait for Dad to fix things, she wanted it done now, so she learned how to do it." TruAnn said, "Mom was a very hard worker and was very skilled at many things. When I came home from school, it was very common to find her staining an antique, reupholstering a piece of furniture, painting a room, or fixing something in the house." Cheri said her mother did a lot so their father could focus on his work. "She allowed Dad to be what he is today," Cheri believed. "I attribute a lot of what Dad is to my mom."

"June loved the Lord and she loved her fellow man," Elder Oaks said. "She was as warm and concerned in conversations with yard workers and artisans as she was with dignitaries. She was often described as 'down to earth,' which I assured her was a sincere compliment—the opposite of pretentious, pompous, or 'stuck up.'" Later, he wrote that "perhaps no quality was praised more frequently by her friends than the fact that June was unaffected by her prominence and was unpretentious to all."

Although most of her public exposure came from being the wife of a prominent husband, she became notable in her own right when Jenny, their last child, entered school and was gone most of the day, and especially after Jenny became old enough to drive. "Now, for the first time in over thirty-five years," Dallin and June wrote to friends, "June is not involved in taxiing children to music lessons and other

Equally yoked

activities." With more personal time, June served the Utah Symphony Guild as a docent, cochair of the outreach program, and then board member. Utah's governor appointed her to the Utah Arts Council, and she eventually served as council vice chair.

In her council capacity, she invited her husband to accompany her to a dinner. "She enjoyed taking me," Elder Oaks wrote, "since the invitation and limelight were hers for a change." She "was so beautiful and charming I was proud to be with her," he noted. Son Lloyd recalled being told that the dignitaries were asked to introduce themselves and their partners. June had been introduced many times as "his lovely wife" and decided to turn the tables. "I'm June Oaks," she said, "and this is my lovely husband, Dallin Oaks."

Nothing about June's status, however, went to her head. She remained down-to-earth, and the next night, the two of them went for a walk. They ended up at a local import market "looking for dead bugs" to help Jenny with a biology project. "I had to laugh," Elder Oaks wrote, "as I contrasted our Wednesday and Thursday night activities!"

Besides being athletic, vivacious, and drawn to the performing arts,

June was deeply spiritual. Susan Lake, a close friend, described her as "a woman who stood with her hands on her hips and eyes ablaze as she invited life in for a romp and a race, followed by a prayer."

On June 16, 1985, June recorded her feelings about attending the Manti Temple rededication. "As I sat through three sessions," she wrote, "I enjoyed each one. As I have sat through similar sessions in Texas, Provo, and Idaho, the Spirit fills my soul. As we join the choir singing 'The Spirit of God Like a Fire Is Burning,' I shed tears of joy as my soul is overflowing. It is difficult to express the feeling one feels as you can feel the Lord's influence so abundant in His house." She acknowledged, "This is probably my favorite privilege so far" in being an Apostle's wife. She added, "It does bother me a bit, however, to walk up to the front, to the nicest seats in the house and be seated. I would like it ever so much better if I could quietly slip into a seat at the back of the room."

One reason June avoided the limelight was that she never felt comfortable being called on to speak. "Those of you who heard her speak extensively here and around the world in the second half of her life," Sharmon revealed, "may be surprised to hear that before she accompanied our father to BYU, I never heard her speak without her voice quaking noticeably in fear. . . . When my parents returned to Utah for our father to be president at BYU, our mother was apprehensive about expectations that she speak publicly. Her desire to serve being stronger than her fears, she accepted speaking invitations and to her surprise was able to speak in her normal strong voice. She recognized the Lord's hand in blessing her with ability to serve others in this way."

Dallin's journal tracked her progress learning to speak before large audiences, at times extemporaneously as Church leaders called on her. She developed her own way of speaking and learned to relate to others on a personal level. "Her pattern," Elder Oaks wrote, "was to present an interesting combination of scripture and/or Church leader quotes mingled with numerous personal experiences to illustrate her point and a fervent testimony to seal its message."

"I feel so blessed as my voice no longer cracks and wavers," she wrote after a regional conference in which she gave two talks. "I know I am blessed." Altogether, Dallin wrote, "her testimony, wisdom, and love have been heard and felt by tens of thousands throughout the world."

June had remarkable stamina. After a day of intensive home remodeling when her husband, who was ill, gave out at 8:00 p.m., June, along with Jenny, labored past midnight, when Jenny went to bed. June carried on until 4:00 a.m. "This kind of dogged, intense, and strenuous *work* when needed is very typical of June, who also *plays* hard," Elder Oaks wrote.

She was also hardly ever sick. Thus, everyone was surprised when in 1997, at age sixty-four, she began to experience muscle pain and diminished energy. At first, no one expected anything serious, and the initial diagnosis seemed innocent enough—a temporary condition that she would eventually overcome. But she didn't get well, and a liver biopsy soon followed. On July 15, 1997, when Dallin got home from work, June met him at the door and announced the grim results: "It's cancer." The biopsy had revealed metastasized cancer in the liver from an unknown source. Her husband gave her a blessing. "June is courageously facing all the implications," he wrote. "I am somewhat in denial, but we both feel strengthened by the Lord to face all the consequences of mortality."

Given her condition, she might have lived only three or four months, but in fulfillment of a blessing, she lived more than a year—a year filled with chemotherapy, nausea, weakness, hope, disappointment, family togetherness, and resolve to face the inevitable. More than anything, June wished to see Jenny happily married—the last of their children to do so. She realized that blessing March 7, 1998, when Jenny married Matthew David Baker in the Salt Lake Temple.

Four months later, a grieving Elder Oaks, feeling "numb all day and little able to work," recorded, "June's mental acuity is fading fast. She is leaving us." The next day, a Sunday, he met with other Apostles on a matter "but could not bear to go to church and answer questions about June." President Gordon B. Hinckley phoned to offer comfort, and as Elder Oaks recounted to June "how he had asked if there was anything he could do, she blurted out of her semiconsciousness, 'Let me go.' When I protested that I did not think it was time for this, she rejoined, 'Yes, it is!'" Even as she lay dying, she was the "same June I have loved forever!" he wrote. The next day, he wrote, "June sinking."

By the late afternoon of July 21, Elder Oaks felt he had an answer to his prayers about when to release Sister Oaks from mortality. He and family members who had gathered turned off the telephone and put a note on the door of the home requesting that no one ring the bell between 4:25 and 4:55 p.m.

"We had prayer," Elder Oaks wrote, "and then at 4:35 I put my hands on her head and tearfully released her by the power of the priesthood. We then sat around her bed and suffered as she struggled so hard to breathe. Then her breathing became more shallow and her hands began to get cold, gradually moving up the arms. We knew she was going." At 5:30 p.m., she "peacefully slipped away."

When June Dixon Oaks died, she left notes from a family meeting less than a year before directing that "in the event of my death . . . I want no tears of sorrow—only tears of joy for a life lived with fulness and purpose, a life dedicated to the Church and committed to following Christ's example." Sharmon remembered, "Mother told us, 'Service is never convenient; you just give it when it's needed,' and then she taught it by her life." Elder Oaks praised her goodness: "She was my best friend, a vital strength to my weaknesses, a loved stimulus to my strengths. In the garden of our marriage, I grew the vegetables and she cultivated the flowers."

CHAPTER 19

"A NEW ERA IN MY LIFE"

Kristen McMain Oaks

With his wife, June, now gone, Elder Dallin H. Oaks mourned. He made it stoically enough through the viewing, the funeral, the family dinner, the cemetery service, and a family meeting to discuss distributing June's things. On Sunday, July 27, 1998, "family attended our ward," he wrote. But he visited another ward "to avoid the emotion I feel when longtime friends express condolences."

The next day, however, he finally succumbed to his emotions. The setting was the Salt Lake Clinic, where he had taken June weekly over the course of a year for chemotherapy. He went there to return some of June's unused medications and happened to see her doctor. "I ran into Dr. Reilly and burst into tears as I tried to express appreciation for his tender professional care of June," Elder Oaks recorded. "I was embarrassed at my lack of control. I guess the spiritual Novocaine is wearing off, and I have more pain and less control."

Gradually, over succeeding weeks, he began to feel "capable of a routine that can be sustained," though he recognized that "there is still much more to be done." He caught up on his journal writing and cried as he reflected on events since he wrote last. By August 17, he had decided to write a history of June's life.

"June often asked me to write her history," he penned in the preface to the volume. "I always told her she should do it herself." But "soon after her death on July 21, 1998, I realized that I must do this, not only because she requested it, but also because this was necessary for me. Writing her history would be a healing experience as I relived our . . . years together and as I kept faith with her wish that our posterity would know her as they would know me."

On August 21, one month after June died, Elder Oaks went through an endowment session in the Salt Lake Temple "and felt her presence with a young June's voice in my mind in the celestial room." He resolved, "I will go again." On October 1, in the endowment session that preceded the Thursday temple meeting, "I felt June's presence," he wrote again, "and had two thoughts communicated peacefully and clearly to my mind from her: (1) she is busy and happy, and (2) she knows why she died at this time. I was comforted."

Near the end of the month, as he was returning from nearly two weeks on assignment in Africa, he had another comforting experience. "While in flight over the Atlantic en route home, I felt June's presence so strongly, comforting me and expressing her love, that I had a strong flow of tears," he wrote. "At that same time, I had a free flow of ideas about how to research and write her history that was pure inspiration. I made notes."

On November 21—the four-month anniversary of June's death—Elder Oaks again attended an endowment session in the Salt Lake Temple. "In contrast to earlier times," he recorded in his journal, "I did *not* feel her presence in the celestial room. I did feel a thought she had left for me, somewhat like a written message: 'Your needs are not so great now, so I will not visit you on a regular basis, but from time to time as you need.' I felt the correctness of this, just as if she had said,

'You are a big boy now and can walk to school alone.'" Elder Oaks wrote that he "went away strengthened for a new era in my life."

In December, as part of his research for June's history, he started reading the journals she kept on their overseas trips together. "This was very tender," he confessed. "I was filled with love for her and her goodness, so clearly recorded there."

On February 1, 1999, after returning from a long trip to Peru and Bolivia, he began editing a chapter of June's history that had been typed up while he was gone. Suddenly, he "broke down and *sobbed* for about five minutes," he wrote. "This was my first at that. I hope this is a watershed, not a trend. I am lonely for June and miss her terribly. The loneliness of this life of mine is beginning to be felt more keenly than anytime so far." Besides going through June's journals, he sifted through his own, finding them "a rich source" for her history.

Meanwhile, his thoughts began to turn to remarriage as a way of filling the hole in his heart. On Thursday, February 11, he attended his regular temple meetings, where he saw Elder L. Tom Perry, who had remarried decades earlier after his first wife died. "I asked Tom Perry what counsel he had received about remarriage," Elder Oaks wrote. Elder Perry passed on advice he received from then Church President Spencer W. Kimball. President Kimball told Elder Perry to marry a woman not a lot younger than himself who had not previously been sealed and to avoid "public 'courting'/dating," which would invade his privacy and his date's and subject them to needless rumor.

On March 5, Elder Oaks was editing one of the final chapters in June's history. "As I saw June's picture," he wrote, "I teared up and felt profound sorrow and discouragement. I cried out for her and instantly felt her presence and felt her comfort me and assure me that all would be okay. What a marvelous, comforting experience!" That spring, he published June's history and delivered copies to their children and grandchildren. About this time, Elder Oaks spoke with a single woman he had known for many years who he thought might be a marriage prospect, but he was disappointed with the response.

He reached a turning point on July 21, 1999, the one-year anniversary of June's death. "I went to the temple this morning and felt a strong impression that it was time to quit mourning and get on with my life," he recorded. Two days later, he wrote further about what he had felt in the Lord's house. "I received these strong impressions: (1) My period of mourning for June is over. (2) I should stop trying to communicate with her and get on with my life. (3) I need a wife to stand by my side in mortality."

He spent that winter pondering and hoping and praying. On December 18, while working at his desk at home, "I suddenly felt June's presence for about five minutes in the afternoon," he wrote. "She was loving, gave me a welcome message, and was gone."

In the meantime, two things took place that prepared him for remarriage. First, all four of their daughters came to him "individually and told me they were ready for me to remarry," he wrote. June had prepared them to do that. "During her yearlong battle with cancer," he recalled, "she came to realize that she would die before me." In that time, "she frequently told our four daughters that she knew I would need to remarry and that when that time came, they should help me find a companion who would fit well into our family and welcome her."[1]

The second preparation grew out of his experience as a lawyer, judge, and Church leader. He had noticed that many children resist a parent's remarriage for fear they might lose a property inheritance. Throughout his marriage to June, Elder Oaks kept careful record "of the gifts and inheritances she received from her parents, including what we purchased with those resources." As one who had degrees in accounting and law, this seemed natural to him. As it turned out, it also made it easier for him, after her passing, to give the children "their inheritance from their mother (and her parents) . . . by transfers of property that had monetary value and by loving division of possessions of sentiment." Later, Elder Oaks would use a prenuptial agreement to assure that his children would also receive what he wanted to give them. These wise steps eliminated concerns about a new wife disrupting any inheritance.[2]

Nearly two years after June's death, he felt "strong pressure from my daughters, confirmed by my own feeling, that it was time to look for a companion."[3] With that encouragement, he decided to become proactive, to exercise faith by doing.

"I went forward to find a wife," he wrote with determination in his journal on July 6, 2000, nearly two years after June's death. He picked up the phone and called three General Authorities to request that they "watch for eligible and qualified women I could consider." One of those General Authorities, Elder M. Russell Ballard of the Quorum of the Twelve, "immediately suggested Kristen M. McMain."

Elder Oaks and Elder Ballard

Kristen McMain was a fifty-two-year-old educational consultant for a large publisher of K-12 books. She lived in Salt Lake City but traveled all over the world in her professional assignments. She had two degrees from the University of Utah (bachelor's in English and master's in special education) and a doctoral degree from BYU (in curriculum and instruction). She had served a mission in Japan and had never married. As Elder Oaks would learn later, she was a gifted professional teacher and faithful Latter-day Saint. Even though she spent quality time with her family in Utah and enjoyed her Church calling as a Gospel Doctrine teacher, she still felt her life lacked balance.[4]

"Most of my life, energy, and time were going to my employment," she realized. "Concerned and feeling unable to change my life, I asked my bishop for a blessing." Her bishop's unexpected counsel surprised her. "If you do not quit your job," he pronounced in the blessing, "you will have your blessings in the eternities but not in this life."

"When I heard his words," she later wrote, "I felt the truth of them. I had to stop traveling and find employment at home. For a single sister, giving up financial security is no easy thing. I had no new job to go to. I had to go on faith to resign from my job."

Over the next few months, she wrote letter after letter of resignation, only to toss them in the trash. "Finally," she said, "I wrote a letter clear enough that no one could doubt my intention to resign. I gave notice and planned to leave on July 1, 2000." Family members, friends, and people at church questioned her judgment, but she had the faith to do what she felt was right.[5]

When her elderly aunts learned she was soon to be unemployed, they arranged an appointment for her to see their nephew Elder M. Russell Ballard because he had connections with Deseret Book and other publishing interests. They thought he might be able to help their niece find employment closer to home in Utah.

For Kristen, meeting with a General Authority about her personal needs seemed rather awkward. "My exposure to General Authorities

Kristen Meredith McMain

had been minimal," she wrote, "and I liked it that way. I had the utmost respect for them. I revered them, but I also understood the line of priesthood jurisdiction and felt confident that my home teachers and my bishop were sufficient to bless my life." Yet she went forward in meeting Elder Ballard anyway. That was just before Elder Oaks called his fellow Apostle to seek guidance in finding a new wife.[6]

Elder Ballard "arranged for me to meet her on her walk Friday in Liberty Park," Elder Oaks noted. He wanted to be properly dressed for the July 7 occasion, and his daughter Sharmon, who happened to be in town, and her husband, Jack, "immediately took me shopping for clothes," he wrote in his journal.

Elder Oaks also followed up Elder Ballard's arrangement with his own personal phone call to Kristen, a call that left her facing "a few daunting circumstances," she later said. "He wanted to bring . . .

Sharmon to meet me before she left town the next day. I did not tell him I had just had a permanent and needed to cover my head. We decided on a walk in Liberty Park," a popular walking location in southeast Salt Lake. "When I met my future husband and his daughter, I was wearing Levi's and a baseball cap (to hide my curls) for our walk"—not exactly what she would have chosen for a first meeting with a member of the Twelve.[7] When Kristen saw Elder Oaks with Sharmon, her first words to him were, "Do you always double-date like this?"

"Looking back," Kristen reminisced, "I would never have planned to meet an Apostle of the Lord and his daughter dressed so casually. But that baseball cap allowed me to just be myself." Feeling surprisingly relaxed, she was able to enjoy their time together. "Our initial meeting and the conversation that ensued," she wrote of her visit with them, "seemed like that of three longtime friends. Elder Oaks told me that he had often taken walks with his wife, June, who had died two years earlier. I asked him to tell me about her. From the beginning we felt calm and relaxed with each other. Sharmon shared much about their family and her mother. We laughed and talked, and our courtship began."[8]

Elder Oaks recorded in his journal the positive reaction to her he felt on this first meeting. "Sharmon and I met and walked with Kristen McMain, who proved to be attractive, intelligent, faithful, and fun," he wrote. "I was intrigued, and Sharmon was impressed." The next day, Elder Oaks spent four hours hiking and having a "deep visit with Kristen M. on the foothills above This Is the Place Park," he recorded in his journal. "I asked her many penetrating questions, and from her answers and questions to me, I continue intrigued."

He felt it was not appropriate yet for them to be seen in public together since that would have spawned rumors, created discomfort, and invaded their privacy. Consequently, he attended church alone on Sunday in his ward. But summarizing the next week in his journal, Elder Oaks wrote, "She has occupied my thoughts and no small amount of time, counting numerous conversations with my children about her."

"My time of getting acquainted with Kristen," he later wrote of their courtship, "was spent in the presence of family—my children, my siblings, June's siblings, and Kristen's family members. I followed the familiar wisdom that it is wise to observe a potential marriage partner in a variety of circumstances. We and our family members came to know one another."[9]

In that time-consuming and rather laborious process, however, things didn't always go smoothly. For example, just three days after they met, Elder Oaks arranged a meeting between Kristen, three of his married children, and their spouses. "I didn't set this up well," he admitted in his journal, "so the exchanges were superficial and not very satisfying for anyone." He and Kristen had a long talk as he drove her home, and he noted, "She has great depth and substance." He even professed, "I could get romantically interested in this lady!"

The next day, he had "numerous phone calls with children, who pleaded that this romance 'not go too fast' (they sense my interest)," he wrote.

Meanwhile, Dallin and Kristen kept seeing each other, often in the company of friends and family. "More visiting with Kristen increases my interest in her (and hers in me, apparently)," he wrote. He took her to see Jeff and Pat Holland, after which they joined some of Kristen's family for a barbecue. "Seeing their loving association helps me know Kristen better," Elder Oaks wrote. One of Kristen's sisters whispered to him that Kristen had lived a "valiant" life. "I was impressed," he wrote, "with that confirmation of my feeling." With each passing day, the relationship seemed to deepen.[10]

The courtship was proceeding toward marriage—Dallin's second, Kristen's first—and he wanted her to be comfortable with that reality. "It was . . . important to both of us that Kristen felt comfortable about becoming a 'second wife,'" he wrote. "She understood the eternal doctrine of relationships" and that "she was becoming part of an existing eternal family unit."[11] To that end, Elder Oaks had Kristen meet with Barbara Perry, second wife of Elder Perry, who could give a candid evaluation of what it meant to enter into such a relationship.

In his July 20 journal entry, Elder Oaks made the key observation, "I enjoy Kristen's company!" She later wrote, "When I met my husband I met my best friend. There was romance, but more important, I found someone I felt comfortable with—someone with whom I could pull weeds in the garden, wash dishes, pray, and confer over problems. I enjoyed his company more than anyone else's and came to depend on his honest feedback and wise advice. I could confide in him, and I had complete confidence in him." And, she added, "He would also laugh at my jokes."[12]

Friday, July 21, 2000, was the second anniversary of June's death, and Elder Oaks used the day to attend a temple session in which he "prayed for guidance and felt peace about my courtship of Kristen, but no clearly confirmed voice from June."

On July 24—the Pioneer Day holiday in Utah—Dallin and Kristen flew to Chicago, where Sharmon and her husband, Jack, met them at the airport. The four of them drove to a condo that Sharmon and Jack owned in Lake Geneva, Wisconsin, "where we spent the most restful three days I can remember," Dallin wrote. They jet-skied, went on walks, enjoyed meals together, and spent a lot of time talking. The best part was that, being outside the Church's strongholds in the West, he could finally enjoy a sense of privacy with Kristen, Sharmon, and Jack. "No one recognized me in the whole time!" he wrote exuberantly.

That quiet time together allowed him to think, ponder, and pray. "I received a feeling of total peace about going forward with marriage to Kristen," he wrote, "and the four of us even discussed possible dates on a 'what if' basis." Sharmon approved of the marriage, and the night before they left for Wisconsin, Dallin had phoned his daughter Cheri, who "said she was at peace" with the idea. On the way back to

Utah, Dallin and Kristen, by accident or divine design, linked up on a Denver-to-Salt-Lake flight with daughter Jenny, "who had instant rapport with Kristen." In Orem that evening, the three attended the Faith Centered Music Association's Pearl Awards ceremony at Utah Valley State College, where Jenny received three awards. Her father felt "proud of her" and also found it "fun to go out in public with Kristen, even in a semi-visible way."

One by one, the children all gave their consent. The next night, Dallin took Kristen to see son Dallin and others. "Kristen is so patient with all these preliminaries!" Elder Oaks wrote. "I met her three weeks ago today and already love and feel sure of her. It seems impossible, but I have the confirmation (and so does she)." He later explained, "We and our family members came to know one another, and by this means I was blessed with the approval of all six of our children before I proposed to Kristen."[13]

On Saturday, July 29, Dallin and Kristen had dinner at the Homestead in Midway, Utah. He had brought flowers for the occasion. "Afterwards, on the beautiful grounds," he wrote, "I told her I loved her and asked her to marry me. She told me of her love for me and said yes." There was no doubt in either of their minds. "We both had a profound feeling of peace and well-being in all of this," he affirmed in his journal. The next morning, he phoned his children to tell them the news. "All were thrilled," he wrote.

Kristen later wrote this revealing insight: "How does one move from living for one to being the matriarch of a tribe? Serving in the Church, coming from a very loving family, and working a job that demanded I be flexible saved me. Being a Primary president, Young Women leader, attending all those homemaking meetings, multiple sleepovers with my nieces and nephews, and having a job that required me to work with large numbers of people was almost like being in a flight simulator to prepare for married life."

On Friday, August 25, 2000, at 10:30 a.m., in the presence of some

Elder Oaks and Sister Kristen Oaks

sixty friends and family members, Elder Dallin H. Oaks and Sister Kristen M. McMain were married in the Salt Lake Temple by President Gordon B. Hinckley.[14] Elder Ballard felt honored to have been "the matchmaker for Dallin and for Kristen," he later said. "When they had their wedding dinner, they invited me, and they gave me an award—the finder's fee—of those little chocolate gold coins."

Elder Oaks had been married to June Dixon Oaks, his first wife, for forty-six years, but only fourteen of those years were during his service as a General Authority. Sister Kristen M. Oaks would now be his wife for most of his service in the senior quorums of the Church. After two years of being single, he felt greatly blessed to have her as his companion.[15]

"She came into the marriage with many gifts and experiences," he later reflected. "Though exposed to Church teachings through Primary attendance in her childhood, she was a convert in her early twenties. She brought into the marriage the fervent testimony of a convert and the marvelous experience of a full-time missionary in a foreign land (to Sendai, Japan, in her late twenties). She was single until her fifties. From these experiences, she has given me many insights that have blessed my ministry as a General Authority. Her mothering instincts and experience were immediately felt throughout the Oaks family, which then consisted of six children and their spouses, twenty-three grandchildren, and two great-grandchildren. As a gifted teacher, speaker, and writer, she has been a great counselor and helper in my ministry. She was truly the ideal woman to join our family and stand beside me in the great responsibilities of my calling."

CHAPTER 20

"ETERNAL SALVATION IS A FAMILY AFFAIR"

The Oaks Family in Action

As the father of six, grandfather of twenty-nine, and great-grandfather of more than sixty, Dallin H. Oaks loves the family. This has been one of the most frequent themes of his apostolic ministry. In his first year as an Apostle, he spoke at a fireside for parents on "parental leadership in the home." "We cannot overstate the importance of parenthood and the family," he said. "The basis of the government of God is the eternal family." He affirmed "that the gospel plan originated in the council of an eternal family, it is implemented through our earthly families, and it has its destiny in our eternal families."[1] These principles were reflected in his family teachings, priorities, and practices.

After his father's death, young Dallin Oaks spent two years on his grandparents' farm. "In my boyhood on a farm," he explained, "every evening was a family home evening, and there was no television to distract us from family activities. Aside from brief hours at school, whatever happened during the day happened under the direction of the family." Now, he recognized, with urban living, "very few of our youth experience the consistent family-centered activities of earlier times."[2]

Elder Oaks working in his yard

Consequently, he and June sought every opportunity for their children to work together under their leadership.

June taught the daughters, and Dallin tried to find meaningful home and yard work and part-time employment for the sons. He practiced what he preached. After the children married, Dallin took over cutting the lawn, which amazed and amused the neighbors. They marveled to see him dressed in old overalls and a baseball cap.

Gardening lent itself easily to teaching gospel principles. "Dad wanted us to know about the principle of sowing and reaping," Lloyd said, "that when we did specific things, . . . there were specific rewards or consequences attached. If we wanted the fruits of labor, we had to labor. . . . He saw the principle of planting and sowing as a general life lesson, and one consistent with eternal principles." Stories of working with Grandpa became legendary.

Elder Oaks's policy had long been to "work first and play later." Even while on a family vacation at a friend's ranch, he had grandsons help cut Canadian thistles to leave the place better than they found it. Working together was not just toil—it was a time to bond, to achieve

With Jenny in the garden, about 1978

goals, to accomplish good, and to experience service. As much as some family members complained at the time, they retained memories of family work projects and remained proud of what they did together.

Daughter TruAnn said her father's motto sometimes seemed like "work first and play never," but it had a positive influence on family members. "He has the most impressive work ethic and gets more done than anyone else I know," she said. "Both he and Mom kept themselves busy working on projects, and many of us follow their examples and take projects with us wherever we go."

Other family activities included trips together (camping when the children were younger and family income was limited), walks in wooded areas, and reading together. They traveled over much of the United States, often stopping at historical markers. "I love that Dad had us stop and read all the historical markers that we encountered, even though sighs could be heard from the back seat," TruAnn said. "He passed to me a real love of learning. He was always eager to learn something new."

Family scripture reading was supplemented by reading from the classic *Hurlbut's Stories of the Bible,* which Dallin had read as a boy on the farm. Dallin and June frequently told stories from their early experiences and their ancestors' histories. Other favorites during family gatherings were selections from the published poems of James Whitcomb Riley, especially his "Bear Story," which Dallin's mother had read to him when he was a child.

"President Oaks's children adore and respect him and desire to be with him whenever possible," Kristen observed. "They love their daddy. He focuses on their welfare and is very proud of their accomplishments. They often call for advice or to report. They respect his wisdom and impressions. They appreciate his work ethic, his love and loyalty to their mother, and his devotion to the Lord. They saw him put the Lord first in his life. Having tasted the joys of the gospel, material things are not important to him. He was still using a fishing pole and waders from the 1980s until fishing friends bought him new ones. Pioneer-like, his motto is 'Use it up, wear it out, make it do, or do without.'"

"Dad was thrifty and frugal because of lessons from his mother and his grandfather Harris while on the farm in Payson," son Lloyd explained. "Dad told me that his grandfather Harris . . . one day tasked him to remove nails from some boards, stack the boards, and straighten the nails for reuse. Dad complained to his grandpa, stating that he should just spend fifteen cents on new nails. Grandpa Harris replied, 'I have never had fifteen cents to spend on nails.'"

Son Dallin D. also remembered that their father created projects for them to instill the work ethic he learned as a youth. "Dad would work alongside of us. He wasn't just saying go out and do all this work. He'd work alongside of us." He wanted his boys to experience the benefits of working with their hands. "We wanted to be with Dad," Dallin said, "and we wanted to have that time with him. . . . I liked being with him, but I didn't necessarily like doing some of that kind of work."

Elder Oaks taught that parents should avoid overscheduling their children with things that were good but not essential. Instead, they should preserve time for a kneeling family prayer every morning and personal prayers every evening, family scripture study, family home evening, and the one-on-one time that binds a family together and fixes children's values on things of eternal worth. He sought to live by those principles in his own home.

In the Oaks family, a meal with Father or Grandfather Oaks became a time of laughter when he could relax and laugh heartily, engage in friendly banter, and offer words of wisdom. "In small groups," son Lloyd said, "he is engaging and funny and has an amazing sense of humor. You don't get to see that from the pulpit when he is talking about weighty things." Son Dallin agreed: "My dad's pretty funny, if you get to know him. He doesn't show that side so much from the pulpit in general conference. But he has a great sense of humor. He loves telling funny stories."

Once when a grandson had a disastrous period in grade school, his distressed parents showed Elder Oaks the boy's report card showing four F grades and one C. Eager for solutions from the wise grandfather, the parents listened intently as he immediately reached a conclusion. Referring to the C, Elder Oaks jested, "He must have concentrated too much on one subject."

One thing that made dinnertime conversation—or any conversation—meaningful for Elder Oaks's family members was that he accorded their opinions great respect. All were expected to speak up, and no one was belittled. By example, Elder Oaks taught that God loves all His children. As a man who grew up with a strong mother and married young to a strong wife, "he was used to very strong women," TruAnn said, "and women being in charge, and women being able to preside and fulfill responsibilities without the aid of a man."

"What your children really want for dinner," Elder Oaks taught in a talk, "is you."[3] As he said in another address, "There is abundant secular evidence that there is no substitute for the traditional family as a means to increase the likelihood of health, happiness, longevity, and prosperity in the parents and the total well-being of children. The family, as someone once said, is the only department of health, education, and welfare that really works."[4]

Over dinner, Dallin and June Oaks naturally blended secular and spiritual topics, teaching by example the importance of being educated about both. "Our dinner conversations were about ideas," daughter Sharmon recalled. "They were about the gospel. The conversations between my mother and father modeled knowing what's going on in the world around you and dealing with it and how the Lord would deal with it."

As busy as he was outside dinner, Elder Oaks gave family members his time when they needed it. During their youth or childhood, if they had minor problems, they would take them to their mother. Major problems were different; those often went to Dad. "You could go in anytime with something that was important," Sharmon remembered, "and he would put down his work and talk."

When serving in the stake presidency in Chicago, he often had to travel long distances to visit local Church units. "When he is not here, . . . you can be proud of that," their mother taught them, explaining that "he will be a better father because of that priesthood service." Besides, just as Elder Oaks's father seemed present in his life after he died, Elder Oaks's children felt his presence even when he was gone.

When family members were away from him, they sometimes wished he were near. "I remember many times on my mission thinking, 'I wish my dad were here, because he'd know what to do,'" son Dallin D. said. "He always seemed to know what to do. He always seemed to be able to make good decisions and act with great wisdom."

As Elder Oaks's father had disciplined him and in the process taught him, Elder Oaks did the same with his children. They were punished and then got what one called "the talk." "It wasn't like he was telling us we were bad," TruAnn said. "But it was 'You know better. I'm disappointed.' And that was so much more intense than if he had just swatted me."

"He gave us space to grow," Dallin D. said. "He didn't hover over us. But he wasn't permissive either. He was very firm in raising us, but . . . he'd let us make mistakes and . . . grow from it."

What he said was how he lived, his children knew. "As a teenager," Dallin D. said, "I may have disagreed with some things. . . . But I don't think I ever had to square in my mind . . . what appeared to be hypocrisy on his part. I always genuinely respected him."

TruAnn told of a time when they lived in Chicago and a fellow Church member bragged about phoning in sick to his employer so he could attend a stake meeting. She said their father came home upset that this man would be dishonest. "That's wrong," he told his children. "Hopefully, you guys will never do anything like that."

His honesty propelled him to address topics others might avoid. "When they see him at the pulpit, he always seems pretty formal and almost untouchable and maybe a little bit less than compassionate," TruAnn said, "just because he touches on some of the harder topics and hits them straight on the head and doesn't mince words." She said, "Those that are looking for criticism" probably feel "that he doesn't care, he's unfeeling, and things like that. But he really does care about people. He's got a very big heart."

"I feel like in all of his talks, he never shies away from the truth," Jenny said. "He doesn't care if it's going to offend anyone or upset anyone as long as . . . he knows he is speaking the will of the Lord." But if he doesn't know the answer to a question, he "is never afraid to say, 'we don't know that,'" Jenny added. He won't "fake a response."

His honesty also extended to meticulously avoiding anything that might look like a conflict of interest. "Sometimes members of his family have to scratch and claw for things despite his prominence, not aided by his prominence," Dallin D. said. He and his siblings recalled many instances in which their father refused to use his position to benefit family members, even when it might have been legal and customary to do so. "He is the chief of anti-nepotism," Lloyd said.

Most important, he taught them faith. In their dinnertime conversations and whenever a natural teaching moment arose, he taught the gospel to his family. "The gospel was a part of everyday life," Jenny said. "I fully trust in the love of the Savior and of Heavenly Father because I've had that kind of love from my father," Sharmon explained.

His children knew he believed not just because of what he said but by what he did. "Daddy taught us the importance of healing blessings," Cheri said. "When I was a baby, I probably should have died. I got penicillin—highly allergic. I know I'm still here because of the priesthood blessing he gave me." Jenny, a violinist, received blessings from him before many performances. "Those blessings are incredible," Jenny said. "They're just so eloquent and so full of profound wisdom and thoughts and promises and blessings. I'm grateful for that."

"We cannot change the evil influences that inevitably press upon us and our families," Elder Oaks taught in one talk, "but we can increase our power to deal with them. We must try to carve out our own islands of serenity and strengthen our barriers against the forces that besiege us in our protected spaces. In short, we should push back against the world."[5]

Kristen furthered that effort. "I have learned that my major responsibility is to create a holy atmosphere at home," she said. "Without the Spirit, Elder Oaks cannot function to his fullest potential. To do his work, he needs peace, free from worldly distractions."

Remembering how extended family members strengthened him as he grew up in a single-parent family, Dallin Oaks made a high priority of attending family gatherings like missionary departures and returns, Boy Scout courts of honor, school graduations, and family reunions.

In Utah mountains, about 1982

He was there for his loved ones. "The best time we had with him was on family vacations," daughter TruAnn said. "We would . . . travel to all different areas . . . in our green station wagon with five kids, parents, and a Great Dane." He frequently pointed out animals to them. "He loved animals," TruAnn recalled. "It instilled in me a real love of animals."

In later years, after his children married and established their own homes, he and Kristen continued to show their love by attending many next-generation gatherings, such as baby blessings, baptisms, grandchildren parties, school plays, music recitals, and athletic competitions. He made himself available for group and individual meetings with his growing posterity. He regularly chose a "grandchild of the month," whose framed picture he displayed in his office. The grandchildren loved this, and many came to his office just to see their pictures.

Family reunions had long been a high priority in the Oaks family,

Elder Oaks and Sister Kristen Oaks at Joe's Valley reunion

first in Dallin's childhood, then with his own children, and finally for grandchildren and great-grandchildren. He saw how family reunions reinforced family traditions and expectations, taught basic values, and inspired members with the examples of their ancestors and peers. For the Oaks posterity, the ultimate reunion has been the one held every two years at the mountain ranch homesteaded in Joe's Valley, west of Castle Dale, Utah, by Abinadi Olsen, Elder Oaks's maternal great-grandfather. Young Dallin first attended it as a boy of about nine years and throughout the rest of his life seldom missed this gathering to which his descendants have also become devoted.

"When I became engaged to Elder Oaks, the first question every family member asked me was 'Will you go to Joe's Valley?'" Kristen recalled. "Of course, not knowing, I simply said, 'Yes.' What I was unprepared for was the gathering of hundreds of people, with their multitudes of cars, camp equipment, tents, trailers, and RVs. Every other year, they gather to honor their heritage. They relish it, and they relish each other."

"It is a forefather's dream come true that his descendants gather in love to celebrate their past and their faith," Kristen said. "The descendants of one of Abinadi's ten children are in charge of the proceedings for that year. In lawn chairs under open skies, families gather to listen to accounts of their ancestors' lives. On sale are a new T-shirt, hat, and emblem specifically designed for each reunion—this family dresses alike, and they celebrate alike.

"There are square dances, reenactments, storytelling, games for the children, and a constant walkabout as people greet relatives they love," she noted. "For the Oaks posterity, this means that grandchildren can go fishing on the stream with Grandpa, go on walks with family members, huddle and tell stories, and get hugs. This family has a heritage of great unity and a sincere joy of joining together to celebrate those they love. It is a mini-RootsTech convention where family tradition and legacy are regaled and celebrated. I have come to love Joe's Valley."

One of these reunions required a large, circus-type tent. When his father tried to help take it down, Lloyd remembered, a relative insisted that he step aside. Elder Oaks then began gathering the tent stakes. "I will organize the stakes," Lloyd heard him say drolly. "That's in my skill set."

Fishing with grandson Matthew Baker, Weber River, 2019

It is hard to overstate the long-range impact of the Olsen reunion. "From the moment our car turns off the gravel road onto the wooden bridge that leads to the ranch, I feel excitement at returning to this place that I love," reflected granddaughter Julianna Ward Recksiek. "The smell of sagebrush and the crisp mountain air always seem to rejuvenate me and remind me of my ancestors who also loved this place. . . . I hear stories of the sacrifices they made, their setbacks and contributions, and their strong faith. I feel gratitude for the legacy and the land they left behind."

"This is where he taught me how to fish," daughter Cheri said of her father. "He was just really good at taking me fishing." "Fishing with Grandpa," Julianna wrote, "was always something special. . . . He would lead us alongside a stream or river as he searched for the perfect spot for us to fish—often a place with a deeper part of the river, that was slower and had shadows. After teaching us how to put the worm on the hook, release the reel, and pull it in again when we felt a tug, he would leave us to place the other grandchild in another ideal fishing spot, not too far away. He would walk between each of us until we caught something. Then, he resumed instruction on how to unhook the fish and clean it afterward. During the whole process, the conversation was minimal, but we still felt his love of the outdoors, the sport, and especially for us." At other times, she wrote, "He is a master teacher. As I look back, he has influenced my life in meaningful ways during some of my most critical decisions and trials."

"Some of my most cherished childhood memories were made at Joe's Valley," wrote another granddaughter, Stefani Ward Steelman. "I learned to fish there. It was a special treat to know it was my turn to wake up very early to meet Grandpa and walk through the woods and along the river. . . . He taught me to speak quietly and to watch the way my shadow crossed onto the water. Sometimes we caught a fish, and sometimes we just got the hook stuck on a branch. Either way, the time spent together was a great memory, and representative of the

Elder and Sister Oaks and family members on cruise, 2015

importance of the reunion—the memories of the people we love in the place we love. . . .

"The generations," she said, "weave together as the older ones tell of the way things used to be, and the younger ones bring a vitality and promise for beautiful things to come. . . . We have a visual representation of what effect two people can have in the lives of hundreds—their posterity. No matter where we are in our spiritual journey, we cannot deny the faith of our ancestors. They continue to strengthen us as we remember their testimony of Jesus Christ, and that knowledge penetrates our hearts and seems to live on in that place and in us."

In the decades since their marriage, Kristen has been an exemplary influence on the growing Oaks posterity. She has sponsored grandchildren parties, sleepovers, and multiple family dinners. She has made it a practice to create every opportunity for grandchildren to be near their grandfather. She loves the family and has also been a superb example of what a second wife can do to join an existing family and unite all who are related to it in any way.

"I came into a large, loving family who still adored their mother, who still had tender hearts from her loss," Kristen explained. "My own mother had lost her mother at age four. She suffered a stepmother who removed all photos of her mother, insisted on no mention of her, and had the children live in a house next door. Sensitized to my own family's suffering, I worked to keep June a part of our family. Every memory, tradition, recipe, and conversation my family wished to have of her I embraced and encouraged. Step by step, we worked to become a forever family."

"She made it clear," daughter Jenny confirmed, "that we could always talk about our mother in front of her, and even though she had never met my mother, she felt great love for her. Kristen also often expressed gratitude that our mother raised us with so much love so we would in turn love and welcome Kristen into our hearts."

Ashley B. Schroeder, another granddaughter, wrote about a grandchildren's party Kristen sponsored to teach family traditions. "One of my most meaningful memories," she said, "is of a party to celebrate my great-grandma Stella H. Oaks. I remember the dinner table was decorated in yellow (because that was Stella's favorite color), and we were all asked to wear hats because Grandma Stella loved wearing hats. At this dinner, my grandfather Elder Oaks gave each of us a copy of her biography. He had marked favorite sections, and as we sat at the table, we read aloud stories from the life of Grandma Stella," who "was a strong-willed and courageous woman and mother. Now, as a mother of four children, I am trying to create traditions within my own family, and I look to my own parents and grandparents as models for establishing those righteous traditions."

Dallin and Kristen Oaks also realized family unity with Kristen's family. She continued the exemplary attention she had always given to her nieces and nephews, and Dallin welcomed them into his family circle. Though Kristen's physician father was not a Latter-day Saint and her mother was not active in the Church, they welcomed and grew to love their prominent new son-in-law, who always tried to be loving, kind, and nonjudgmental.

Dallin and Kristen encouraged their family members to memorize sacred texts whose words would strengthen and protect them. Their first challenge was to memorize the entire family proclamation. Later, they challenged family members to memorize "The Living Christ." More than thirty family members fulfilled this challenge. Most recently, in anticipation of the April 2020 general conference's focus on the First Vision, they challenged family members to memorize Joseph Smith's account of the appearance and words of the Father and the Son. Fifty-six family members completed this memorization. Most important, when various conference speakers quoted those sacred words, many grandchildren recognized them and joined like a chorus as they were recited. One of their mothers described the experience of memorization as "an event in our family history that I'm sure we will remember and talk about through the years."

Family members also remember revelatory experiences with their father and grandfather. "Another gift that he has is tremendous foresight," Jenny said. "He can see the end from the beginning." This gift, TruAnn said, "is that he is able, with the help of the Spirit of the Lord, to see possible outcomes before they occur."

Kristen offered an example. "Soon after June's funeral, Elder Oaks and his grandson Brent Ward went on a road trip to southern Utah," she related. "Brent drove, and Elder Oaks stared at scenery or read. On an isolated road, while looking down at a paper, Elder Oaks suddenly asked Brent to slow down. Much to Brent's surprise, a deer immediately ran in front of the car. Later that week, again while his grandfather was buried in a book, he suddenly again cautioned Brent to slow down. Brent did so, and immediately and to his surprise a small child ran across the road."[6]

"One of our favorite times together is after general conference," Kristen said. "The family gathers for dinner and discussion of the talks given. From the oldest to the youngest, we gather in a circle and, using modern technology (phones and iPads), those from far away join to share testimonies, words that touched us and what we have learned. These times allow us to testify to one another, reinforce our faith, and build testimonies of Christ. The best part is at the end when Grandpa bears his testimony and gives fatherly advice."

Despite the busyness of Church assignments, Elder Dallin H. Oaks, along with Sister June Oaks and then Sister Kristen Oaks, has made family a key priority, recognizing that families are the basic unit of society not only in this life but also in the celestial kingdom of God. The Oakses sought to weave family and Church together in a way that strengthened both.

CHAPTER 21

"ACCOMPLISHED WONDERS"

Philippines Area President

The two years following Dallin and Kristen Oaks's marriage were a happy and comfortable time as they adjusted to their new life together. Elder Oaks continued with his many assignments as a member of the Quorum of the Twelve, joined by Sister Oaks when possible. They enjoyed activities with family members, including parties to help grandchildren become better acquainted with their grandparents. Sister Oaks enjoyed serving in the Primary, working in the garden, and volunteering at school. Near the end of those two years, inspiration to Church President Gordon B. Hinckley sent Elder and Sister Oaks on an assignment together that drew them even closer to each other and to the Lord.

In 1995, President Hinckley told reporters that the Church's number-one challenge was "the challenge that comes of growth."[1] In the spring of 2002, after many years of battling some growth challenges without major improvement, he decided on a bold move. "I've wanted to do this for a long time," he told the Twelve one day, according to Elder Jeffrey R. Holland. "I'm going to send two of you. I'm not telling you who it is, but I'm going to send two of you to the field. I'm going to send one of you to Chile, and one of you to the Philippines."

More than a half century had elapsed since a member of the Twelve had been sent to reside and serve outside the United States. Shortly after alerting the Twelve to his plan, President Hinckley called Elder Oaks into his office and asked if either Dallin or Kristen had any health issues that might interfere with their serving overseas.

"Well," Elder Oaks replied, "I have been diagnosed with celiac disease."

"What is that?" President Hinckley asked, appearing dismayed.

"An allergy to wheat," Elder Oaks answered, "but I can eat rice."

"Good," President Hinckley laughed, "because there will be plenty of rice where you are going."

Instantly, Elder Oaks realized he was about to be assigned to the Philippines.

The Philippines was an area where Church growth had been explosive, providing an ideal setting for testing solutions to the problems that accompany growth. President Hinckley told Elder Oaks the new assignment would give him "needed experience." Elder Oaks had not served a full-time mission in his youth, and his unusual career path and direct call to the Twelve meant he had not served as a mission president or a member of the Seventy like some of his fellow Apostles. Nor had he ever lived outside the United States.

When Elder Oaks told Sister Oaks about the new assignment, she responded positively, as he had. "I was thrilled at her reaction," he wrote. They were happy to be able to serve together in this challenging responsibility.

At the same time, President Hinckley assigned Elder Holland to go to Chile, another area of intensive growth. In many ways, Elders Oaks and Holland were ideal for such assignments. Both had strong administrative skills, each having served as president of BYU, and both were in good health. Elder Oaks had visited the Philippines many times before and had a sense for the land and its people, which contributed to his excitement to serve there. "I don't know whether you'll do any good out there or not," Elder Holland remembered President Hinckley saying to the two of them. "You probably won't. But I believe that you'll come back and forever see your work in the Twelve differently because of what you've done."

On August 9, 2002, the Oakses met with President Hinckley, who gave Elder Oaks a blessing. It included the promise, "You will hear the whisperings of the Spirit in the quiet hours of the night, and you will be prompted to do that which will help move the work forward."

Elder Oaks's two counselors in the Area Presidency, Elders Angel Abrea of Argentina and Richard J. Maynes of the United States, were both gifted leaders.[2] Elder Abrea was remarkable with numbers and at one time had been considered to be the finance minister in Argentina. "He had the nose of an accountant," Elder Oaks said, "and could spot an error in a spreadsheet just by glancing at it." Elder Maynes, having been a mission president in Mexico and a successful businessman, was very adept at solving problems, including developing self-reliance programs specific to Filipino needs. Together, they proved to be a great team.

On August 16, the day after the Oakses' arrival in Manila, two feelings struck Elder Oaks as he was examining missionary applications. The first was sympathy for the poverty faced by some of the Philippine Saints. By American standards, many lived humble lives, though circumstances varied by family. At the same time, he felt bothered that many of those applying for missions and their parents offered to contribute only the minimum financial amount required by the Church for their own support.

Given the variations in their situations, he expected to see greater variation in their contributions. Even more important, he worried that they might be depriving themselves of blessings by excusing themselves from sacrificing adequately because of straitened circumstances. "We need to foster spiritual growth through sacrifice," he wrote, "but not set the bar so high that few can serve." The calling, preparation, and work of missionaries, along with the retention of converts, would be major themes of his service in the Philippines.

Soon Elder Oaks held his first formal Area Presidency meeting with his counselors. "We have good rapport," he wrote in his journal. The men spent their initial meeting making decisions on some routine matters and identifying key issues on which to focus their ministry. Elder Maynes became impressed with Elder Oaks's skill in running meetings. "He was incredibly open and transparent and listened with actual interest to different opinions within the room, especially his counselors," Elder Maynes said. "Even though he was an Apostle, as well as the president, he worked with great unity and didn't move forward until we were all united on whatever the topic was at hand."

On August 22, Elder Oaks was awakened from sleep with a powerful impression: "We should approach the retention/conversion challenge through the mission presidents." More thoughts flowed: "We should determine how much of the retention problem fits directly under their responsibility, since they preside over the member districts (almost as numerous as stakes in the Philippines), including the very poor record of ordaining male converts. We should consider reallocating missionary time to reactivation and retention—a 'mission to the baptized but unordained or unconverted.'"

Such revelatory thoughts gave Elder Oaks a good start in figuring out how to turn around the Church in the Philippines. But that was something he had to manage along with the heavy, routine tasks of running an area of the Church that was largely unfamiliar to him. The routine tasks included daily meetings, interviews, and weekend conference assignments that by themselves equated to a full-time job.

He and Sister Oaks soon settled into their assignment. "The Philippines has warm weather, and its people have a warm disposition," Sister Oaks wrote. "They have a sincere love of Jesus Christ and a natural affinity for religion. Their humility is exceptional. They are easy to convert, but in many cases need to learn the diligence the restored gospel requires to stay active. Their sweet friendship, generosity, and caring natures made our time there a joy. They were always 'very much grateful' for every blessing, and we loved having them in our home for family home evenings."

The Area Presidency members' wives, including Sister Oaks, were encouraged to teach, and the Filipino women were eager for instruction. When Elder Oaks could, he took Sister Oaks with him as he traveled to stake conferences. A gifted teacher, she taught the sister leaders, and her teaching was essential in that matriarchal culture. The other wives in the Area Presidency also taught and enjoyed it. Seeing a need, Kristen Oaks led out in encouraging young women and their leaders to complete their Personal Progress programs.

Up until the Oakses' arrival, most wives of the North American General Authorities assigned to the Philippines were women who had gray or blonde hair. By contrast, Sister Oaks's hair was very dark. After her first leadership teaching opportunity, a local sister came up to her and said, "We love you because you have Philippine hair." Sister Oaks related the story to her husband, and Elder Oaks repeated it in the Saturday evening conference meeting, joking, "But what about me?"

As new residents of the Philippines, Elder and Sister Oaks had to navigate a culture that was unfamiliar to them. When they were able to travel together, they sometimes found the hotel conditions primitive by American standards. Once when Elder Oaks traveled alone to a remote area, Sister Oaks reported: "The only place for him to overnight was a small home rented by missionaries. To make him more comfortable, the mission president bought a new mattress, but the apartment had no shower, so Elder Oaks joined the missionaries in using a bucket of water." Sister Oaks summed it up: "He was in the field."

On another occasion, Elder Oaks related, "A young missionary in the Philippines told me they had trouble with retention because after work some of the men they baptized had a tendency to join their neighbors to 'drink gin and eat dogs.'" Not knowing that many Asian peoples eat the creatures kept elsewhere only as pets, Elder Oaks replied, "I didn't know they had 'hot dogs' in the Philippines." Later, he wrote, "That missionary must have thought me pretty naïve."

Despite the culture shock people often experience when they move to a new country, Elder and Sister Oaks remained focused on why they had been called to the Philippines. Elder Oaks and his counselors saw that despite large numbers of baptisms, the number of Melchizedek Priesthood holders and adult full-tithe payers had increased only negligibly in the area. They noted also "an alarming loss of youth" from the Church, especially during their teenage years. Finally, unbridled Church growth had resulted in weak congregations without adequate leadership or strong members to fill key callings.

In September, the new Area Presidency set goals on how to advance the Church significantly in the Philippines. "We agreed," Elder Oaks wrote, "that the three things we will stress this year are (1) teaching doctrine and building faith; (2) rebalancing the balanced effort;[3] and (3) establishing programs of activity for youth." Elder Maynes noted how Elder Oaks focused them on "the fundamentally important things versus just important things." He knew, Elder Maynes recognized, that "the fundamentally important things would drag the important things along with them."

A week after formally establishing their goals, the Area Presidency held a mission presidents seminar. "I summarized what we need," Elder Oaks recorded, "in words something like this: We need to have an entirely new balance between baptisms and retention/reactivation, and we are willing to accept a reduction in the first if it is necessary to produce the needed sharp increase in the second. This was well received by everyone."

His counselor Elder Maynes summarized "what we will do differently, effective immediately." This included no longer assigning missionaries to "places where we can't have a viable unit for many years, if at all," instead emphasizing the "concept of growing from centers of strength."

Back in Salt Lake City for the October 2002 conference, Elders Oaks and Holland gave reports to Church leaders on their areas. "We both were very candid about the dangerous state of the Church in our areas," Elder Oaks recorded. "I used the phrase 'the Church in the Philippines is in liquidation,' referring to the continued input of tens of thousands of baptized persons with very little real growth in the critical areas of active Melchizedek Priesthood and full-tithe payers. I also expressed alarm at the drastic fallout of youth, who are the future leaders. We both attributed this dangerous condition to baptizing more than we could retain with the critical mass of active people and also to the weakening effect of premature creation or division of units so that we do not allow most units to reach the critical mass to conduct the Church program and have activities attractive to youth."

Elders Oaks and Holland not only identified problems but also proposed solutions. "We summarized what we intended to do about the subject," Elder Oaks recorded. "At the conclusion, President Hinckley said soberly, but with obvious pleasure at the content of our reports, 'It is in your hands. You do what you need to do to turn it around.' We were both thrilled." Elder Oaks also noted, "Our presentations were very popular with the Seventies, who felt that they opened new options for them in guiding the organizations under their direction."

President Hinckley drew on these findings when he spoke at a General Authority training meeting on October 1. Having Apostles in the Philippines and Chile was starting to impact the worldwide Church leadership.

In early January 2003 in Manila, Elder Oaks opened a letter from the First Presidency that he did not know was coming. Dated December 4, it read, "After giving the matter prayerful consideration, we have decided to have you continue as President of the Philippines

Area for an additional year. The contributions you have made thus far have been greatly appreciated. It is felt that your continued efforts will prove to be a great blessing to the Saints and the Brethren as the challenge of rapid growth and leadership continues to be an area of significant concern in this worldwide Church."

When Elder Oaks shared the extension news with Sister Oaks, she first thought he was teasing.

"These men don't tease," her husband assured her.

"Then, to my delight," Elder Oaks wrote, "she reacted very positively." She "was delighted and immediately began to talk about how this would permit us to do more effective work here in the Philippines, to help the members and the Church. I was thrilled with her reaction."

The succeeding months until the April 2003 general conference were exhausting ones for Elder Oaks as he and his counselors worked mightily to turn around the work in the Philippines. In all this, he was deeply grateful for Sister Oaks's support. "Through all the extra time this has taken, early in the morning, all day long, and late at night, Kristen has been admirably patient and supportive," he wrote. "What a blessing she is to me!"

During the April 2003 general conference in Salt Lake, Elders Oaks and Holland again reported to the First Presidency. They were granted even greater authority in their responsibilities than they had expected. Elder Oaks wrote with satisfaction, "The whole meeting had a great supportive spirit, and Elder Holland and I went forth feeling reinforced in our responsibilities."

The conference period also had a light moment for the Oakses. Church leaders appointed long-time University of Utah graduate, faculty member, and administrator Elder Cecil O. Samuelson of the Seventy to be the new president of rival Brigham Young University. Sister Oaks and a friend made a cake to celebrate—and kid him about—his appointment, and Elder Oaks went down the hall with them to present it. The frosting on the cake was BYU blue. "But when you cut into the cake," Elder Oaks wrote, "it was bright red," the color for the University of Utah. Everyone had a good laugh.

Over the succeeding weeks and months in the Philippines, Elder Oaks and his counselors continued to focus on missionary work, consolidated weak units to form strong ones, worked with the First Presidency on how to deal with cohabiting couples, and trained local leaders. They held an area meeting with ten local Area Authority Seventies to "report on things that had happened at April conference," Elder Oaks wrote, "notably the fact that Church departments and the First Presidency and Quorum of the Twelve are looking to us in the Philippines to show the way for the Church in the developing world. I, therefore, suggested as the theme of our area council: 'The Philippines Shows the Way.'"

Early in June 2003, Elder and Sister Oaks experienced what they felt to be a miracle. A stake president was scheduled for release that month after serving almost eleven years. His release had previously been postponed because it was thought unsafe for a General Authority to travel to his stake in Zamboanga in southwest Mindanao. Because

Elder Oaks with Filipino children

of reports about many kidnappings and bombings by local Muslim separatists, no General Authority had visited the region since the stake president was installed in August 1992. Determined to avoid further postponement, Elder Oaks assigned himself. Two months before the conference, he felt impressed to schedule it for June 7 and 8, but for security reasons, he kept his participation and travel plans confidential.

Two days before his departure, a Philippine newspaper announced that Admiral Thomas Fargo, U.S. commander in the Asia Pacific, had just arrived in Zamboanga for a three-day visit "to observe joint efforts to fight terrorism in the country" and that "security was tight for [his] entire visit." Elder Oaks noted in his journal, "The Lord takes care of His servants when they are on His errand." During Elder Oaks's visit, Zamboanga was "quiet and peaceful" with "no spirit of fear among the people." The stake conference took place without disruption, and despite over a decade with no General Authority visitors, the stake proved to be one of the strongest he had visited in the Philippines.

The second year of Elder Oaks's service as Philippines Area President formally began on August 15, 2003. "Today," he wrote, "is the effective date of our new Area Presidency, with Richard J. Maynes first counselor and Rex R. Gerratt second counselor." Elder Gerratt was from Idaho, had been a mission president in the Philippines, and was a strong addition to the Area Presidency.

Planning for the coming year, the Area Presidency kept its earlier goals but added two more. "We [added] (1) getting more young elders on missions and (2) getting more people to the temple," Elder Oaks wrote. "We determined to hold five to eight cluster meetings during 2004 to reach all of the stake presidencies and district presidencies in the Philippines, tentatively choosing the various areas where we will assemble."

From time to time, the Oakses had visits from family members. To their delight, in 2003, two of Kristen's sisters visited for a few days, and in January 2004, three of the Oakses' four daughters visited. When the

Elder Oaks with visiting daughters Cheri, Sharmon, and TruAnn

daughters left for their homes, Elder Oaks wrote, "I believe our two weeks with the girls are as happy a time and as emotionally resting and family-bonding a time as we have ever experienced."

On January 24, 2004, Elder Oaks led perhaps the most important leadership training meeting of his time as Area President. It included Area Seventies, the Manila temple president, the presidents of missions near Manila, and as many as could attend from the presidencies of twenty-nine stakes and nineteen districts. The Area Presidency gave blunt and direct counsel and felt good reactions from those in attendance. "The brethren were extremely attentive," Elder Oaks wrote. "Almost all of the questions from the floor were excellent." He declared it "a milestone in our leadership teaching here in the Philippines."

President Gordon B. Hinckley also saw the progress from his vantage point in Salt Lake City and wrote to Elder Oaks. "I received a wonderful complimentary letter from President Hinckley," Elder Oaks noted. "It contained this line: 'You have accomplished wonders while you have been there.'"

In February, a pouch of mail from Church headquarters brought a First Presidency letter releasing Elder and Sister Oaks from their Philippines assignment, "effective August 15, 2004." With the date now set for their release, Elder Oaks reflected on their service in his journal. "Kristen and I," he wrote, "consider ourselves very blessed to be in the Philippines to assist in the growth of the Church in this wonderful land. I am having some very positive feelings about what is happening here. . . . I am also feeling that I need to do more to praise the people for what is happening to build their confidence. Part of this—already undertaken—is to enhance the stature of the Area Seventies both in their own minds and in the eyes of the people."

By May 1, Elder Oaks was able to journalize, "Kristen and I feel very peaceful and fulfilled at our forthcoming release. It was good to come here when called by the Lord, and it is good to return at the same direction. We only pray that we can finish with honor and do the concluding things in a way that will secure the work we have done in the furtherance of the work of the Lord and to the benefit and blessing of the wonderful people of the Philippines."

Additional inspiration on June 4 left him with a more sober feeling. "In the night," he wrote, "I had a troubling dream about Neal Maxwell not being able to get through a fence when we were walking together. I called President Packer and found that Elder Maxwell is, indeed, failing. We increase our prayers for his benefit."

Over the next month, Elder Oaks worked at fulfilling final speaking assignments, writing reports, tying up loose ends, packing, and preparing to return to the United States. Then on July 6, he received a phone call from Elder Maxwell. "He was alert but subdued, and it was soon apparent that he considered this phone call a final goodbye," Elder Oaks wrote. "We discussed how we wanted to work with one another on the Leadership and Training Committee, but he said this 'may not be possible.'"

He asked Elder Oaks when he and Sister Oaks would be returning to Utah. "I could see," Elder Oaks concluded, "that he was calculating whether he would still be there. I told him I could not accept the fact that I would not see him again but observed that we would be working together on whichever side of the veil the Lord assigned us."

Elder Maxwell's response touched Elder Oaks deeply. He said he would give Elder Oaks's deceased mother "a good report about you." Elder Maxwell had known her early in his life. "This is so emotional," Elder Oaks wrote later, "that I can't write much about it."

On Sunday, July 11, 2004, Elder and Sister Oaks had the capstone experience of their two years in the Philippines at an area conference originating from the Fairview stake center in Quezon City and telecast to buildings throughout the area. Many came to the stake center three hours early. "Their powerful spirits," Elder Oaks wrote, "inspired everyone." The speakers focused on the subjects the Area Presidency had emphasized over the prior two years. "I was the concluding speaker," Elder Oaks wrote, "and gave an overview of our goals and the progress we have made in the Philippines.

"The Spirit was extremely strong," he noted. "Kristen commented that this was the most powerful meeting she had attended in the Philippines, and I felt the same. She said that this was an occasion where spiritual food was being served and the audience was partaking to the fullest. It filled our hearts." About earlier meetings and this one, Sister Oaks wrote, "I remember multiple times large crowds of Filipinos surrounded President Oaks as we left. They came to his chest and encircled him as if in one big group hug."

"One cannot serve in the Philippines without acquiring a profound love and respect for the people," she later wrote. "Their humility, warm smiles, thankfulness, and desire to please make preaching the gospel there a delight. We made so many dear friends. Under the direction of President Oaks, those serving in the priesthood blossomed in their capacity to serve. Seeing their potential, he demanded many things from them. He expected them to keep the commandments, hand in their reports on time, and as Church leaders to speak out about

Elder Oaks on assignment in the Philippines

keeping Church standards. The result of these expectations was quite miraculous."

On Elder Oaks's last day in the area office, he scrambled to finish assignments and reports, clear off his desk, and say goodbyes. Then a 3:30 p.m. phone call brought President Packer's solemn voice reporting, "We have just lost Neal."

"We both choked up," Elder Oaks recorded, "but I must admit that it was not unexpected. . . . I had many minutes during the rest of the afternoon when I pondered the sweetness of his association, the greatness of his contribution, and the sadness of not being able to work with him again on this side of the veil."

The next morning, Elder and Sister Oaks left for Utah. "When we arrived home," Elder Oaks wrote, "we were surprised to see two vans in front of our home, a big banner and ribbons welcoming Dad and Kristen back." Family members "came running out of the house for a joyful welcome. Inside there were balloons and welcomes and an incredible stuffing of the refrigerator with every food imaginable. . . . What a dear welcome home!"

A few days later, they attended Elder Maxwell's funeral, which took place on July 27—the birthday of Elder Oaks's mother. Four days later, around 5:15 a.m., Elder Oaks arose from a sound sleep to answer another call from President Packer. "Well," he announced somberly, "we've lost David"—meaning Elder David B. Haight of the Twelve.

"What a remarkable circumstance, after over nine years of no changes in the Quorum of the Twelve, to lose two of our dear brothers within ten days," Elder Oaks reflected. "I . . . lay awake with many sweet memories of Neal and David and with heavy mortal forebodings about what this would mean as we readjust our positions and responsibilities in the Quorum of the Twelve."

As President Hinckley had promised, Elder Oaks gained great experience in the Philippines as he worked to turn around the Church in that country. He returned home just as the loss of two senior Apostles meant he would shoulder even more responsibilities than ever before in the senior quorums of the Church. His two-year Philippines experience provided important perspective he would need in an increasingly global church. It was a precious time for bonding, as Dallin and Kristen taught and labored together. Years after his experience in the Philippines, Elder Oaks would say he learned more in those two years than in any other two-year period of his ministry.

CHAPTER 22

"GO YE THEREFORE AND TEACH ALL NATIONS"

A Worldwide Ministry

As the Lord Jesus Christ prepared to leave His disciples near the end of His post-resurrection ministry, He commanded them, "Go ye therefore, and teach all nations, baptizing them in the name of the Father, and of the Son, and of the Holy Ghost" (Matthew 28:19). In this last dispensation, the Lord called twelve Apostles to be "special witnesses of the name of Christ in all the world" (D&C 107:23). As an Apostle, traveling the world to testify of Christ's name and His gospel became a vital part of Elder Oaks's ministry both before and after his call to serve in the Philippines.

Global travel broadened his understanding of the world, its peoples, and their cultures, and he recorded impressions of what he saw, often in elegant prose. But his main purpose for travel was not sightseeing, and he sometimes lamented how little time he had to enjoy the beauties of the earth and its people. Instead, he focused intently on the apostolic purpose of his travel, which included the scriptural command to strengthen the stakes of the Church (see Isaiah 54:2), a commandment fulfilled in major part by teaching and training.

Yet as a new General Authority in the mid-1980s, Elder Oaks had his own steep learning curve, and he felt the pain of climbing it. "No one says anything to me about my talks," he worried in his journal. "This is eerie to have no feedback, but I suppose I will just have to get used to it as a consequence of the reluctance of people to speak with an Apostle about his performance. . . . But the respect for the position is such that I am tolerated with love and respect."

At a mission presidents seminar in Europe in late 1991, he shared with his audience "how inadequate I felt in my own calling because of deficiencies in my preparation." Then he offered this caution: "The natural tendency in such a circumstance is to fall back on doing what we know how to do, regardless of the requirements of our calling, but we should shape ourselves to our calling rather than trying to conform our calling to our own experience or preference."

Over time, he progressed, and at a mission presidents seminar in 1996, he "felt very blessed in the ninety-minute keynote address" that he gave. Still, the pattern of a slow start remained. "As is always true on my trips," he wrote in late 1999, "as each day passes I get more in tune with the Spirit, and I clearly finish more strongly than I begin."

Success in his speaking and training depended on the preparation of both the audience and the speaker. In 1985, just a year after his call to the apostleship, he addressed a well-prepared audience in Brazil, "and although I had only a few notes for my remarks," he observed, "the Spirit was so strong and directive that I felt this was one of the best talks I have given during our travels." Twenty years later, after a training meeting for priesthood and auxiliary leaders, he concluded, "What we can do in training is dependent as much on the audience as it is on us."

Sometimes effectiveness hinged on other circumstances, too. At a leadership conference in Washington state, Elder Oaks encouraged leaders "to use the proper full name of persons they were submitting for a sustaining vote, forgoing nicknames such as 'Butch.'" Afterward, Elder Oaks's son Lloyd, counselor in a local bishopric, came up and introduced his ward elders quorum president as "Butch." "Embarrassed,"

Elder Oaks recounted genially, "I asked 'Butch' whether that was his true name. In response, he provided his full name—which helped me understand why he went by 'Butch.'" They had a good laugh together, and Elder Oaks resolved to be more careful in the future with his illustrations.

Early in his ministry, he met a husband-wife doctor team who had traveled more than six hundred kilometers "to see the Apostle" and hear the Lord's words communicated through him. "This sobered me with the magnitude of the members' and the Lord's expectations of me in my calling," Elder Oaks wrote, and he labored hard to do what he felt the Lord wanted of him.

A duty he performed frequently was speaking to missionaries. In 1985, near the start of his apostolic ministry, he spoke to some in Ecuador. "These are sweet meetings," he wrote, "and I hope we are as helpful to the missionaries as they are heartening to us." Most of the time, he found missionaries humble and teachable, susceptible to the Spirit. When that happened, Elder Oaks felt personal rejuvenation and

Elder Oaks with missionaries

rich inspiration in his messages. "The spirit of the missionaries surely makes a difference in what speakers can do!" he observed.

Over time, he grew in his ability to assess and address an audience. He prepared the best he could for each occasion and sought to be in tune with the Spirit. On a trip more than two decades after his call, he gave a series of firesides and "depended on the Spirit to lead me where it would, so the fireside talks were quite different in each location." The next day, he wrote, "I gave a different message than I have given to any of the missionary audiences on this trip, but felt inspired and blessed in doing so."

"I have witnessed multiple times and have been told by people that as he spoke, he answered the prayers of those in the audience," Kristen Oaks said of her husband after many years of serving with him. "They had concerns for family, spouses, death, divorce, sickness, or even finances, and his words directed them and provided them comfort. He spoke under the influence of the Spirit and blessed those who came to hear the word of the Lord.

"He has the gift to see danger from afar," she said of him. "He was one of the very first to speak on the dangers of pornography, alternate voices, and the attacks on traditional marriage. He sees the danger in terms of damage done to members spiritually and also how legislation will affect freedom of religion in years to come. This is the reason he is often so adamant in his teaching against certain movements, arguments, and activities. When some others only think of the present and personal feelings of those involved, he sees the future effect on the many. He is valiant in supporting the laws of God. He is truly a seer, and I am so proud of him."

Throughout his life, thorough preparation had been his hallmark. As one called to the Twelve without the typical experiences of having been a full-time missionary, mission president, or member of the Seventy first, he sought to make up for the lack of experience by diligent study, which was what he had learned to do as a lawyer and academic. Over time, he prepared well and learned to let go of what he prepared if the Spirit moved him in a better direction.

Yet, like all Church members, he had times when he struggled. "I felt quite out of tune with the Spirit and had to pray fervently before speaking for over an hour," he admitted in Taiwan in 2002. "My prayers were answered, and I believe my talk was at least adequate." His hectic schedule sometimes made preparation difficult. In 2004 he wrote, "I arose at 4:30 a.m. to work intensively on the four-hours' worth of messages I need to give at this mission presidents seminar. I had not prepared these prior to my coming (too busy)."

When he was a junior Apostle, he felt self-conscious at times when speaking on the same program as those more senior. "This morning I was the first speaker at the mission presidents seminar, for two hours," he wrote in the Philippines in 1988. "This is difficult. A talk to mission presidents is the most difficult talk I give, and to be the first speaker at the seminar when I am 'cold' and they are 'cold,' is the hardest spot of all. I felt flat and struggled and completed my assignment with relief"—especially since President Gordon B. Hinckley, then a counselor in the First Presidency, arrived in time to hear the last part of the talk.

Elder Oaks recognized that his role was to expound and exhort, not entertain. At a conference in New Zealand in 1988, he spent forty-five minutes telling stories and, he wrote, "the audience seemed to love it." Some contrasted the serious style of his general conference addresses with his "good-natured and happy" style in their meeting. "I suppose that is okay if I get my messages across," Elder Oaks begrudged, "but here I think I went a little too far with stories and shorted the message content."

Sister Kristen Oaks later identified this experience as a turning point in his ministry. "As he sat down," she said, "the Spirit whispered to him, 'Never do that again.' From that point on, like his mentor Elder Bruce R. McConkie (who had a tremendous sense of humor), he became very solemn and serious when teaching doctrine. So intense was Elder Oaks when he spoke of sacred things that his daughters said to him, 'Daddy, you look like you are mad sometimes when you speak.' He was never angry or irritated, just somber as he shared sacred truths. The lesson taught him in New Zealand has directed his teaching to this day."

In Guam the year after his New Zealand experience, he spoke informally to gathered members and wrote, "The people seemed to enjoy it, and I hope I will be forgiven if I share the happiness as well as the doctrine of the restored gospel." Over time, he learned to fit the tone to the nature of the meeting. With practice, he also learned to speak more spontaneously and personally in his talks, often saying things he had not thought about ahead of time as he prepared.

He also found humor in unexpected responses during serious teaching moments. "In a Saturday evening meeting in a conference in the United States," he recalled, "I was trying to encourage families to hold a family home evening. I saw the teenage son of a counselor in the stake presidency in the audience and called him to the stand. Without warning I asked him what his family did for home evening. He surprised everyone and embarrassed his father by saying, 'What's home evening?'"

Frequently, he repeated President Harold B. Lee's statement that "this Church is not a retirement home for the righteous but a hospital for sinners." One of Elder Oaks's traveling companions, he remembered, "told me he had also used that story, and afterwards a recent convert said, 'Thanks for explaining that principle. Now I finally understand why our Church calls its units wards.'"

Besides worrying about the contents of his talks, Elder Oaks came to see how important one-on-one interactions were with his audience, whether simple eye contact, a wave, or especially shaking hands. "I can feel the power of a personal 'touch,'" he wrote. "I feel the Lord is exercising influence on people through my personal contact with them, and I am coming to feel that this is at least as important as what I say from the pulpit."

Certain personal interactions proved especially memorable. In New Zealand, some Maori members "wanted to involve me in the traditional Maori nose-to-nose greeting (hongi)," he noted. "I complied." In England, a ten-year-old girl handed him a note that included a sketch of his head in pencil and the words, "I know you are an aposal because you are clean and your head is shiney."

Elder Oaks found the reference to his baldness particularly amusing. Much of his humor was self-effacing. "Perhaps," he explained, "I inherited this kind of humor from my beloved grandmother Harris, who delighted in telling how a young grandchild asked her, 'Grandma, did you used to be pretty?'" Often, at the pulpit, he quoted an earlier General Authority who, patting his bald head, said, "The noble and great always come out on top."

He also liked to tell the story of a mother who wrote saying "that her young son was an admirer." The boy wearied his parents with repeated requests for "a haircut just like Elder Oaks." "His parents finally relented," Elder Oaks said, "and cut his hair bald on top with fringes on the side." They sent Elder Oaks a picture, which he enjoyed showing to others.

In Bordeaux, France, in 1991, Elder and Sister Oaks had lunch with the mission president, Neil L. Andersen, his wife, Kathy, and their children. Fifteen-year-old Camey said, "I expected to sit there while the Oakses talked to my parents, but Elder and Sister Oaks began asking questions about all of us and made us part of their conversation. They were so much fun, and we laughed throughout the lunch." In her journal, she wrote, "The Oakses are such neat people!"

During his assignments, Elder Oaks met many members who were suffering from serious illness or struggling with important personal problems. While unable to give many requested blessings, he often prayed by name for those who sought relief. He sometimes learned later of miraculous blessings in their lives. Mindful of teachings and counsel about sharing sacred experiences, however, he has not talked about such experiences publicly.

Years of ministering helped Elder Oaks realize that helping listeners connect with the Spirit was often more important than giving instruction. "There was a very strong, sweet spirit in the meeting," he wrote in 2000, "and many said it was one of the best meetings they had ever attended. I doubt that anyone will remember long what was said, but they will probably remember how they felt."

A skill Elder Oaks had to learn as a General Authority was enduring the grind of long and frequent international travel. Besides dealing with jet lag and sluggishness at the start of a trip, he had to handle exhaustion and emotional weariness at the end of it and on very long days. At times he could become "desperately tired," he wrote. Fatigue could also make his remarks fall flat. After one such experience, he lamented, "I left that meeting feeling I wish I could have done better."

For someone who had spent most of his career in the English-speaking United States, a major challenge was the language barrier between him and his audiences. "This was my first experience holding a stake conference in a country where I needed the aid of a translator," he wrote in Brazil not long after he was called. Because he had excellent translators, "I seemed to get along all right with my talks," he wrote. "The people were very warm and loving, and I tried to return that feeling across the language barrier." On one trip, his translator "was so touched that he broke down and wept and was unable to continue for several minutes."

At times, Elder Oaks tried giving a few lines of a talk or testimony himself in the language of his audience. He felt his first efforts were poor, though with Spanish he improved over time. In addition, the Spirit helped him over some linguistic hurdles.

Although reorganizing stakes was a duty frequently delegated to members of the Seventy as the Church grew in size and complexity,

Elder Oaks enjoyed the strong witness of the Spirit that came when he fulfilled that responsibility. Two members of the Seventy assisted him in organizing the first stake in one country. They quickly narrowed the candidates to "two men, whose qualifications were so equal that we could not choose between the two on any objective grounds," Elder Oaks wrote. "We knelt in prayer, with each one of us praying in turn." Then each took a slip of paper on which both candidates' names were written and privately checked the name he felt impressed should be called. "When this was done," Elder Oaks wrote, "I turned them over one by one. All three of us had checked the same name" and were "thrilled by this evidence that the Lord was directing the choice."

One of the main purposes of his global travel was leadership training. In his lifetime, the Church had grown from predominantly a United States institution to a global one, with membership expanding most vibrantly south of the equator. The key to the Church's growth

Elder Oaks hugs Elder Won Yong Ko of the Seventy, Seoul, Korea, 2001

was leadership, which varied from weak and thin in some areas to strong and plentiful in others. As Elder Oaks traveled the world, he saw progress in the spiritual maturity and skill of the leaders called to serve in many countries, and he tried to tailor his training to fit his audience.

One principle he taught was the importance of having the Church grow from centers of strength. "We want stakes in the capital cities before we try to salt and pepper branches all across the landscape in a way that we cannot supervise adequately," he explained.

One of the best parts of his worldwide travel was his traveling companions, usually other General Authorities, and he often commented on how much he enjoyed working with them. As often as he could, he liked to travel with his wife, June, during the first part of his ministry, and with Kristen after his remarriage. June disliked public speaking but dutifully did what was asked of her, giving remarkable talks that reached audiences well. Her feedback and guidance helped him grow in his ministry.

Kristen was highly experienced and adept at public speaking, spoke frequently, and helped train women leaders around the world. Speaking at a fireside in Cusco, Peru, in 2014, Elder Oaks had her in mind when he advised his hearers to "choose a spouse that made them want to be better than they were." He declared, "Though I had been an Apostle for sixteen years at the time I married her, she was still showing me ways I could be better, and she always made me want to be better."

"Our time in the mission field improved my vision of my purpose as the wife of an Apostle," Kristen wrote. "We were truly 'equal partners' in family matters, but the great reality of priesthood authority unfolded itself before my eyes as Elder Oaks arose in the night to pray and record impressions, as he labored daily in the mission field and instructed Church leaders. His was a distinct and separate God-given responsibility to build the kingdom of God on earth.

"On a personal level," she added, "I am forever grateful that I could testify of my Savior, Jesus Christ, visit members' homes around the world, teach the sisters, and distribute Testimony Gloves for children—over 100,000 in twenty languages.[1] These were glorious opportunities as I stood at my husband's side. I will always remember and rejoice in them. I also came to understand that my greatest contribution was to ease my husband's burdens by listening to his impressions, supporting his ideas, and creating happy moments along the way—gathering our families, relishing our grandchildren, making time for recreation and laughter, and even enjoying unexpected diversions such as a train ride to Machu Picchu while on Church assignment. Those moments have made our life joyous."

Kristen became a keen observer of her husband during their ministry together. "I remember in Nigeria as he spoke, he slowed and his countenance changed," she recounted. "He was speaking as a prophet and told the audience that 'Nigeria would become one of the leading nations in the world.' Earlier in his service, he also spoke and told members in Ukraine that they would have a temple, which then seemed impossible." Yet it came to pass.

Kristen's life experience also suited her well to accompany her husband in meeting prominent leaders. For example, Elder Oaks worked with the Church's Family History Department in completing a family history that could be presented to First Lady Michelle Obama. On Wednesday, March 17, 2010, Senator Harry Reid took Elder and Sister Oaks and General Relief Society President Julie Bangerter Beck and her husband to meet with Mrs. Obama. "We presented the volumes," Elder Oaks wrote, "and demonstrated the electronic version. I had Julie Beck read the letter of presentation I had prepared, which she did with emotion. The Spirit was there, and all felt it. Mrs. Obama was touched and thrilled, and could not have been more gracious and grateful."[2]

During the decades of his apostolic ministry, Elder Oaks helped the Church grow in some of the largest countries of the world where it previously had few members, including China, India, and some countries of the former Soviet Union. For this and other reasons, he

Elder Oaks and Sister Kristen Oaks visit with Michelle Obama

frequently met with government officials. By policy, the Church enters countries through the front door, obeying the laws of the land.

Chinese officials permitted the Church to function in China so long as Chinese members and expatriates worshipped separately. Without missionaries in that country, the Church's growth occurred gradually through word of mouth, family growth, and particularly the return to China of members who joined in other countries. Guiding him in this work, especially early in his ministry, was fellow Apostle Russell M. Nelson, who had impressive prior experience in China. "He is a man of great faith and wisdom," Elder Oaks wrote admiringly.

During the early years Elder Oaks traveled in China, he met frequently with Gerrit W. Gong, president of the Beijing Branch, whom he had first met when Gerrit was a freshman at BYU. Later, Elder Oaks tracked Gerrit's impressive career, noting in his journal when he became a Rhodes Scholar at Oxford. Their meetings continued when Gerrit was called to the Quorum of the Twelve. "We would talk about the things that were happening in China or in Asia in general,"

Elder Oaks and Sister Kristen Oaks at the Taj Mahal, 2007

remembered Elder Gong. "He had this voracious ability to understand things and to put them into perspective."

As in China, the Church had a small number of members in India. Elder Oaks was assigned to dedicate the land and help develop "a master plan for establishing the Church there." Dedicating the country in 1989, he felt divine inspiration. "I had not formulated any phrases in my mind," he wrote, "but after I got started the words came strong and fluent, and the Spirit of the Lord was present and felt by all." Sister June Oaks told him afterward that it "was a powerfully inspirational experience for her," and he affirmed, "It surely was for me."

In 1991, Elder Oaks and Elder Nelson traveled to Armenia to dedicate that country. Elder Nelson asked Elder Oaks to be voice for the prayer. "Without preparation," Elder Oaks wrote, "I was entirely dependent upon the Spirit of the Lord to guide me." Elder Nelson later explained, "With my arm around his waist, we knelt under the shadow of Mt. Ararat and Dallin gave a dedicatory prayer that was just eloquent. He had no idea fifteen minutes before that he was going to dedicate that country. It was a matchless, eloquent dedicatory prayer."

In April 1993, Elder Oaks dedicated Albania on a hillside east of the nation's capital. "In preparation," he wrote, "I had studied, fasted, and prayed, and I felt very blessed in this prayer." His dedication of Cape Verde in 1994 also went well as he "was blessed with fluency in the dedicatory prayer." When he dedicated Pakistan in 2007, he "felt very blessed and inspired" in what he said, "and the spirit was very sweet" during the proceedings.[3]

To accomplish all that was required of him over decades of travel, Elder Oaks and his companions endured long absences from home, uncomfortable accommodations, flight delays, missed connections, snarled traffic, cancelations, lost luggage, power failures, illness, and accidents. "I do not enjoy sitting on planes and buses and in airports," Elder Oaks moaned on an unduly long trip, adding philosophically, "But it is all part of travel." And then there was the heavy weight of the many difficulties brought to him by local leaders. "Oh, the problems of a worldwide Church!" he once wrote.

Yet, in general, he took everything in stride. As he wrote during a visit to Europe, "So far our trip has been strenuous but purely delightful." After difficulties during an Asian trip, he wrote optimistically, "It all worked out." To keep in good spirits, he thought of the nineteenth-century Apostles. "What a contrast," he wrote, "between the comfort and speed with which we travel and the circumstances when the early Apostles took their journeys east across the plains and by sail to England, taking about two months on their trip."

The most challenging aspect of global travel was weariness. Entry after entry in his travel journals describes his falling into bed exhausted after a long day. Yet he accepted tiredness as a price of doing his duty, and it did not dissuade him. As with other challenges, he just worked through it the best he could and counted the spiritual blessings that came with the grueling schedule. The older he got, the more difficult travel became, and he had to learn to pace himself.

He summed up his feelings best while on a trip to Africa in 2006. "As I reflect on what I have been doing on this trip," he wrote, "I have been impressed with the fact that I am working so hard that I would not possibly do this for money. I love doing this for the Lord, and I love the people with whom I work and those I meet on these trips. . . . Falling into bed exhausted at the end of the day, I do not contemplate or dread another day, but only have a wonderful feeling about having done my very best in the day just concluded. I love working for the Lord and His children."

CHAPTER 23

"A MUTUALLY REINFORCING RELATIONSHIP"

Priesthood Authority in the Family and the Church

One of the most important topics Elder Dallin H. Oaks addressed in the decades after his call to the Twelve was the authority that operates in the Church and the family. His ponderings on the subject began after his widowed mother was left to raise three small children. When he was ordained a deacon, young Dallin thought he would be in charge of spiritual matters at home. His mother told him "how pleased she was to have a priesthood holder in the home," he remembered, but she "continued to direct the family, including calling on which one of us would pray when we knelt together each morning." Having been "taught that the priesthood presided in the family," Dallin was puzzled.[1]

"When my father died, my mother presided over our family," he came to realize. "She had no priesthood office, but as the surviving parent in her marriage she had become the governing officer in her family. At the same time, she was always totally respectful of the priesthood authority of our bishop and other Church leaders. She presided over her family, but they presided over the Church."[2] The two institutions supported one another.

With this background, he taught that as the children of Heavenly Parents, "our highest aspiration is to perpetuate [our] family relationships throughout eternity. The ultimate mission of our Savior's Church is to help us achieve exaltation in the celestial kingdom, and that can only be accomplished in a family relationship."[3]

Elder Oaks repeatedly quoted Spencer W. Kimball, the twelfth President of the Church, who helped define what it meant to be an equal partner in marriage. "We have heard of men who have said to their wives, 'I hold the priesthood, and you've got to do what I say.' Such a man should be tried for his membership," President Kimball declared. "Certainly he should not be honored in his priesthood. We rule in love and understanding."

On another occasion, President Kimball said, "When we speak of marriage as a partnership, let us speak of marriage as a full partnership," not one of "silent partners or limited partners." He implored, "If we desire the Lord's blessings in our efforts, we must use our priesthood authority in the Lord's way, in the family and in the Church," with the patience, kindness, long-suffering, and other qualities mentioned in section 121 of the Doctrine and Covenants.[4]

Around the time of young Dallin's deacon ordination, he saw a violation of that principle: unrighteous dominion by one who held priesthood authority. "We had a neighbor," Elder Oaks recalled, "who dominated and sometimes abused his wife. He roared like a lion, and she cowered like a lamb. When they walked to church, she always walked a few steps behind him. That made my mother mad. She was a strong woman who would not accept such domination, and she was angry to see another woman abused in that way."[5]

In contrast, Elder Oaks witnessed equal partnership in his home growing up. "The faithful widowed mother who raised us had no confusion about the eternal nature of the family," he related in 2005. "She always honored the position of our deceased father. She made him a presence in our home. She spoke of the eternal duration of their temple marriage. She often reminded us of what our father would like us to do so we could realize the Savior's promise that we could be a family forever."

Because of the way she talked about her deceased husband, Stella Oaks helped her son Dallin feel his father's constant presence. "Just before Christmas one year," Elder Oaks remembered, "our bishop asked me, as a deacon, to help him deliver Christmas baskets to the widows of the ward. I carried a basket to each door with his greetings. When he drove me home, there was one basket remaining. He handed it to me and said it was for my mother. As he drove away, I stood in the falling snow wondering why there was a basket for my mother. She never referred to herself as a widow, and it had never occurred to me that she was. To a twelve-year-old boy, she wasn't a widow. She had a husband, and we had a father. He was just away for a while."[6]

Elder Oaks distinguished the way priesthood functions in the hierarchical government of the Church. To understand that distinction fully requires understanding the meaning of *priesthood,* a term he defined in several talks. "What we call priesthood authority," he taught in one, "is the authority to act for God in a function that will be recognized not only in the activities of mortal life, but in the activities and requirements of eternal life. Mortal authority, which all of us have in some measure from our family, our community, and our employment, pertains only to mortal life. Priesthood authority pertains to time and eternity.

"The great significance of priesthood authority," he explained, "is that it authorizes its holder to act for God in ways necessary to the government of his kingdom, the performance of his ordinances, and the saving of his children. Priesthood holders act as authorized representatives of the Lord Jesus Christ in functions that will be recognized and have effect in the lives of the children of God in time and throughout all eternity."[7]

The government of the Church depends on priesthood keys, which are defined as the powers to direct the exercise of priesthood authority. "In the controlling of the exercise of priesthood authority, the function of priesthood keys both enlarges and limits," Elder Oaks pointed out in an April 2014 conference address. "It *enlarges* by making it possible for priesthood authority and blessings to be available for all of God's children. It *limits* by directing who will be given the authority of the priesthood, who will hold its offices, and how its rights and powers will be conferred.

"For example," he illustrated, "a person who holds the priesthood is not able to confer his office or authority on another unless authorized by one who holds the keys. Without that authorization, the ordination would be invalid. This explains why a priesthood holder—regardless of office—cannot ordain a member of his family or administer the sacrament in his own home without authorization from the one who holds the appropriate keys.

"With the exception of the sacred work that sisters do in the temple under the keys held by the temple president," he further clarified, " . . . only one who holds a priesthood office can officiate in a priesthood ordinance. And all authorized priesthood ordinances are recorded on the records of the Church."[8]

Other differences in the way priesthood authority is exercised in the family and Church are boundaries, duration, call and release, and partnership, Elder Oaks taught. Local Church officers "always have geographic boundaries that limit" their authority, whereas "family relationships and responsibilities are not dependent upon where different family members reside."

As to duration, Church callings end, "but family relationships are permanent." Church leaders with keys may call and release members and even terminate their membership if misbehavior warrants it. "In contrast," Elder Oaks taught, "family relationships are so important that the head of the family lacks the authority to make changes in family membership. That can only be done by someone authorized to adjust family relationships under the laws of man or the laws of God." Parents, for example, cannot disown children whose choices or lifestyles vary from those taught by the Church.

Finally, he explained, "the concept of partnership functions differently in the family than in the Church," with husbands and wives being equal partners in ways that Church officers are not.[9]

In April 2014, Elder Oaks noted, "Since the scriptures state that 'all other authorities [and] offices in the church are appendages to this [Melchizedek] priesthood' (D&C 107:5), all that is done under the direction of those priesthood keys is done with priesthood authority." Then he asked, "How does this apply to women?"

Citing President Joseph Fielding Smith, he answered that "the Church work done by women or men, whether in the temple or in the wards or branches, is done under the direction of those who hold priesthood keys," and "Relief Society is not just a class for women but something they belong to—a divinely established appendage to the priesthood.

"We are not accustomed to speaking of women having the authority of the priesthood in their Church callings," Elder Oaks acknowledged, "but what other authority can it be? When a woman—young or old—is set apart to preach the gospel as a full-time missionary, she is given priesthood authority to perform a priesthood function. The same is true when a woman is set apart to function as an officer or teacher in a Church organization under the direction of one who holds the keys of the priesthood. Whoever functions in an office or calling received from one who holds priesthood keys exercises priesthood authority in performing her or his assigned duties."[10]

Elder Oaks quoted Elder M. Russell Ballard, who said, "Our Church doctrine places women equal to and yet different from men. God does not regard either gender as better or more important than the other. . . . When men and women go to the temple, they are both endowed with the same power, which is priesthood power. . . . Access to the power and the blessings of the priesthood is available to all of God's children." Elder Oaks testified that "the power and blessings of the priesthood of God" are "available for His sons and daughters alike."[11]

"In our theology and in our practice," he summarized, "the family and the Church have a mutually reinforcing relationship. The family is dependent upon the Church for doctrine, ordinances, and priesthood keys. The Church provides the teachings, authority, and ordinances necessary to perpetuate family relationships to the eternities."[12] After long decades of study, he had laid to rest the questions he first considered as a twelve-year-old deacon and, with the approval of the First Presidency, shared what he learned for all to hear.

CHAPTER 24

"AN APOSTLE, NOT A JUDGE"

The Church and the Law

When not traveling the world, members of the Quorum of the Twelve work at Church headquarters in Salt Lake City. During his thirty-three years as a member of the Twelve, Elder Dallin H. Oaks had the typical rotating assignments given General Authorities to oversee the Church's units in specific areas of the world and to serve on general Church councils and committees. In addition to these assignments, Apostles sometimes receive additional responsibilities peculiarly suited to their backgrounds and experiences.

In the twentieth and early twenty-first centuries, some Apostles had backgrounds as attorneys. The University of Chicago Law School graduated the largest number of these men: Stephen L Richards, Albert E. Bowen, Henry D. Moyle, and Dallin H. Oaks. When Elder Oaks entered the Quorum of the Twelve, four General Authorities senior to him were also attorneys: Marion G. Romney, then First Counselor in the First Presidency, and three members of the Twelve—Howard W. Hunter, Bruce R. McConkie, and James E. Faust.

When Elder Oaks received his call as an Apostle, President Gordon B. Hinckley told him to avoid giving legal advice to the

Church or practicing law privately. But Elder Oaks's long experience in the law was useful in identifying legal issues for referring to Church lawyers and in defining law-related issues, such as religious liberty, that needed to be understood by Church leaders and members and could be worked into his talks.

Elder Oaks's career as a legal practitioner, law professor, legal historian, and judge also made him a natural recipient of assignments to represent the Church at outside proceedings in which legal expertise was important. It further qualified him to revise and update the Church's handbooks for leaders. Moreover, it helped him tackle difficult and complex doctrinal topics and explain them in a systematic way. Finally, as changes in the law incorporated values that increasingly conflicted with the Church's, his experience helped him in being a point person for defending the Church's values.

Among the many assignments he received to represent the Church was his testimony at a hearing of the Subcommittee on Civil and Constitutional Rights of the House Committee on the Judiciary, part of the United States Congress. He went to express Church support for a bill to overturn a U.S. Supreme Court decision that lowered religious freedom standards.[1]

"As a general rule," Elder Oaks began, "our church does not take positions on specific legislative initiatives pending in Congress or state legislatures. Our action in this matter is an exception to this rule. It underscores the importance we attach to this congressional initiative to restore to the free exercise of religion what a divided Supreme Court took away."

He offered some background on why this was important to the Church. "I know of no other major religious group in America that has endured anything comparable to the officially sanctioned persecution that was imposed upon members of my church by federal, state, and local government officials," he told the subcommittee. "In the 19th century, our members were literally driven from state to state,

Elder Oaks addresses House subcommittee

sometimes by direct government action, and finally expelled from the existing borders of the United States."[2]

In his testimony, he mentioned numerous instances of religious persecution of the Latter-day Saints, including his own ancestors. "I have a personal feeling for these persecutions, since . . . most of my ancestors suffered with the [Saints] in their earlier persecutions," he noted. He gave as an example his third great-grandmother Catherine Elmira Prichard Oaks, a member of the Church who was driven from Missouri and later Illinois. "Fleeing religious persecution," he testified, "she died on the plains of Iowa, a martyr to her faith." He also explained that his great-aunt Belle Harris was imprisoned at age twenty-two for refusing to testify against her husband, who was being prosecuted at the time for cohabitation.

During the nineteenth century, "Congress and some state legislatures," he explained, "passed laws penalizing the religious practices, and even the religious beliefs, of Latter-day Saints. Under this legislation, the corporate entity of The Church of Jesus Christ of Latter-day Saints was dissolved, and its properties were seized. Many church leaders and members were imprisoned. People signifying a belief in the doctrine of my church were deprived of the right to hold public office or to sit on juries, and they were even denied the right to vote in elections."

Unfortunately, "most of these denials of religious freedom received the express approval of the U.S. Supreme Court," he noted. "It was a dark chapter in the history of religious freedom in this nation." "If past is prologue," he warned, "the forces of local, state, and federal governmental power, now freed from the compelling governmental interest test, will increasingly interfere with the free exercise of religion. We fear that the end result will be a serious diminution of the religious freedom guaranteed by the U.S. Constitution. . . .

"Most of the court cases involving government interference with religious freedom involve religious practices that appear out of the ordinary to many," he pointed out. "By their nature, elected officials are unlikely to pass ordinances, statutes, or laws that interfere with large mainstream religions whose adherents possess significant political power at the ballot box. But political power or impact must not be the measure of which religious practices can be forbidden by law. The Bill of Rights protects principles, not constituencies. The worshipers who need its protections are the oppressed minorities, not the influential constituent elements of the majority."[3]

Besides testifying in such legal proceedings, Elder Oaks also represented the Church in public forums when an officer with a substantial legal reputation was needed. On February 5, 2006, for example, he participated on a distinguished panel for a program on personal ethics called "My Brother's Keeper," which was taped for the *Ethics in America* educational video series. He felt disappointed at the situational ethics expressed in the answers of some participants but was pleased that he could join a Protestant educator in declaring "the existence of right and wrong, in contrast to expediency and political correctness."[4]

Six and a half years later, Elder Oaks represented the Church at Notre Dame University in South Bend, Indiana, for "A More Perfect

Union: The Future of America's Democracy," another panel discussion, this one made up of religious and educational leaders. "These prominent religious leaders," a preprogram advertisement announced, "will address the ways in which religious values inform political decisions, the role of religious leaders in debates over public issues, and political diversity among adherents of the same faith."[5] "I had prepared intensively and prayerfully and felt very blessed in my participation," Elder Oaks recorded. But he felt the greatest significance of the trip was the relationships he built with other religious leaders.

Besides contributing to public discourse on topics of Church interest, Elder Oaks also played a key role in defining issues for discussion by the members of the Quorum of the Twelve and other Church leaders. His ability to reduce complex topics to their essence—a skill he developed through legal study and practice—contributed to focusing discussions in ways that were highly productive. "He had a wonderful way of defining what the issues were in a way that it would open up discussion, not shut off discussion, and allow everybody to express their view," said Elder Quentin L. Cook. "He's able to take a very complex set of circumstances and facts and organize those facts in a way that makes it much easier to make a judgment or to make decisions about those facts," explained Elder Gary E. Stevenson. "I think that much of that must have been refined in his role as a judge."

A good example was when he served on the Missionary Executive Council of the Church. Experience had taught him that missionaries too often focused on faith and baptism, neglecting repentance, and that, as a result, people were baptized without fully repenting of their sins and becoming converted. "We should be careful that we are teaching repentance, not just faith," Elder Neil L. Andersen remembers Elder Oaks teaching. He focused the council and those under its direction using the words "Teach repentance, baptize converts," a phrase that was easy to understand and remember.

Elder D. Todd Christofferson admired Elder Oaks's ability to "help set the stage for a useful discussion" in quorum meetings by offering a few observations and inviting everyone to contribute. "I think that's a great talent to contribute and stimulate a healthy discussion, counseling together without controlling or trying to steer it." Elder Gerrit W. Gong admired that Elder Oaks "always tried to look at things from a very broad, global, and churchwide view." "We've served together extensively," said Elder David A Bednar. "I consider it one of the great learning experiences of my life to watch him in action."

Besides helping others frame discussions, Elder Oaks was ideally suited by his legal experience to prepare Church handbooks for internal Church use by leaders. The First Presidency gave him assignments to work on the handbooks, Elder Russell M. Nelson explained, "because of that methodical mind of his." In Elder Oaks's work on handbooks over the decades, he would be aided, among others, by Elder Cook and Elder Christofferson, two other members of the Twelve who had legal backgrounds.

In January 1988, less than four years after Elder Oaks's call to the apostleship, he received an assignment "to oversee the final approvals for the new edition of the *General Handbook of Instructions,*" he recorded in his journal. His role was to propose and gather suggestions for handbook changes, oversee their drafting, and steer them through a complex approval process. As with his other important assignments, he invested himself fully in the task.

Aided by very capable staff, he worked systematically through the handbook section by section, submitting proposed changes to his brethren for comment as he did so. Section 8, dealing with Church "courts" (as they had traditionally been called) was the one to which he devoted the most effort, informed by a balance of his legal training and spiritual responsibilities. He took the topic into a temple meeting in early April. "Today," he wrote, "my thirty-minute discussion on 'Church Discipline' (the new title I proposed) went very well. All were enthusiastic about my proposal to broaden the focus and legitimize probations and handling transgressors according to their needs instead of affixing 'penalties' or 'punishment' according to the gravity of the sin."

Elder Boyd K. Packer complimented him on a later presentation, "referring," Elder Oaks wrote, "to my proposal that we abandon the legal terminology and talk in this section like shepherds of a flock instead of wardens of a penal institution. He said I was showing my earlier-stated determination to be an Apostle, not a judge."

By June 23, he had worked his way through most of the sections of the handbook. As of July 11, during what should have been his summer break, he had gotten through much of what remained and commented, "This drafting of very difficult material goes so easily that it is a testimony that we are going in the right direction." He worked on and off to complete the first draft over the next few days, again observing, "The work flows out smoothly, surprising for intermittent work on a difficult subject. It must be something I am supposed to do, for me to get so much help."

But as the work dragged on over the next months, the number of hours, drafts, and approvals required to complete the task seemed almost overwhelming at times. On August 18, after receiving several more suggestions for improving what he had done, he sighed, "More long hours! I wouldn't work this hard for any cause but the Lord's!" On November 21, he wrote, "I felt the spirit of inspiration in making changes previously overlooked but important for the guidance of participants."

By mid-December, he received another heavy assignment that would take years to complete. He looked forward to working with the team assigned to the new project. "But in the midst of my sprint to finish the handbook in these next few days," he wrote, "I felt like a runner in the last lap of one long race who suddenly learns that he is beginning another long race in the last few steps of his finish of the current one. There is no rest for those who do it and get it done."

And that's the kind of man he was—someone the First Presidency could depend on to shoulder heavy tasks and get them done well, no matter how much time and effort they required. After venting briefly in his journal, Elder Oaks lunged ahead, describing the day as "extraordinarily difficult" and "stressful" but ultimately "rewarding." Two days later, in the final temple meeting of the year, the First Presidency and Quorum of the Twelve approved nearly all the sections of the new handbook. "I feel," Elder Oaks wrote with relief, "like a hiker who has been over the mountain and is close enough to home to see the lights and smell supper."

During his time in the Twelve, Elder Oaks would also be responsible for a second and a third major handbook edition, laboring with his very capable partner, Elder Cook. Working on the second edition in 1995, Elder Oaks wrote, "We are making good progress toward consolidating about forty handbooks into only two." The next year, the First Presidency and Twelve approved what he, his committee, and the staff had done. "Now," Elder Oaks wrote, "we can go forward to finish this five-year effort on our proposed course." The two consolidated handbooks, published in 1998, included one for stake presidencies and bishops and a second for priesthood and auxiliary leaders.[6]

In November 2001, Elder Oaks, along with fellow Apostles Henry B. Eyring and Dieter F. Uchtdorf, recorded a training video on some additions to the handbook. When President Packer saw it, he gave them a rare compliment. "I pronounce it," he proclaimed, "one of the best things I have seen in all the years I have been here. . . . Enjoy the certainty that it was a double A+ presentation."

During the annual general conference in 2006, Elder Oaks helped train General Authorities and Area Seventies on the purpose and use of a new revision of the handbook. In his presentation, he sought "to draw the distinction between the needed precise adherence to some parts ('uniformity') and the need for selective revelatory adaptations to local circumstances in other parts ('flexibility')." Afterward, President

James E. Faust, Second Counselor in the First Presidency, told Elder Oaks, "You threaded the needle," meaning that he had described the balance perfectly.

That comment was a relief to Elder Oaks. "I have worried and prayed much over this one," he confided to his journal. The goal of the members of the Twelve responsible for handbook training had been "to change thinking and pave the way for more local flexibility without yielding the necessary uniformity." After the training, President Packer, Elder Oaks, and Elder David A. Bednar met and "concluded we did as well in this new more open and flexible way of training as we could in a first effort," Elder Oaks wrote.

During the time he served as Area President in the Philippines, Elder Oaks conferred regularly with Elder Holland in Chile about vastly simplifying the handbook for the developing world. "Elder Oaks and I were on the phone to each other about every week," Elder Holland remembered. "We were the pioneers, and we were comparing notes." They recognized that areas where the Church was still in its formative stages needed handbooks that focused on essentials and not on details primarily of value in locales with highly developed wards and stakes.

After they returned to the United States, Elders Oaks and Holland continued to discuss these concepts. But the subject was postponed in the need to get out a third edition of the main handbook for the whole world, though their ideas would help shorten and shape that edition and emerged more fully again years later under the direction of Elder Christofferson.

The third edition on which Elder Oaks labored came out in 2010.[7] In preparing these handbooks, he consulted with others who had headquarters and field experience to aid him in the simplification effort, including Elder Holland and Elder Cook. In his journal, Elder Oaks wrote that the purpose of the new edition was "to promote flexibility and simplification," especially at the local level. Revising the handbooks, however, was a complex task, "hard and painful" for those assigned to the job.

Besides helping with the handbooks, Elder Oaks's experience with the law helped him tackle difficult and complex doctrinal topics and derive conclusions to help guide Church members in their lives. Beginning with the death of Elder Bruce R. McConkie in 1985—and accelerating with the passing of other major authorities on Church doctrine, including Elder Neal A. Maxwell and President Boyd K. Packer—Elder Oaks felt drawn to give greater and greater attention to the content and application of the doctrine of the Church. Though this was a task assumed by prophets, seers, and revelators generally, Elder Oaks over the years drew significant numbers of assignments requiring his work on doctrinal topics.

Laboring as an appellate judge before his call to the Twelve proved particularly helpful in fulfilling these challenging assignments. "Popular opinion often considers," he wrote, that the role of an appellate judge means "merely voting on how a case is decided, but lawyers and many others understand that the most important role of an appellate judge is to declare what the law is and how it is to be applied in difficult factual situations." Over the years, he applied these skills in tackling tough doctrinal assignments.

"These assignments have borne heavily on my time and concerns," he wrote. "People sometimes say to me, 'You seem to take all the hard subjects.' I can only answer that I do not volunteer but respond to the strong impressions of the Spirit or the assignment of my senior brethren." The result has been some of his best-known and most widely noted talks, including several on important social issues. His long legal experience blessed the Church and would continue to do so throughout his tenure as a General Authority, especially in the realm of religious freedom.

CHAPTER 25

"A LIFELONG INTEREST"

Religious Freedom

Religious freedom is a lifelong interest of mine," Elder Oaks explained in a talk at St. John's College, Oxford, in 2016. "My first publication as a young law professor at the University of Chicago fifty-three years ago was an edited book on the relationship between church and state in the United States."[1] Church and state were two areas in which he spent much of his life, and he understood each and how it related to the other. The topic of religious freedom was also one on which the Church's Public Affairs Committee urged him to speak, furthering the desires of the First Presidency.

"I have viewed the boundary between church and state from both sides," Elder Oaks related at the Sacramento Court-Clergy Conference in 2015. "I viewed it from the state side as a law clerk to Chief Justice Earl Warren of the United States Supreme Court, as a prosecutor in the state courts in Illinois, and still later as a justice on the Utah Supreme Court. From the church side, I have been a lifelong believer, teacher, counselor, and leader in my denomination. For me, questions about the relationship between government and religion are not academic, any more than the fate of Christian martyrs or the events of the Holocaust are academic to persons associated with them."[2]

Elder Oaks's family history made him acutely aware of what happens when religious freedom is curtailed. "My great-grandfather Harris—through whom I have my middle name—served time in the Utah Territorial Prison for violation of a federal law intended to punish him for acting on his religious belief," he explained. "Before that, my wife's great-great-grandfather Hyrum Smith was murdered in Illinois by an anti-Mormon mob."[3] Not surprisingly, then, as he later told the Argentina Council for Foreign Relations, "My lifelong advocacy of religious freedom is grounded in my religious faith."[4]

"When I first studied this subject in law school about sixty years ago," he told his audience in Sacramento, "the popular metaphor of the relationship between church and state was that of a 'wall of separation.'" Six decades of study drew him to a different conclusion. "I reject the idea of a wall between church and state," he contended. "The more appropriate metaphor to express that relation—reinforced by various decisions of the United States Supreme Court—is a curtain that defines boundaries but is not a barrier to the passage of light and love and mutual support from one side to another."[5]

Years before becoming an Apostle, Elder Oaks had already developed a reputation as a knowledgeable church-state scholar. While serving as president of Brigham Young University, he helped lead independent colleges and universities in legal battles against government bureaucrats who would saddle them with restrictions that could limit religious freedom.[6]

In March 1985—less than a year after his call to the Twelve—Elder Oaks spoke in Chicago at DePaul University's Center for Church-State Studies, giving what he later called "my last legal lecture."[7] "For me," he recalled at a symposium on religious freedom in 2014, "that was a transition from my service on the Utah Supreme Court, in which capacity I had accepted the invitation, to my service in my present calling, in which capacity I delivered the lecture."[8] The lecture's title, "Separation, Accommodation, and the Future of Church and State," gave him an opportunity to predict how church-state relations would play out in the United States.

He concluded that the government would increasingly accommodate religious activities and at the same time seek to regulate them. If that proved true, then "churches and religious practitioners," he advised, would "need to protect their interests more frequently through legislative lobbying."[9] Three decades after making this prediction, Elder Oaks concluded that although experts might cite individual exceptions, he had given "a generally accurate forecast of the movement of church-state law in the thirty years since I offered it."[10]

Watching his prediction come to pass proved unsettling. In 1988, for example, when the actions of the U.S. Congress threatened to extend the government's full regulatory authority to institutions receiving federal aid, he penned a one-word editorial in his journal: "Regrettable." The gradual fulfillment of his forecast made his talks progress over time from criticizing the current situation to offering suggestions about what organizations and individuals might do about it.

On Friday, June 24, 1988—Dallin and June Oaks's thirty-sixth wedding anniversary—Elder Oaks flew to Washington, DC, where he spoke by assignment at the unveiling of the Thorvaldsen *Christus* statue at the temple visitors' center there. The next morning, he took part in a ceremony outside the Williamsburg, Virginia, courthouse with an audience of some two thousand present and an educational television film crew on hand. Many prominent people from a wide range of backgrounds signed the Williamsburg Charter, summarized by Elder Oaks as reaffirming "the preeminent importance of religious liberty in the Constitution." Representatives of many American faith groups—Elder Oaks among them—gave brief statements as part of the ceremony. It was an opportunity to stand shoulder to shoulder in defense of religious freedom.

In early May 1990, Elder Oaks learned that the *Wall Street Journal* had accepted an abbreviated version of one of his recent speeches as an op-ed piece for the paper. "I relish firing a salvo in favor of public prayer and against those who seek to eliminate the name of Jesus Christ in public prayers," he wrote.

On September 18, 1992, Elder Oaks was back in Washington. "This morning," he wrote, "I testified before the Senate Judiciary Committee in support of S. 2969, the Religious Freedom Restoration Act. Senators Kennedy and Hatch present. Did OK."

Friday, February 4, 2011, was "one of the most stressful days in memory," Elder Oaks wrote. He was in Los Angeles that day to deliver a university lecture and do media interviews. He interviewed with a *Los Angeles Times* reporter and then delivered a lecture on preserving religious freedom at Chapman University to a crowd of some seven hundred, who gave him a standing ovation. Finally, he gave a two-hour interview to host Hugh Hewitt for his program on a radio network of some 120 conservative stations.

In the fall, he was once again in Washington, DC, at the invitation of Senator Orrin Hatch to testify before the Senate Finance Committee on the topic of modifying charitable deductions. "I introduced Catholic Bishop Timothy Senior of Philadelphia," Elder Oaks wrote, as well as Dean Russell D. Moore of Southern Baptist Theological Seminary. They each agreed with Elder Oaks's testimony, and he "called on each to answer the questions put to me by senators. The hearing was cordial and informative, and I believe will help our long-term ('coalition') relations with Catholics and Baptists." His testimony was broadcast on television news and via the internet.[11]

In January 2012, when the U.S. Supreme Court unanimously ruled that federal employment discrimination laws do not apply to hiring and firing ministers, Elder Oaks rejoiced, "The Lord has intervened to reinvigorate the prospects for religious freedom!" The next day, coincidentally, he hosted U.S. Attorney General Eric H. Holder Jr. in his

Elder Oaks with Cardinal Francis George at Becket Fund dinner

office, a meeting Elder Oaks characterized as "exemplary in cordiality, candor, and good feeling as we spoke of immigration and the Church's position of nonparticipation in political campaigns."

At a black-tie dinner in New York attended by religious dignitaries from many faiths in 2013, the Becket Fund awarded Elder Oaks the Canterbury Medal for his lifetime of defending religious liberty. Speaking to what he termed "the most influential audience I have ever addressed" on the topic, Elder Oaks gave a landmark address on religious freedom, its meaning and importance, the forces eroding it, and what can be done about it. "Unfortunately," he told the Becket dinner participants, "for about a half century the role of religion in American life has been declining. In this same period, the guarantee of free exercise of religion seems to be weakening in public esteem."[12]

Addressing a BYU audience in 2016, he elaborated, "I believe religious freedom is declining because faith in God and the pursuit of God-centered religion is declining—worldwide. If one does not value religion, one usually does not put a high value on religious freedom. . . . I believe the freedoms of speech and assembly are also weakening

Elder Oaks speaks at Utah's Constitution Day celebration, 2010

because many influential persons see them as colliding with competing values now deemed more important."[13]

Speaking again at Claremont Graduate University in California that same year, Elder Oaks mentioned government growth as another reason for the decline. "As citizens look to government for more and more and to private initiative for less and less," he said, "the unregulated room for religious activity is reduced and the likelihood of government regulation of religious activities increases." Added to that, he said, is "the increasing complexity of our society and diversity of our population. . . . With the increasing diversity of religious beliefs, including non-Abrahamic denominations, the scope of protection under the Free Exercise Clause began to change. When a constitutional right covers more and more, the scope of its protection is likely to become less and less."[14]

One of the largest threats, Elder Oaks said at a Utah constitutional symposium in 2014, was "the way various official actions at the state and federal level are overshadowing the free exercise of religion by making it subordinate to other newly found 'civil rights.'" Elder Oaks singled out one argument as an example. "As it happens," he said, "the argument I have chosen for comment has figured in various recent court decisions on same-sex marriage, but that is not the reason I have chosen it. I comment on this particular legal argument because of its relationship to free speech and because of its obvious importance to your constitutional symposium on religious freedom."

The argument he criticized was the assertion that any position founded on religious belief was *by definition* illegitimate. When Elder Oaks first heard the argument years earlier in an abortion case, he thought it "preposterous, since it would make illegitimate most of western society's criminal laws and family laws." But recently, he noted with dismay, "the incredible claim that laws cannot be based on religious morality seems to be gaining respectability," including the notion "that public debate should be limited to so-called public reason," defined to exclude religion as a private matter. "Religion is being marginalized to the point of censorship or condemnation," Elder Oaks lamented.

"A companion technique for pushing religious values off the public square is to dismiss them on the ground that they are irrational or that they reflect impermissible animus [hatred]. Part of that technique is to magnify the allegations of animus with sufficient rhetoric to conceal or omit consideration of the very real secular reasons that support the position." One result of this technique "is not only to diminish religious freedom, but also to diminish freedom of speech." Advocates of one position simply use "accusations of bigotry or animus" to rhetorically shout down anyone with a different point of view.

"Both freedom of speech and freedom of religion are jeopardized when their advocates are disparaged as being motivated by hatred," Elder Oaks noted. "Those who have sincere questions about the wisdom of a particular proposal—questions unrelated to religious doctrine or values—will be strongly deterred from rational dialogue if they perceive the risk of being branded as bigoted or hateful. . . .

"Religious leaders and religiously motivated persons should have the same privileges of speech and participation as any other persons or leaders," Elder Oaks argued, and "churches should stand on at least as strong a footing as any other corporation when they enter the public square to participate in public policy debates. The precious constitutional right of free speech does not exclude any individual or any group, and the exercise of that right with religious speech is especially protected in view of the companion guarantee of the free exercise of religion."[15]

"Some public policy advocates have attempted to intimidate persons with religious-based points of view from influencing or making laws in our democracy," Elder Oaks said at the Claremont conference in 2016. "One part of this effort is the recent characterization of the free exercise of religion as limited to the privilege of worshiping in the protected space of our own homes, churches, synagogues, or mosques. Beyond those protected spaces, the argument goes, religious believers and their organizations have no First Amendment protection—not even normal free speech guarantees."

Backed by this misguided thinking, some people become upset any time a religious person or organization attempts to express political views or lobbies government officials. "How is it 'un-American' and a 'serious threat to a free society' for a religious organization and its members to participate in a public process of lawmaking?" Elder Oaks asked. Such "arguments leave me wondering why any group of citizens with secular-based views that make up a majority is free to impose their views on others by a democratic lawmaking process, but persons or their organizations with religious-based views are not free to participate in the same democratic lawmaking process."[16]

In several addresses, he talked about the value of religion to society generally. Society "is not held together primarily by law and its enforcement," he observed, "but most importantly by those who voluntarily obey the unenforceable because of their internalized norms of righteous or correct behavior." Among those norms, "religious belief in right and wrong is a vital influence to produce such voluntary compliance by a large number of our citizens."

Elder Oaks quoted George Washington, first president of the United States, who recognized that principle in his farewell address.

"Of all the dispositions and habits which lead to political prosperity, religion and morality are indispensable supports," Washington said. "Reason and experience both forbid us to expect that national morality can prevail in exclusion of religious principle."[17]

In an address at Oxford University, Elder Oaks reminded his listeners that "in the United States, our enormous private sector of charitable works—education, care for the poor, and countless other charities of great value—originated with and is still sponsored most significantly by religious organizations and religious impulses." He noted that "religion inspires many believers to service to others, which, in total, confers enormous benefit on communities and countries."[18]

In addition, he pointed out in his Argentina address, "many of the most significant moral advances in Western society have been motivated by religious principles and persuaded to official adoption by pulpit-preaching." These include "the abolition of the slave trade in England," the Emancipation Proclamation in the United States, and "the Civil Rights movement of the last half century." "These great advances," he pointed out, "were not motivated and moved by secular ethics or persons who believed in moral relativism. They were driven primarily by persons who had a clear religious vision of what was morally right."[19]

Speaking at the Johns Hopkins School of Advanced International Studies, Elder Oaks observed how religious freedom advances "countless other social objectives." Therefore, "it follows that religious freedom is not just the concern of religious persons. Others have a strong interest in religious freedom because it is necessary for peace and stability in our pluralistic world. The protection of conscience is a vital ingredient for stability because it helps people from a wide spectrum of beliefs feel assured that their deepest concerns and values are respected and protected."[20]

Given all these benefits from religion, what needs to happen in an increasingly pluralistic society to preserve and balance the rights of believers and nonbelievers? "My thesis," Elder Oaks said at the court-clergy conference, "is that we all want to live together in happiness, harmony, and peace. To achieve that common goal, and for all contending parties to achieve their most important personal goals, we must learn and practice mutual respect for others whose beliefs, values, and behaviors differ from our own. As Justice Oliver Wendell Holmes observed, the Constitution 'is made for people of fundamentally differing views.' . . .

"Second," he added, when it comes to the most divisive issues, "both sides should seek a balance, not a total victory. For example, religionists should not seek a veto over all nondiscrimination laws that offend their religion, and the proponents of nondiscrimination should not seek a veto over all assertions of religious freedom. Both sides in big controversies like this should seek to understand the others' position and seek practical accommodations that provide fairness for all and total dominance for neither. . . .

"Third," he pointed out, "it will help if we are not led or unduly influenced by the extreme voices that are heard from contending positions. Extreme voices polarize and create resentment and fear by emphasizing what is nonnegotiable and by suggesting that the desired outcome is to disable the adversary and achieve absolute victory. Such outcomes are rarely attainable, and never preferable to living together in mutual understanding and peace."

What about "extremist and even terrorist groups that attempt to use religious beliefs to justify illegal incitements or violent or destructive actions"? he asked. "Those excesses," he answered, "can and should be rejected by our understanding of the limits on any constitutional right. . . . We all understand the common-sense principle that the prospect of abuse of a constitutional right must not be used to veto that right. We resist that tendency for speech and press, and we must also resist it for religion."[21]

"In this country," he noted at Claremont, "we have a history of tolerant diversity—not perfect but mostly effective at allowing persons with competing visions to live together in peace. Most of us want effective ways to resolve differences without anger and with mutual understanding and accommodation. We all lose when an atmosphere of anger or hostility or contention prevails. We all lose when we cannot debate public policies without resorting to epithets, boycotts, firings, and other intimidation of our adversaries. We need to promote the virtue of civility. . . .

"When our positions do not prevail," he said, "we should accept unfavorable results graciously and practice civility with our adversaries. In any event, we should be persons of goodwill toward all, rejecting persecution of any kind, including persecution based on race, ethnicity, religious belief or nonbelief, and differences in sexual orientation."[22]

Sister Kristen Oaks remembered an experience with civility. "When we visited Claremont College," she said, "I spoke to an audience and shared the pain I felt from a cartoon that misrepresented us. It was touching to me that many of the LGBTQ population came up and surrounded me and apologized. We saw each other as real people, capable of real feelings, and there was no desire to hurt anyone. I realized we just need to communicate and see each other as people with needs."

"I believe one important way to move forward," Elder Oaks said at the 2014 constitutional symposium, "is to minimize talk of rights and to increase talk of responsibilities. From the standpoint of religion, I urge my fellow believers to remember that the scriptures contain very little talk of rights, only commandments that create responsibilities. Others, who choose to reason in pragmatic terms, should remember that we strengthen rights by encouraging the fulfillment of responsibilities."[23]

His talks included invitations to work for improvement. "In expressing this expectation of mutual understanding and statesman-like lawmaking," he said in one, "I hope I am not an unrealistic dreamer. I invite you to join me in the hope that in time, with patience and goodwill, contending constitutional rights and conflicting personal values can be brought into mutually respectful accommodation."[24]

"Such hopes," he said in another, "can only be realized by concentrating on what we have in common, by striving for mutual understanding, by treating all our neighbors with goodwill, and by exercising patience. It is a time of hope for mutual respect and accommodation, but it is up to you and me to make it happen."[25]

Having expressed himself on this topic, over time Elder Oaks curtailed the number of talks he gave on religious freedom for two reasons. First, he felt he had delivered the essential messages he had been encouraged to give. Second, and even more important, he had received many opportunities over the years to address the subject and wanted to share future invitations with other members of the Quorum of the Twelve—especially those with legal backgrounds or public affairs responsibility. The talks he had given, however, continued to reflect his feelings on a topic he considered of great importance to the Church and to the world.

CHAPTER 26

"ALWAYS LOOK TOWARD THE MASTER"

Proclaiming the Gospel through Talks

As an Apostle, Elder Dallin H. Oaks had a duty to proclaim the gospel around the world, something he did to a great extent through the talks he gave. Even before he became an Apostle, he had opportunities to address groups on gospel subjects, and those talks helped refine his speaking style and establish his focus on doctrinal topics.

One of the best-loved talks he gave before his call was a 1981 devotional address at Brigham Young University that he titled simply "Revelation." "Revelation," he told the students and faculty, "is communication from God to man. It can occur in many different ways." After giving examples of the ways revelation occurs, he identified "eight different purposes" for these divine communications: "(1) to testify; (2) to prophesy; (3) to comfort; (4) to uplift; (5) to inform; (6) to restrain; (7) to confirm; and (8) to impel." He described each of these purposes in order, with examples.

This was a doctrinal address of the kind that would become standard for him after his call to the apostleship: like all his talks, it focused on a single subject and had a specific purpose. "My purpose in suggesting this classification and in giving these examples," he told his listeners in the 1981 talk, "is to persuade each of you to search your own experience and to conclude that you have already received revelations and that you can receive more revelations because communication from God to men and women is a reality."[1]

Just as he had before his call to the apostleship, he relied heavily on revelation to guide him in what he said to audiences after he became a member of the Twelve. He felt the heavy responsibility of spiritually feeding those who came—or tuned in—to hear him, and he wanted to align his will with God's in selecting, developing, and addressing topics of importance in advancing the Lord's purposes.

As an Apostle of the Lord Jesus Christ, Elder Oaks testified frequently about the Savior and His attributes. At the October general conference in 1987, three years after his call, he gave an important doctrinal talk titled "The Light and Life of the World." Like many of the doctrinal addresses he would give during his ministry, this one analyzed and built on scriptural passages. Citing holy writ, he spoke about why Christ is the light and the life of the world and invited all to come unto the Savior.

Three years later, at a BYU devotional, Elder Oaks gave another talk related to the Atonement of Christ, titled "Sin and Suffering." It aimed at those who sinned with premeditation, hoping "to experience the sin, but avoid its effects." Elder Oaks warned that a necessary "condition of repentance is suffering or punishment for the sin." Sinners trying sincerely to repent "will not experience the full 'exquisite' extent of eternal torment the Savior suffered," but they will suffer as a necessary part of their repentance and a natural consequence of their sin. "All of our personal experience confirms the fact that we must endure personal suffering in the process of repentance," he warned, "and for serious transgressions that suffering can be severe and prolonged."[2]

A June 1992 address at BYU proved to be among his most memorable. Titled "Our Strengths Can Become Our Downfall," it was later

Elder Oaks at general conference with President Thomas S. Monson, 1992

excerpted for the *Ensign* magazine. He noted that Satan will often tempt people by aiming at their weaknesses. "But weakness is not our only vulnerability," he noted. "Satan can also attack us where we think we are strong—in the very areas where we are proud of our strengths. He will approach us through the greatest talents and spiritual gifts we possess. If we are not wary, Satan can cause our spiritual downfall by corrupting us through our strengths as well as by exploiting our weaknesses."[3]

In 1998, Elder Oaks gave another address at BYU, this one on the topic "Judge Not and Judging." "I have been puzzled that some scriptures command us not to judge and others instruct us that we should judge and even tell us how to do it," he noted. "I am convinced that these seemingly contradictory directions are consistent when we view them with the perspective of eternity.

"The key," he explained, "is to understand that there are two kinds of judging: final judgments, which we are forbidden to make; and intermediate judgments, which we are directed to make, but upon righteous principles." Final judgments are God's, not ours, he taught, and "whenever we proclaim that any particular person is going to hell (or to heaven) for a particular act or as of a particular time . . . we hurt ourselves and the person we pretend to judge."

In making intermediate judgments, he said, "we should take care to judge righteously," seeking "the guidance of the Spirit in our decisions" and limiting judgment "to our own stewardships." We should avoid judging others "until we have an adequate knowledge of the facts" and "should judge circumstances rather than people," applying "righteous standards." Finally, "in all of this, we must remember the command to forgive."[4]

At the October 1997 general conference of the Church, Elder Oaks gave a talk about personal choices that became one of his most long-remembered addresses. According to his son Lloyd, the talk had its origins in a visit to Grandmother Stella Oaks's home. In the basement, Lloyd found an old Sears mail-order catalog from his father's childhood on the farm and ran upstairs to show him. Dallin showed the catalog to his brother, Merrill, pointing out how it listed good, better, and best versions of items for sale. "After a moment," Lloyd recalled, "Dad reflected to his brother, 'Good, Better, Best.' I think that there is a talk in there somewhere." And indeed there was.

In Elder Oaks's talk "Good, Better, Best," he observed: "Most of us have more things expected of us than we can possibly do. As breadwinners, as parents, as Church workers and members, we face many choices on what we will do with our time and other resources. . . . We should begin by recognizing the reality that just because something is good is not a sufficient reason for doing it. The number of good things we can do far exceeds the time available to accomplish them. Some things are better than good, and these are the things that should command priority attention in our lives."

He used the analogy of the Sears catalog and gave numerous examples of how good things should give way to the best in our lives. "Consider how we use our time in the choices we make in viewing television, playing video games, surfing the Internet, or reading books or magazines," he advised. "Of course it is good to view wholesome entertainment or to obtain interesting information. But not everything of that sort is worth the portion of our life we give to obtain it. Some things are better, and others are best."

When it comes to family activities, "many breadwinners worry that their occupations leave too little time for their families," he said, reflecting his own experience. "There is no easy formula for that contest of priorities. However, I have never known of a man who looked back on his working life and said, 'I just didn't spend enough time with my job.'"[5]

At April general conference in 2011, Elder Oaks gave a talk on the related topic of personal desires. "Desires dictate our priorities, priorities shape our choices, and choices determine our actions," he taught. "The desires we act on determine our changing, our achieving, and our becoming." We all have basic needs like food and sleep that we must control to achieve our greatest desires. "Readjusting our desires to give highest priority to the things of eternity is not easy," however. "We are all tempted to desire that worldly quartet of property, prominence, pride, and power. We might desire these, but we should not fix them as our highest priorities," he admonished.[6]

Elder Oaks delivered some of his most important talks at leadership training meetings—talks that were not published for general readers. "Apostles hold all the keys of the priesthood," he told members of the Fourth Quorum of the Seventy in April 2015. Others—such as temple presidents, mission presidents, stake presidents, bishops, and elders quorum presidents—also receive keys when they are set apart. "But note," he said, "that these keys are withdrawn when the person is released from the particular office that caused them to be bestowed. This is necessary to preserve order in the Church.

"There is only one office in the Church and in the priesthood," he explained, "where keys are inherent in the office, and that is the office of an apostle who has been set apart as a member of the Quorum of the Twelve Apostles." The Twelve receive "all of the keys of the priesthood" and "'officiate in the name of the Lord, under the direction of the Presidency of the Church' (D&C 107:33)." The Twelve, in turn, "authorize the Seventy to confer keys even though the Seventy do not have them.

"Why this cumbersome method of conferring keys?" he asked. "As I have pondered this question, it has occurred to me that it is an essential corollary of the fact that, unlike Apostles, who serve for life, the Seventy are called for a season and then released. If keys were inherent in their office, it could create the same kind of confusion that would exist if keys were inherent in the office of a bishop, but because of the worldwide jurisdiction of the Seventy the confusion would be far more troublesome. Unlike a bishop, whose office and calling is limited to a single geographic ward, the Seventy's office and calling is worldwide—wherever he is assigned. He will always hold his priesthood office, but it is necessary that keys are not inherent in that worldwide office."

In April 2014, Elder Oaks gave a powerful address on leadership at a training meeting of the General Authorities and Area Seventies. "Like the Savior, a Christlike leader will be full of love for those whom he has been called to serve," Elder Oaks taught. "Love is the first principle of leadership. Its effect magnifies the effects of every other principle of leadership. Leaders who love those that they lead enhance the impact of their leadership and the duration of their influence.

"A Christlike leader should teach the flock that they should always look toward the Master," Elder Oaks instructed. "One who teaches this to the flock should never obscure their view by standing in the way, such as by seeking the limelight himself or by casting a shadow of self-interest, self-promotion, or self-gratification."

Being a Christlike leader may be uncomfortable at times. "There is a strong tendency in most of us to spend our time and fulfill our responsibilities through activities in which we feel a sense of qualification and comfort," he related, again from his own experience. "We must resist that tendency. We should turn from that which is familiar and comfortable and work to do that which is required, spending our time and exerting our efforts to qualify ourselves for what we have been called to do. That is the way to have the spirit and power of our callings."

Good leaders are also good teachers. "The Savior was the supreme teacher," Elder Oaks pointed out. One way He taught so effectively was by telling stories using easy-to-understand words. "He shared simple stories, parables, and real-life examples that made sense to those He taught. His simple language enabled Him to reach and hold hearers from every class and condition."

Elder Oaks practiced what he preached. Elder Neil L. Andersen remembered Elder Oaks visiting his mission years earlier and speaking to his missionaries in terms they could remember "long after he is finished." Elder Oaks told the missionaries simply, "Be worthy, be obedient, and be busy," elaborating on each idea in turn. Elder Andersen marveled that "a man with his kind of mind" would say "something so simple."

"The Savior led by example," Elder Oaks noted in his 2014 talk. "No single principle of leadership is more powerful in its effect on followers than a leader setting the right example, and Jesus did that. In the conclusion of His direct teachings on this continent He said, 'Therefore, what manner of men ought ye to be? Verily I say unto you, even as I am.' . . . Example pervades all principles."

Like the Prophet Joseph Smith, Elder Oaks has a naturally cheery temperament. The Church leaders in a position to know him best have all remarked on his meekness, his affability, and his remarkable sense of humor. "His eyes twinkle," said Elder Gerrit W. Gong. "He smiles in a way that reflects his whole being. Sometimes when he laughs, the chuckles just envelop his whole body." Elder Oaks's fellow Apostles describe him as humble and teachable—always eager to learn, acknowledge mistakes, and grow. "He's not a dominating presence, because he's meek," said Elder David A. Bednar. "But there is a competence in him that can be intimidating."

"He has a soft heart," said Elder Dieter F. Uchtdorf. But once he feels he has received divine direction on a talk topic, he goes forward without fear of how others in the world might feel. "On ideas that he believes in, he is very determined," Elder Uchtdorf explained. Elder Andersen agreed, saying, "He's very serious about revelation, and when he gets it, he's not heavily influenced by other people." President M. Russell Ballard observed, "He's got a happy heart, a happy disposition. And at the same time he can be very, very serious when the issues require it." "He is fearless, absolutely fearless," said Elder Bednar. "He draws a lot of fire . . . , but he couldn't care less. All he wants to do is please Him whom he serves."

In an October 1995 *Ensign* article, Elder Oaks broached a subject of growing importance not previously treated at length by any other General Authority. In a doctrinal exposition, he declared that feelings of same-gender attraction were not sinful, but that sexual relations between people of the same sex were violations of God's law of chastity. He discouraged men and women from labeling themselves as gay or lesbian and from arguing they were "born that way." At the same time, he declared that members of the Church were responsible "to show forth love and to extend help and understanding" to persons who faced these challenges.[7]

"In the decades that followed," he later wrote, "I continued to study doctrine relating to LGBT issues. I was encouraged to speak and write about it. As laws and popular culture moved farther from our Church doctrine, I received much opposition in the media and in private correspondence. I tried never to speak of this subject without speaking of love as well as law."[8]

Although he himself was not personally discouraged by the

Sister Kristen Oaks blowing a kiss to her husband in general conference

response, his wife Kristen felt it keenly. "There is a price to be paid for protecting religious freedom," she wrote. "Cartoons in the news, articles on the internet, and negative comments were initially very hurtful. There were days of a few tears, fears, and frustrations. Elder D. Todd Christofferson put this in context for me and many others when he spoke of this as 'a day of sometimes merciless attacks in social media and in person against those who seek to uphold the Lord's standard.'[9]

"It was not easy for me to rise above this," she said, defending her husband. "I had to dig deeply into the recesses of my soul to realize the truth of Peter's assurance that if we are 'reproached for the name of Christ, happy are ye; for the spirit of glory and of God resteth upon you' (1 Peter 4:14). I know those words to be true, and I am proud of my husband."

"He is honest to the point of being blunt if he has to be," Elder Jeffrey R. Holland said of Elder Oaks. "You look at his sermons. You look at some of the tough issues that he's dealt with, some of the social issues of the day, whatever. Nobody has any question where Dallin Oaks stands. And he isn't doing that out of vanity. He isn't doing that out of self-aggrandizement. He's doing it because he thinks it needs to be done. He's doing it because he thinks that goes with his calling. I don't suppose he likes the subjects any better than anybody else. But he believes that's incumbent on him to do it."

During his years in the Quorum of the Twelve, Elder Oaks gave thousands of talks in diverse settings to audiences totaling many millions. People came to know him as a doctrinal speaker boldly addressing groups in formal settings, often on serious subjects without heed to public opinion. But he also reached out directly and more quietly to individuals in need of help through a personal ministry of letters.

CHAPTER 27

"I WILL UNDERTAKE TO ANSWER"

Ministering through Letters

In addition to their public ministries, which are highly visible to Latter-day Saints and include addressing large groups, many of the Church's General Authorities carry on quiet, personal ministries, reaching out to individuals in need. President Thomas S. Monson, for example, began ministering to widows in his ward while serving as a young bishop and continued that private ministry throughout his life.[1] From the beginning of Elder Dallin H. Oaks's service as a General Authority, he ministered to others by writing letters to people who might benefit from his counsel, guidance, or expressions of gratitude and support.

As a general rule, Church leaders have encouraged members not to write to General Authorities but instead to counsel with their local leaders.[2] When letters from members raised matters best discussed at the local level, Elder Oaks generally referred them back to their local leaders for aid or guidance. In matters that were not of that type, however, he spent long hours writing letters that ministered to those in need.

Aiding him in the work over the years were several capable secretaries, none whose service outshone or outlasted that of Margie

McKnight. In 2020, she celebrated fifty years of Church employment, the last twenty-two as senior executive secretary to Elder Oaks. She superbly managed his busy schedule, his extensive files, and, most of all, his voluminous written work, including typically ten to fifteen drafts of each talk and thousands of letters. He felt she was "an extension of my personality and working methods"—a high compliment from someone with his exacting standards. His family members also came to love and appreciate her for her helpfulness to them.

Margie learned to work with him as he relied on well-tested tools for doing his work: a dictaphone, a manual typewriter, number 2.5 lead pencils, and yellow legal pads. Working from drafts that he prepared or edited with these tools, she typed the final versions of what he wrote for distribution. As technology evolved, Margie asked him why he continued to use a manual typewriter, and he responded with a twinkle in his eye, "Well, I can keep working if there's a power failure, and you can too."

Once, when one of his typewriters wore out, he went out hunting for a new one but had a hard time finding a salesperson who knew what he was talking about. "Finally," he said, "I found a small shop with a grizzled old proprietor who knew what a portable manual typewriter was. He still had one in the back room, and I was thrilled to purchase it. The proprietor was a little puzzled about what I was going to do with it. He was too polite to ask but made a guess. As he handed me my new portable typewriter, he said, 'We don't sell many of these. You must do a lot of camping.'"

Though he smiled at that response, Elder Oaks's letter-writing ministry was something he took seriously. "He's very concerned about the individual," Margie said. "He personally answers almost all of the correspondence that he receives." He would continue to do so throughout his decades in the Twelve.

"Mortality is a great challenge, and there are many tragedies over which we have no control," he wrote to someone struggling with the effects of sin. "In addition, we all make mistakes that need to be corrected, and we are all guilty of transgressions that need to be repented. It all adds up to a bumpy road through mortality." To a person facing affliction, he recounted the similar challenges facing his widowed mother, whose favorite scripture included the promise that God "shall consecrate thine afflictions for thy gain" (2 Nephi 2:2).

To a person suffering from depression, he wrote, "Some people have greater challenges than others, and having depression does make facing the trials of life more difficult. If you are not already getting professional help for your depression, perhaps your bishop could consult with LDS Social Services to assist you in finding someone in your area that can help you." To a mother grieving over a wayward child, he consoled, "My first impression is for you and your husband to stop grieving over the past and second-guessing decisions you made. As I read what you did and why you did it and how you prayed for and received guidance, I believe you have done what you should have done."

Some people wrote to criticize or correct him. One woman pointed out that in referring to senior missionaries at a conference, he used the husbands' first names but not the wives'. "If you did not know their first name, which I suspect you did," she wrote, "you could have used their missionary title of Elder and Sister, thus giving respect and honor to both members of the companionship."

"I have received the rebuke contained in your letter," Elder Oaks replied, "and wish to tell you that I have taken it in good spirits. I believe you are right. I should surely have referred to the sister missionaries by their names. In fact, I did not have their names . . . , but I should have been in possession of that information, and I should have used it. In the future I will be more careful. Thank you for calling this to my attention."

"In view of the enormous responsibilities of my office," Elder Oaks replied to another person, "I am not able to respond in detail to your seven-page single-spaced letter that essentially disagrees with a talk I prepared prayerfully to fulfill the responsibilities of my calling in the circumstances of the present." Elder Oaks acknowledged he was aware of the many quotations from previous leaders that the writer used to justify his position but urged him "to be more sensitive to the promptings of the Holy Spirit about the meaning of the words of *living prophets.*"

To another person who criticized a talk, Elder Oaks recounted the deep, prayerful study that went into preparing it. "For that talk I felt a strong impression as to the subject and the content," he wrote. "I can only follow that impression and hope that my remarks will be heard or read with the same kind of prayerful consideration with which they were prepared."

To a correspondent who disagreed with him on several points, Elder Oaks suggested that their disagreement sprang from "the different premises from which we begin to think about the matters." Still, he wrote, "I wish you well and hope you will succeed in finding some happiness in the course you have outlined." In responding to another similar letter, he wished the writer "well as you seek to find the truth without the faith that I consider fundamental."

To someone who alleged improprieties in a Church member's business dealings, Elder Oaks wrote, "We teach principles of honesty and Christian love and responsibility, and we are distressed whenever anyone feels that a member of our church has not lived up to these responsibilities." He agreed to forward the letter to the alleged offender's local Church leader and encouraged the offended man "to obtain professional assistance in pursuing whatever your legal rights may be."

To a mission president and his wife who invited Elder and Sister Oaks to a dedicatory event in their area, he expressed gratitude for the invitation, noting, "June and I would love to be with you on that occasion, but we are not masters of our own time. We only travel when we are assigned by the First Presidency." Consequently, he wrote, "we will just have to be with you in spirit," adding, "it means much to us to know that you thought of us and would like us to be there."

Not all letters Elder Oaks wrote were in response to ones he received. Elder Neil L. Andersen of the Twelve was only thirty-seven years old when he was called to be a mission president. He sold his advertising business to answer the call, and as he and Sister Andersen were returning after their mission, uncertain about their future, Elder Oaks wrote to them, assuring them all would be well. "It was just a very thoughtful thing, that letter that reassured us and told us the Lord would be with us," Elder Andersen said. "It came out of the blue." Elder Oaks "didn't have to do it" but did it of his own free will to minister quietly to a young couple in time of need.

Long after Elder Oaks released a stake president, he received an impression to write and ask what was happening in the former president's life that would cause the Lord to bring him into his thoughts. The man replied that his wife had unexpectedly left him, and he was in deep depression. Elder Oaks wrote a letter of comfort and counsel that, many years later, this man acknowledged as a testimony that the Lord knew him and reached out and inspired His servant to help one of His suffering children.

A former BYU student wrote to Elder Oaks, admiring his many achievements and coming down hard on himself for not achieving his own "lofty goals." Elder Oaks encouraged the writer to focus "on strivings rather than on accomplishments," observing that "strivings are better indexes of accomplishment than any worldly measure, such as position, power, or prestige." Moreover, "focusing on strivings is also helpful to put in perspective the fact that no one is perfect, that we all fall short, and that we are, therefore, all in need of repentance and the atoning sacrifice of our Savior."

A returned missionary who had ceased Church activity wrote to Elder Oaks because he felt years of prayer and scripture study had not given him an absolute knowledge that God exists. "I wonder," Elder

Oaks inquired gently, "what you expect as an answer to your prayers?" Referring to the still small voice Elijah heard, he suggested, "Perhaps your prayers have been answered again and again, but you have had your expectations fixed on a sign so grand or a voice so loud that you think you have had no answer." He reminded his correspondent "that people have different spiritual gifts," including the gift of believing on the words of those who know, "'that they also might have eternal life if they continue faithful' (D&C 46:13–14)."

On another occasion under similar circumstances, Elder Oaks offered four suggestions. The first was about reading from varied sources in searching for truth. Sometimes, Elder Oaks observed, those who say they read broadly exclude reading sources "that will sustain and nourish faith." Second, he explained, "while doubt can be a virtue when it moves people to seek knowledge, it is also an eternal principle that faith precedes the receipt of knowledge from above." Third, knowing the Church is true does not require "the kind of transcendental experience the Prophet Joseph Smith had." That knowledge can come from simply keeping the Lord's commandments (see John 8:31–32). Fourth, we must avoid judging godly things "according to what seems 'godly' according to our standards or culture or experience." Instead, "we are to learn from Him, not teach Him or confine Him within our criteria." Finally, Elder Oaks wrote, no one can pass the responsibility for personal conversion to another. "The whole case is in your hands," Elder Oaks concluded, "and its resolution is between you and your Heavenly Father."

In 2017, he responded to a woman who felt estranged from the Lord. "As one who you know cares deeply for you," he wrote tenderly, "I feel to ask you this question: Do you really believe that the Lord does not approve of you or that He has 'left' you because He has not answered your prayer by giving you what you want? All of us have prayed for things that were righteous desires (in my case, it was to pray for the preservation of my wife June's life when she was afflicted with cancer), and all of us have had the experience of not having the Lord give us what we ask for. Trust in the Lord is the key to our relationship with Him. He knows how our own lives fit into His eternal plan for us and for all of His children."

Some people wrote Elder Oaks with doctrinal questions. When appropriate, he provided straightforward expositions of well-settled doctrine. Other letters merited counsel as well. "I believe you have become a specialist in one aspect of the gospel to the exclusion of other things, and that this specialty is dragging you down spiritually," he wrote to one correspondent. To another, he offered, "It is apparent that you and I read the scriptures differently and understand the gospel of Jesus Christ differently. I respect your right to hold the opinions you hold, but respectfully suggest that you are mistaken in the things you say you believe." Another standard response he gave afforded recipients the personal growth that comes through wrestling with a subject: "The doctrinal question you asked is one that each member is expected to work out through study of the scriptures and personal prayer."

Some people questioned why the Church did not give money to good causes valued by the writers. "The Church's mission is to preach righteousness, but not to give financial support to every organization involved in good works," he typically replied. "That would be impossible, and it would deplete our resources from those things that must uniquely be done under priesthood authority," such as "proclaiming the restored gospel" and "building temples."

He offered similar counsel to someone who wrote to ask that the Church take a more active role in environmental preservation. Elder Oaks thanked the writer and called the matter one "fitting the instruction given in D&C 58:27–28," which encourages members to exercise their own initiative in doing good. "There are many good causes in the world," Elder Oaks pointed out, "and that is surely one of them," again explaining the Church's need to focus on "those subjects that require priesthood authority." He concluded by wishing the writer well "in the important work" in which he was engaged.

To a woman wrestling with whether there is plural marriage in the next life, Elder Oaks wrote, "It is true that we don't know everything about this subject, but we do know that plural marriage is not necessary for exaltation." He observed, "People take the circumstances of mortality and try to translate them, unchanged, into the next life, which causes some problems." Because "agency is eternal," he wrote, she could be confident "that no one is going to be forced into *anything* in the next life." He assured her that if she put her speculations aside, kept the commandments, and trusted in God, all would "turn out right and happy."

To a man who wrote on reconciling science and religion, Elder Oaks responded, "Because our knowledge of the truths of the gospel is still evolving with continuing revelation, and because the 'truths' of science are also very dynamic, I am skeptical about bringing them together at present, though I know that they will each be gloriously consistent when all truths are known."

A man wrote asking whether he should refrain from promoting new concepts that came to him about Christ's Atonement. "The Lord has given us a prophet and his two counselors," Elder Oaks replied, "and they are the ones to whom we look for 'new concepts' on our doctrine. The rest of us should refrain."

A young couple getting ready to leave for professional schooling worried about the worldly pressures they would face and wrote to Elder Oaks, seeing him as someone who had confronted such pressures and emerged unscathed. "The problems you outline about a professional life are there," he acknowledged, "but they are not unique. In any field of activity, a person faces problems of this sort. My advice to you is to pursue your interest and talents, under the direction of the Spirit of the Lord. Once you have made your choice for any occupation, you will have the lifelong problem of practicing that vocation in a way consistent with the standards of the gospel and the dictates of the Spirit. Some fail at this, but many succeed. With your attitude, you can succeed."

As one with a sterling professional career in the law and the insights of a senior Church leader, Elder Oaks was particularly prepared to respond to a question about church and state. "Everyone has personal principles," he wrote, "and for most of us these come from religious beliefs. For a public official to act on personal principles based on religious belief is no violation of the separation of church and state. If we were going to purge all moral considerations out of the law, we would have very little left, as any thoughtful person should recognize.

"Second," Elder Oaks taught, "the idea that laws cannot interfere with someone's freedom or else they have impaired his free agency is also a fallacious idea. There are all kinds of coercive requirements in the law. The fact that you cannot take someone's property without risking a jail sentence or a civil judgment, and the fact that one is not free to choose whether or not to pay taxes, are just two examples. Hundreds more could be given. Almost every exercise of lawmaking involves a judgment about the extent to which the laws should interfere with the freedom of one citizen in order to serve the larger good represented by the interests of citizens as a whole."

To a letter writer who posed several examples of dishonesty, Elder Oaks replied, "You are, of course, right that the standard of honesty and integrity is the same whether a person is in business or in the political arena. I have seen plenty of examples of untruthfulness and deceit in both of those areas, and some of those examples have involved members of the Church. Some have even involved Church leaders.

"I try not to be discouraged by this," Elder Oaks wrote, "since I remind myself that for every bad example we notice, there are hundreds of conscientious people who are doing their best, and are deserving of praise." The writer wanted to know the solution to the problem, and Elder Oaks suggested, "The correction in the marketplace is to cease dealing with people whom we do not trust. The correction in the political arena is to perform our duties as citizens to see that they are replaced."

From time to time, Elder Oaks received letters from Church members who claimed to receive revelation for others. Elder Oaks sometimes spoke publicly on order in the Church and how members may receive revelation for their specific areas of responsibility but not for those outside of it. "A neighbor does not receive revelation for a neighbor," he wrote in one book.[3] One man challenged this idea, writing Elder Oaks a letter with personal examples he felt disproved the statement. In responding to this letter, Elder Oaks wrote, "It asks important questions. Because it also manifests a receptive spirit, I will undertake to answer.

"First and foremost," he testified, "the principles I have taught about revelation are true. 'A neighbor does not receive revelations for a neighbor.' This means that if we have no stewardship responsibility for a person (comparable to what a bishop has for his ward or a person he is counseling), we will not receive revelation 'for' that person. We may receive a revelation for ourselves pertaining to that person. For example, we may receive inspired guidance on what we should say to that person in response to their question. We may be inspired to lead them to something they might read or do that would be helpful to them. But we will not receive revelation in which the Lord directs them or communicates to them what they should do. They must receive that revelation for themselves.

"Second," Elder Oaks warned, "I know of *many* instances where the adversary has misled well-meaning members of the Church into circumstances where they turned to another member of the Church who was not entitled to receive revelation for them and began to look to that person as the oracle of God to give them *directions* from their Heavenly Father. Some of those instances escalated innocently from a perfectly appropriate trusting relationship. All of them turned out to be a spiritual and (ultimately) a financial disaster for the persons who followed this so-called 'revelation.'"

One correspondent was bothered that a family member talked openly about purported spiritual manifestations, causing considerable frustration in the family. "Have you noticed," Elder Oaks asked in response, "that General Authorities, fifteen of whom are sustained as prophets, seers, and revelators, rarely speak about personal and sacred spiritual experiences?

"That cannot be a coincidence," he taught. "It is also true that there are many miracles and sacred spiritual experiences among the Latter-day Saints, and we rarely hear of them across the pulpit or in classes. That cannot be a coincidence either.

"True," Elder Oaks agreed, "some individuals speak of their personal and sacred spiritual experiences, but I have noticed that those individuals are cautioned not to do so, and if they persist, they are generally released from their Church positions or requested not to speak in Church meetings.

"What explains all of this?" Elder Oaks inquired of the writer. "A person has only to read the directions in the Doctrine and Covenants to see that the Lord has told us that our sacred experiences are personal and are not to be shown before the world." He concluded, "If every person would be careful to limit the use of their spiritual experiences to their own personal benefit, instead of using them for other purposes, the adversary would have less occasion to mislead us by counterfeit spiritual experiences."

To a despair-filled woman worn down with personal troubles and the requirements of Church membership, Elder Oaks wrote a letter of encouragement. "You are worried about all that you have to do," he summarized, then counseled, "Just live each day the best you can, and know this. Our Heavenly Father does not expect us to do all things all the time every day. We must live the commandments to the best of our ability every day, but there are many things like those mentioned in your letter that we do at one time of our life, but we do not have time at another time."

One brother wrote a letter to Elder Oaks full of skepticism about scripture. Not long afterward, the man wrote again. "Throw my letter away," he pleaded in a penitent tone. "I found the answers to my questions in reading and contemplating."

"I liked your second letter better than your first," Elder Oaks commented in writing back. "I congratulate you on your increased understanding."

"There *are* many things we need to take on faith," Elder Oaks affirmed. "When we reach out for knowledge, and when we are willing to humbly put difficult questions (which all of us have) on the shelf to wait for answers, our Heavenly Father is able to teach us through His Holy Spirit. Our questions give way to a sweet feeling of assurance as we mature in the gospel." He assured the man, "If we have faith and do our best to keep the commandments, the Lord will bless us, and in time we will know the answers to all things."

Over the course of his time in the Quorum of the Twelve Apostles, Elder Oaks wrote thousands of letters spanning a wide range of topics, providing counsel, direction, guidance, comfort, and consolation to many people around the world from all walks of life. Through this personal ministry, he helped to "succor the weak, lift up the hands which hang down, and strengthen the feeble knees" (D&C 81:5). In this way, he sought to emulate the Savior, whose servant he was.

CHAPTER 28

"WHOM THE LORD HAD PREPARED"

Call to the First Presidency

On New Year's Day in 2018, Elder Dallin H. Oaks was eighty-five years old and had served as an Apostle for more than a third of a century. During that time, he had grown in spiritual maturity and experience, gradually increasing in seniority until only two other Apostles sat ahead of him: President Thomas S. Monson, the President of the Church, and President Russell M. Nelson, the President of the Quorum of the Twelve. When President Monson passed away on January 2, 2018, the orderly tradition of succession made it clear that President Nelson would be the Church's new President and that Elder Oaks's role and life would also change.[1]

On Friday, January 12, funeral services were held for President Monson in the Tabernacle on Temple Square in Salt Lake City. Because of Elder Robert D. Hales's death three months earlier, thirteen living Apostles now remained. On Sunday, these Apostles met in the Salt Lake Temple consistent with the pattern of succession that had been followed since the death of the Prophet Joseph Smith. In a spirit of fasting, they voted to organize a new First Presidency and to sustain the senior Apostle, Russell M. Nelson, as the President of the Church. The next most senior Apostle, Elder Oaks, ordained and set apart President Nelson, with the other Apostles laying their hands with his on the new Church President's head during the ceremony.[2]

"The significance of that moment settled upon me with great power as I laid my hands upon his head," Elder Oaks recalled. "I remember feeling an impression on the words I should speak in *setting him apart,* but being far less fluent *in blessing him* than I had desired or anticipated. It was, nevertheless, a very sacred and historic moment." Elder Dale G. Renlund had felt the Spirit's confirming witness that the presidency should be reorganized. When Elder Oaks began by saying, "Russell M. Nelson," Elder Renlund again felt "the same Pentecostal feeling," he said. "I wish everybody could have been there. But it just melted me. It made me weep." He felt Elder Oaks's blessing was "beautifully inspired."

Across the circle from him was Elder Quentin L. Cook, who likewise felt the experience was "incredibly powerful." He glanced across the circle at Elder Renlund and noticed "tears running down his eyes, and they were running down my eyes at the same time," he remembered.

President Nelson said, "Words are inadequate to tell you what it felt like to have my brethren—brethren who hold all the priesthood keys restored through the Prophet Joseph Smith in this dispensation—place their hands upon my head to ordain and set me apart as President of the Church. It was a sacred and humbling experience." He explained, "It then became my responsibility to discern whom the Lord had prepared to be my counselors." That choice proved emotionally wrenching. "How could I choose only two of the twelve other Apostles, each of whom I love so dearly?" he worried.[3] He, of course, sought divine direction in his choice.

Elder Henry B. Eyring, who had served as First Counselor in the First Presidency under President Monson and Second Counselor to President Gordon B. Hinckley, recalled what President Nelson did next. "Excuse me," he told his brethren. "I need to go and pray." Then the new Church President announced, "I would like to meet each member of the Twelve alone."

As part of the process leading to revelation, President Nelson wanted to interview each of the Apostles before deciding who his counselors in the First Presidency would be. This was an unprecedented move as far as selecting counselors for the First Presidency but a familiar one to everyone there when it came to choosing local leaders. President Nelson told them, "I want to have your best thinking on my counselors and the two empty chairs in the Quorum of the Twelve." He later explained, "It's the same pattern we've used all these years in selecting new stake presidents. You go to the people who know the people best and ask them what they think. So that's what I did."

As President Nelson interviewed each one individually, the rest sat reverently. "There was no chatting, no passing the time with any kind of interaction," Elder D. Todd Christofferson recalled. "Everyone was there with his own thoughts and prayers." Elder Dieter F. Uchtdorf had served in the First Presidency with President Monson, and when he met with President Nelson, he recommended two other men to be counselors in the First Presidency. "Elder Oaks was one of my recommendations," he later explained.

"Through the course of those interviews," President Nelson recounted, "it became very clear to me, as I prayed about it, that Dallin should be First Counselor because, upon my demise, he's the next President of the Church. That's the kindest thing I could do to the Church and for him . . . to give that exposure."

President Nelson's thinking was driven in part by what President Spencer W. Kimball had told him. "I remember when President Kimball was called to be the President of the Church," President Nelson related. "I was his surgeon. He confided in me a lot. He said, 'Brother Nelson, I don't know anything about the work of the presidency of the Church.' He'd only been in the Quorum of the Twelve. . . . Members of the

Quorum of the Twelve do their work well and know their work well, but it does not include any apprenticeship for the items that are only done by the First Presidency. So, I thought, for the good of the Church, Dallin should be in the First Presidency."

Still, after interviewing all the Twelve, President Nelson made his choice a matter of deep and reflective prayer before announcing it. "He was alone for a long time after the last person" was interviewed, Elder Eyring remembered.

Finally, after a long period of interviewing, pondering, and praying, President Nelson returned to the other twelve Apostles and announced to the group that his two counselors would be Dallin H. Oaks and Henry B. Eyring. As the Apostle second in seniority to President Nelson, President Oaks would also serve as President of the Quorum of the Twelve, with M. Russell Ballard serving as Acting President. President Nelson called for a sustaining vote on these matters, and all thirteen Apostles' right hands went up. "That's the first Dallin knew" of his call to the First Presidency, President Nelson noted. "I had not asked him" ahead of the vote.

The way President Nelson wrestled with choosing his counselors and then announced the Lord's will revealed to him on the subject "was just sweet beyond imagination," President Eyring recalled. "Just sweet. . . . It was a lovely moment."

After their sustaining, President Nelson set apart President Oaks, President Eyring, and President Ballard. "This was a deeply sacred and special experience, with an abundance of the Spirit in attendance," Elder Gary E. Stevenson of the Twelve testified, adding his "absolute witness that the will of the Lord, for which we fervently prayed, was powerfully manifest in the activities and events which took place that day."[4]

Two days later, on Tuesday morning, January 16, 2018, the members of the First Presidency and Quorum of the Twelve met at the Salt Lake Temple annex for a broadcast announcement to the members of the Church and the world. As President and Sister Oaks were being transported to the annex, they were filled with emotion. "I had a feeling of excitement and anticipation to participate in a historic announcement from a location never used before," President Oaks recalled. "Instead of gathering in the Church Office Building, as was the custom," Sister Oaks wrote, they were gathering "in the holiest building on earth to make the holiest announcement."

Because President Nelson had told his fellow Apostles to keep the events of Sunday confidential, President Oaks had not yet told his wife about his new role. As they reached the temple, he felt he was now "released from President Nelson's Sunday request" and so leaned over and whispered in her ear "that I was to be a counselor in the First Presidency." Kristen felt "stunned," later writing, "Our world changed in a moment."

In the temple, Elder D. Todd Christofferson of the Quorum of the Twelve, chairman of the Public Affairs Committee at the time, conducted the meeting and gave some historical background for viewers on how the senior Church leadership is organized after the death of a President. "As Elder Christofferson gave the historic background," Elder Oaks wrote, "I remembered explaining this process to members of the Chicago South Stake in 1970 when President Joseph Fielding Smith was sustained as President of the Church. I was struck with the fact that *now* I was part of the process being explained by someone else."

Following that explanation, Elder Christofferson announced the new First Presidency. President Nelson then spoke, recalling the events of two days earlier when the living Apostles voted to organize a new First Presidency and ordained and set him apart as the new Church President. "It then became my responsibility," he recounted publicly, "to discern whom the Lord had prepared to be my counselors." President Nelson thanked the Lord "for answering my fervent prayers."

"I am very thankful that President Dallin Harris Oaks and President Henry Bennion Eyring are willing to serve with me as First and Second Counselors, respectively," President Nelson said. "As the Apostle second in seniority, President Oaks also becomes President of the Quorum of the Twelve Apostles. However, given his call to the First Presidency and consistent with the order of the Church, President M. Russell Ballard, next in seniority, will serve as the Acting President of that quorum.

"Now each day of an Apostle's service," President Nelson explained, "is a day of learning and preparing for more responsibility in the future. It takes decades of service for an Apostle to move from the junior chair to the senior chair in the circle. During that time, he gains firsthand experience in each facet of the work of the Church. He also becomes well acquainted with the peoples of the earth, including their histories, cultures, [and] languages as assignments take him repeatedly across the globe."

That was certainly the case for President Oaks. Decades of experience had prepared him for service in the First Presidency. During the decades he served in the Twelve, he traveled the world, testifying to groups in seventy-five countries. Fifteen countries he visited between five and twenty times: Argentina, Brazil, Chile, Mexico, Peru, England, Germany, Italy, Ghana, the People's Republic of China, Japan, Korea, the Philippines, New Zealand, and Samoa. In addition, he fulfilled many important roles at Church headquarters on councils and committees that gave him a view of the Church and its increasingly global scope.

"My dear brothers and sisters," President Oaks began when it was his turn to speak, "I have sat beside President Nelson in the Quorum of the Twelve for almost thirty-four years. I know his love of the Lord Jesus Christ and his commitment to our Heavenly Father's plan of salvation.

"I know his love of the people," the new counselor in the First Presidency testified. "I know of his wisdom. I feel privileged to be called as a counselor to President Nelson in the First Presidency. I likewise feel

New First Presidency is ONE at news conference: Presidents ***O****aks,* ***N****elson, and* ***E****yring*

privileged for the opportunity to work with President Henry B. Eyring, whom I love and respect. With all my heart, I pledge my loyalty and support for President Nelson's loving and inspired leadership. I rejoice in the opportunity to give my full efforts to bear witness of Jesus Christ and to proclaim the truth of His restored gospel."

When President Eyring spoke, he echoed those sentiments and added, "Every association I have had with President Nelson and President Oaks has increased my ability to remember the Savior, keep sacred covenants, and find joy in the influence of the Holy Ghost. I am so grateful for the increase of that blessing in my life."[5]

Later that morning, the First Presidency met the media at a news conference in the lobby of the Church Office Building in downtown Salt Lake City. Both the temple broadcast and the subsequent news conference were carried in twenty-nine languages on many news platforms across the globe. Before taking questions from media representatives, each member of the First Presidency spoke, beginning with President Nelson.

When it was President Oaks's turn to speak, he said, "I'm thrilled to participate in the leadership of this worldwide church, and to do so with President Henry B. Eyring under the direction of President Russell M. Nelson, who knows that worldwide membership and our worldwide concerns. We are thrilled with his leadership. I love working with the Quorum of the Twelve and our other leaders, men and women, local and general. Our Savior Jesus Christ has called each of us, and He will guide and bless each of us. I know that to be true."[6]

From the behavior of the members of the new First Presidency, viewers could see how much they loved each other and were in total unity. The three "gathered at a small table shoulder to shoulder," Sister Oaks observed. "From day one, they appeared to function as one, big smiles on their faces and genuinely joyful. They were one in purpose. They huddled together in unity."

On Saturday morning, March 31, 2018, as part of the Church's annual general conference, President Eyring, under President Nelson's direction, conducted a solemn assembly in which members of the Church throughout the world voted to sustain the new First Presidency and other General Authorities.[7] "The Conference Center had a tangible energy as every member readied to sustain the new prophet," Sister Oaks wrote. "Spiritual power seemed to ripple across the center" as each group in turn stood and offered a sustaining vote. "First to rise was the First Presidency," she remembered, then the "Quorum of the Twelve, the Quorums of Seventy and Presiding Bishopric, the remaining Melchizedek Priesthood holders, followed by the Relief Society (a change made by President Nelson), the Aaronic Priesthood, the Young Women, and the Church at large."

In the Saturday afternoon session of the conference, President Oaks led the semiannual sustaining of Church leaders in addition to the members of the First Presidency and Twelve sustained in the morning's solemn assembly. He also made a significant statement showing the new First Presidency's consciousness of the growing global presence of the Church. "With the sustaining that has just taken place," he noted, "we now have 116 General Authorities. Nearly 40 percent of them were born outside the United States." The sustaining also gave him a chance to express his gratitude to the members of the Church who voted that morning to accept him as a new member of the First Presidency. "Brothers and sisters," he said, "thank you for your continued faith and prayers in behalf of the leaders of the Church."[8]

President Oaks labored long to prepare his two conference addresses. He had "always prayed fervently to know what talks I should give in general conference," he wrote, "but this time was different." Sister Oaks remembered that he "spent many hours on his knees" pleading to know what he should say, "longing to bless the members." He received "sacred instructions," she said, that helped him know what to say.

In Saturday evening's general priesthood meeting, President Oaks taught that the Melchizedek Priesthood "is sacred and powerful beyond our powers to describe." It "is a divine power held in trust to use for the benefit of God's work for His children." Men "are *not* 'the priesthood,'" he emphasized. "It is not appropriate to refer to 'the priesthood and the women.' We should refer to 'the *holders* of the priesthood and the women.' . . .

"The principle that priesthood authority can be exercised only under the direction of the one who holds the keys for that function is fundamental in the Church but does not apply to the exercise of priesthood authority in the family," he declared. "A father who holds the priesthood presides in his family by the authority of the priesthood he holds. He has no need to have the direction or approval of priesthood keys in order to counsel the members of his family, hold family meetings, give priesthood blessings to his wife and children, or give healing blessings to family members or others.

"If fathers would magnify their priesthood in their own family, it would further the mission of the Church as much as anything else they might do," he said. "Fathers who hold the Melchizedek Priesthood should keep the commandments so they will have the power of the priesthood to give blessings to their family members. Fathers should also cultivate loving family relationships so that family members will want to ask their fathers for blessings. And parents should encourage more priesthood blessings in the family."[9]

As he explained earlier in the talk: "The most important principle for all priesthood holders is the principle taught by the Book of Mormon prophet Jacob. After he and his brother Joseph were consecrated priests and teachers of the people, he declared, 'And we did magnify our office unto the Lord, taking upon us the responsibility, answering the sins of the people upon our own heads if we did not teach them the word of God with all diligence' (Jacob 1:19)."[10]

In a nutshell, that scripture captured the way President Oaks saw his role as a Church leader. His leadership was not about himself; it was about representing the Lord and being personally responsible for teaching God's word in a clear way that would not be misunderstood. To that end, he subordinated his own interests to knowing and understanding the Lord's will.

President Eyring, his fellow counselor in the First Presidency, had watched him function since 1971, when both were called to serve as presidents of Church institutions of higher learning—President Oaks as president of Brigham Young University in Provo, and President Eyring as president of Ricks College, which later became BYU–Idaho. A respect grew between the two men, and President Eyring came to view President Oaks not simply as an intellectual giant but also as a deeply spiritual man. "He would pray very, very hard and feel that he got revelation," President Eyring recalled of their time together in Church education. "And of all the things that I thought he ought to be struggling with" as a university president, "that was the kind of thing he did."

Not only that, but unlike some remarkably bright people President Eyring had known, President Oaks was wide open to suggestions from others, a characteristic Brother Eyring came to admire, especially as the two served together in the Quorum of the Twelve. Elder Oaks would listen carefully to others, thoughtfully consider what they said, and change his mind if he felt their views were better than his.

Twice during their many years in the quorum together, Elder Eyring disagreed with Elder Oaks, who was his senior, and after the discussion, the quorum voted in favor of Elder Eyring's position. Both times, he recalled, Elder Oaks approached him afterward and gently said, "Thank you very much. You helped me see it."

"He would not remember probably," President Eyring said in 2019 after they had been serving nearly two years together in the First Presidency. "It's probably just natural to him. But to me it was just stunning because I like to win arguments. Most people do. But it was never an argument with him. It's a different kind of thing. He didn't have to win an argument. He'd try to find the truth." And it wasn't just when they were in the Twelve together. "He's that way now," President Eyring said. "He'll turn to me as if my opinion mattered. I just think it's incredible."

After working in the First Presidency with them, President Eyring considered President Oaks and President Nelson to be "the most wonderful persons to work with that I've ever worked with in the Church." In fact, he considered the President and his First Counselor to be like "twins," two men who "are dear friends," were called "at the same time," and are "very much alike." President Eyring had watched them for decades as "they've worked so well together, so long, side by side."

Elder Ulisses Soares, who was sustained as a new member of the Twelve at the March 31, 2018, solemn assembly, echoed what President Eyring said about President Oaks's willingness to listen to others. "He's a great listener, and I admire him, I love him, for that," Elder Soares said. "He never comes with a solution into a conversation. He always comes willing to learn, to listen, and then he makes conclusions. And I think that's the right way the Lord gives revelation and inspiration to his servants. We have to learn things first. We have to listen. And so he's a perfect example of that."

On Easter Sunday, April 1, 2018, President Oaks spoke during the morning session of general conference. As a special witness of Jesus Christ, he wanted to "concentrate on the Savior and His Atonement," he wrote. He felt impressed he should testify of "the literal nature of His resurrection and its significance for the literal resurrection of all who have lived upon the earth." Sister Kristen Oaks remembered his spending long hours in prayer and rewriting the talk many times to get it right. As a man "who had felt the sting of losing a beloved wife," she said, the Resurrection was particularly meaningful to him.

"Because we believe the accounts in both the Bible and the Book of Mormon about the literal resurrection of Jesus Christ, we also believe the numerous scriptural teachings that a similar resurrection will come to all mortals who have ever lived upon this earth," he declared. "That resurrection gives us what the Apostle Peter called 'a lively hope' (1 Peter 1:3). That lively hope is our conviction that death is not the conclusion of our identity but merely a necessary step in our Heavenly Father's merciful plan for the salvation of His children. That plan calls for a transition from mortality to immortality. Central to that transition is the sunset of death and the glorious morning made possible by the resurrection of our Lord and Savior that we celebrate on this Easter Sunday."

He then transitioned to an important topic related to how men and women become true disciples of the Lord Jesus Christ. The impression to address this topic surprised him. He and Sister Oaks were on one of their daily walks when "I saw the cracks in the pavement," Elder Oaks later explained, "and felt the impression to use that as an illustration of what each one of us needs to do to fulfill our destiny under the great plan of salvation."

"This morning," he told his audience, "I have felt to use as my text Alma's teaching to his son Helaman, recorded in the Book of Mormon:

'By small and simple things are great things brought to pass' (Alma 37:6). We are taught many small and simple things in the gospel of Jesus Christ. We need to be reminded that in total and over a significant period of time, these seemingly small things bring to pass great things."

He showed photographs he and Sister Oaks had taken of heavy concrete sidewalks cracked and lifted by the slow but inexorable growth of tree roots. "The thrusting power that cracked these heavy concrete sidewalks was too small to measure on a daily or even a monthly basis," he observed, "but its effect over time was incredibly powerful. So is the powerful effect over time of the small and simple things we are taught in the scriptures and by living prophets."

The same could be said of the path that led him to becoming a member of the First Presidency. He had not aspired to that position. Rather, he had led a steady life over many decades of consistently making one small, good decision after another that prepared him for this new role in his later years. Not that he was perfect. Neither he nor any of the leaders of the Church claimed perfection. Instead, they found strength and growth in the repentance made possible by the atoning sacrifice of the Savior.

"Another source of spiritual uplift and growth," he said in his Easter address, "is an ongoing practice of repenting, even of seemingly small transgressions. Our own inspired self-evaluations can help us see how we have fallen short and how we can do better."

As a member of the new First Presidency, Dallin H. Oaks would join Presidents Russell M. Nelson and Henry B. Eyring in pushing the Church forward one step at a time and through small and simple means would significantly advance the Lord's work. As President Oaks reminded his conference listeners, the Book of Mormon prophet Alma taught, "And the Lord God doth work by means to bring about his great and eternal purposes; and by very small means the Lord . . . bringeth about the salvation of many souls" (Alma 37:7).[11]

CHAPTER 29

"A CONSTANT JOY"

Serving in the First Presidency

Serving in the new First Presidency with Presidents Nelson and Eyring proved energizing to President Oaks. After one of their first meetings together in January 2018, he recorded, "President Nelson strong in inspiration and courageous in tackling long-delayed and difficult issues. Counselors supportive and harmonious. This service is joyful!" The new First Presidency operated as a true council. In April, President Oaks wrote, "Our First Presidency meetings continue to be very revelatory for all three of us: open discussion of different points of view followed by sweet coming together in unity."

Likewise, when they met with the members of the Quorum of the Twelve, a body in which each had served for many years, they also worked as a council on important issues. Under President Nelson's leadership, there were fifteen fully functioning Apostles in the Council of the First Presidency and Quorum of the Twelve, and this was "thrilling to all!"

President M. Russell Ballard agreed. "President Nelson doesn't see the First Presidency independent of the Twelve, and the Twelve don't see the First Presidency independent of us," he said. Likewise, as

President Oaks watched how President Ballard carried out his responsibilities presiding over the Quorum of the Twelve and worked together with the First Presidency, he felt great admiration for him. They had sat side by side in the Twelve for more than three decades and maintained a close bond. The new First Presidency "have full confidence in President Ballard," observed Elder Dale G. Renlund of the Twelve. "There is excellent communication."

Besides working well together and with the Twelve, the members of the First Presidency carried out their assigned individual duties. President Oaks extended calls and transfers to General Authorities, "a new kind of responsibility with my new calling," he noted. He also called mission and temple presidents, observing that many who accepted calls did so at great personal sacrifice. "We have miraculously faithful members!" President Oaks admired after making one such call.

In a meeting of the First Presidency in which they were clearing new mission presidents, President Oaks saw a name on the list that prompted him to look up a journal entry of twenty-seven years earlier. The entry recorded his impression back then that a young missionary

President Nelson, President Oaks, and President Eyring

he met would someday be mission president in the language region where he was serving. "Miraculous!" he now observed at the impression's fulfillment. He felt grateful for the sweet experience of extending the call to this man.

Two days a week, President Oaks had the responsibility of reviewing recommendations to have repentant persons readmitted to Church membership or their blessings restored. This proved painful duty because of the need to review why they had been excommunicated years earlier. "Hard to hear but merciful to do," he wrote tenderheartedly.

Church education—an area in which he had made major contributions as a member of the Twelve—also occupied his attention as a member of the First Presidency. Elder Kim B. Clark of the Seventy, a former dean of the Harvard Business School who served as Church Commissioner of Education, emphasized the key contributions President Oaks made in advancing Church education over the years, especially as chairman of the Church Education System Executive Committee. These included expanding education globally, establishing BYU Pathway, emphasizing religious education at BYU–Provo, and enhancing BYU Broadcasting. "President Oaks is one of my great heroes," Elder Clark said. "Working with him that closely for that many years was just a gift from heaven."

With Elder Oaks's new responsibilities in the First Presidency, he was able to shed some duties he had carried while in the Twelve, giving him better control over his time. On Tuesday, January 30, 2018, he had a rare free afternoon to get organized. "I finished getting settled," he rejoiced, "and looked across a totally clean desk for the first time in my professional/Church life." At the same time, the weight of his new responsibilities necessitated cutting back on his letter writing and individual travel assignments. He now belonged to a quorum responsible "to receive the oracles for the whole church" (D&C 124:126).

"In First Presidency meeting, we had an outpouring of revelation to all three of us," he wrote in early 2018. "The Lord is in charge, and with His direction we can make big changes." A month later, he recorded, "President Nelson is receiving . . . inspiration, and it is always confirmed to President Eyring and me. Thrilling!" In February 2019, more than a year after the new presidency was formed, President Oaks wrote that the presidency continued in a "remarkable period of President Nelson's rapid and inspired decisions on important matters for future refinement and implementation/announcement. I feel privileged to be part of this."[1] In all of this rejoicing in his journal, he discreetly avoided giving details or violating confidences.

In the October 2019 general conference, President Oaks quoted President Russell M. Nelson's teaching that the Church was restored "so that families could be formed, sealed, and exalted eternally," adding that President Nelson's teaching "has important implications for persons who identify . . . as LGBT." President Oaks explained, "The laws [of God] that apply most significantly to [this group] are God's law of marriage and its companion law of chastity." Nevertheless, he concluded with his constant counsel that "those who follow lesbian, gay, bisexual, or transgender teachings and actions should be treated with the love our Savior commands us to show toward all our neighbors."[2]

The changes the new First Presidency made in its first two years together were breathtaking. The new presidency made great progress in each of the four "divinely appointed responsibilities" described in the general handbook of instructions: "helping members live the gospel of Jesus Christ, gathering Israel through missionary work, caring for the poor and needy, and enabling the salvation of the dead by building temples and performing vicarious ordinances."[3]

To help build faith in the members and encourage them in living the gospel, President Nelson embarked on an aggressive travel schedule, beginning with a world ministry tour.[4] With President Nelson gone, President Oaks and President Eyring became responsible for the day-to-day management of the Church. They worked well as a pair during President Nelson's frequent absences, and on one such occasion,

President Oaks remarked, "President Eyring and I are united and a good team." They also worked well with the Twelve.

When President Nelson returned from his world tour, President Oaks found him "full of energy and inspiration." Later, when President Nelson went to speak to a stadium full of Church members and visitors in Arizona, he took President Oaks with him, and they and their wives spoke to a live audience of some sixty thousand people.[5] Such travels put the leaders face-to-face with local members, helping them feel the pulse of the membership.

President Oaks also had his own way of making those connections. "He knows that people put on a dog and pony show for a visiting General Authority," son Dallin D. said. "So on his free Sundays, . . . sometimes he just drops in at wards. They don't know he is coming." Once he dropped in on a ward in Virginia, and the ward mission leader asked him to visit the apartment of the local missionaries, who had not been at church. The young elders were surprised when an Apostle showed up. He gave them counsel to clean up their apartment and told them their mission president needed to know about the visit. Would they like to tell him, or should he? They agreed to report. Soon Elder Oaks received a letter from the mission president asking him to confirm their story of his visit.

Besides helping members live the gospel by meeting with them face-to-face, the members of the new First Presidency instituted numerous changes during their first two years together. They promoted a home-centered, Church-supported model of worship with new gospel study resources for home use. The presidency reduced the Sunday meeting block from three hours to two, consolidated high priest groups and elders quorums at the ward level, and replaced home and visiting teaching with personal ministering. They announced a new hymnal and children's songbook and new Book of Mormon videos. They also made the Saturday evening women's session an integral part of the general conference weekend.[6]

In making all these changes, they tried to envision the breadth of Church members. Speaking at a devotional for young marrieds in Chicago, President Oaks said Church leaders always tried to remember its members in humble economic circumstances and young couples with small children. "For example," he told them, "the voices of young mothers who had great difficulty managing children during a three-hour block of meetings on Sunday was an important consideration in reducing our worship meetings to two hours and Primary's duration commensurately."[7]

In May 2018, President Oaks recorded that President Nelson had strong impressions that "we must use the revealed name of Church, not substitutes." This became one of his key emphases for the Church.[8] The First Presidency also created Area Presidencies in the United States, introduced new global programs for children and youth, changed the timing on when youth advance in their classes, focused the curriculum on growing in faith through living a balanced life, introduced programs to protect youth from abuse, aligned seminary study with the adult curriculum, revised policies regarding LGBT members (allowing children of such couples to be blessed and baptized), and introduced resources to reduce suicide and to battle pornography.[9]

In the midst of these changes, President Oaks urged members to focus on what matters most. "Change is almost always exciting," he told the large audience in Arizona. "But as I have thought about the many recent changes in the Church, I have felt some caution. The changes we have experienced in our Church meetings and policies should help us, but by themselves they won't get our members to where our Heavenly Father wants us to be. The changes that make a difference to our position on the covenant path are not changes in Church policies or practices, but the changes we make in our own desires and actions."[10]

One change regarding Church members that the new First Presidency did not implement but celebrated in an unprecedented way was the revelation on priesthood received by President Spencer W. Kimball in June of 1978. That revelation was revolutionary to the Restored Church, similar to the revelation the Apostle Peter received as recorded in Acts 10 that helped expand the New Testament Church. The First Presidency sponsored a celebration of the fortieth anniversary of the revelation in which President Oaks was the keynote speaker.[11]

The revelation, he said, was a "divine call to abandon attitudes of prejudice against any group of God's children," including on the basis of race, ethnicity, culture, nationality, education, and economic circumstances. "Even as we unite to abandon all attitudes and practices of prejudice," he reminded his audience, "we should remember that it is not prejudice for the Church to insist on certain rules in furtherance of the Lord's requirement of worthiness to enter a temple. The Lord has declared that obedience to covenants and commandments is an essential requirement to enjoy sacred blessings."[12] He would return to this theme again and again, focusing on the two great commandments: first, to love God, and second, to love our neighbors as ourselves.[13]

In November 2019, President Oaks returned to Chicago, where he had lived for many years, and spoke at a devotional for Spanish-speaking members in eight stakes. Recalling his own family's immigrant history, he told his audience, "We want you to know that the leaders of the Church are very aware of the special difficulties so many of you face in being separated from family members who are in many other countries." He spoke with them about their employment difficulties and the Church's efforts to "help immigrants—including refugees—meet basic needs, such as food, housing, schooling, and medical and legal services."[14]

The new First Presidency also made significant changes in missionary work, the second of the four divinely appointed responsibilities. They merged old missions and opened new ones; issued a revised version of *Preach My Gospel*; began delivering mission assignments online; updated interview questions for missionary preparation; and made it possible for service missionaries to be called in the same way as proselyting missionaries, opening up service opportunities for more young people. The First Presidency also updated dress guidelines for missionaries, issued a new missionary handbook, and announced that missionaries could contact their families electronically or by phone on weekly preparation days.[15]

Speaking at the June 2018 mission leadership seminar, President Oaks said, "We never go wrong in following the direction and counsel of our prophet. President Eyring and I love working under the direction of President Nelson. Working with him is a constant joy."[16] The next year, President Oaks called on mission leaders to look beyond the current changes to eternal principles that are unchangeable. "We are having some important changes in the ways we do missionary work," he told them, "but the most important things about leading missionaries who are preaching the gospel have not changed and will not change." He encouraged them to "teach and model these eternal fundamentals," giving priority to them "in your personal learning, your teaching of missionaries, and your personal administration." The most fundamental of these, he said, "is our understanding of and our commitment to our Savior Jesus Christ. Our most important possession is our testimony of the risen Lord and His central role in the plan of salvation and in His restored gospel."[17]

As a member of the new First Presidency, President Oaks helped reach out to people of other faiths and backgrounds around the world. He met with Muslim leaders, a Native American leader, Hindu priests, the leadership of the National Association for the Advancement of Colored People,[18] and national officers of the Anti-Defamation League. He gave a blessing requested by a Jewish friend who had a serious health concern. He met with ambassadors from Africa, Asia, Europe, and South America, and showed concern for Hispanics of other faiths living in the United States who hailed from many countries.

The concern the Savior showed for others gave rise to the third

First Presidency meeting with Philippine ambassador

of the Church's four divinely appointed responsibilities, caring for the poor and needy, a subject on which the new First Presidency focused significant attention. Just twelve days after the presidency was formed, the Church issued a statement on immigration that observed, "Most of our early Church members emigrated from foreign lands to live, work, and worship, blessed by the freedoms and opportunities offered in this great nation." The statement recognized the divisive nature of the subject but declared that the Church's "first priority is to love and care for one another as Jesus Christ taught." It called on governments to create solutions providing "for strengthening families and keeping them together."[19]

Almost two years later, President Oaks joined the other members of the presidency in issuing another statement on immigration. Expressing compassion for the millions of refugees globally fleeing "violence, war, or religious persecution," it encouraged people everywhere to volunteer "their time, talents, and friendship to individuals and families who are integrating into our societies."[20]

After a hurricane devastated parts of the southeastern United States, President Oaks and Sister Kristen Oaks visited the area to lift and strengthen those affected by the storm. They and their traveling companions met with civic leaders, who expressed gratitude for the

Church's aid in the wake of the destruction. They also held meetings with thousands of Church members.[21] "An outstanding memory of this trip," President Oaks wrote in his journal, "was the comment of a mother of young children. When asked what she had learned from the ruining of her home, she replied, 'I learned the difference between what is important and what is not important.'" This was a repeated theme of his ministry—the difference between the temporary and changeable things of mortality and the unchangeable things of eternity.

Such service activities came naturally to Kristen, whose outreach spanned cultures and nationalities and drew her husband into friendships that continue to this day. Included in these were families they met in Uruguay and Brazil, some of whom later moved to the United States. While volunteering at a local school, Kristen befriended a young girl and her family who came from Burundi and into the Oakses' hearts. Teaching English as a second language to Church-sponsored groups at the University of Utah endeared Kristen to a Turkish family that remains close to them. Her work with the young women of the

President and Sister Oaks in North Carolina, 2018

Nepali Ward included annual Christmas functions. For all involved, their world became more joyous.

The last of the four divinely appointed responsibilities on which the new First Presidency focused was temple and family history work. Within the first month of the presidency's formation, President Oaks wrote in his journal that during their meeting that morning, "we had an outpouring of revelation to all three of us" on subjects related to temples. The inspiration continued throughout their months and years together.

In an article President Oaks wrote for the Church magazines of May 2018, he reminded readers that temple work had been a key theme of this new First Presidency from the beginning. "On January 16, 2018, two days after President Nelson was set apart as President of the Church, he announced that the new First Presidency would begin its ministry 'with the end in mind,'" President Oaks wrote. "That 'end' is the salvation of individuals and the sealing of families in the house of the Lord."[22]

President and Sister Oaks gave the keynote presentation at the RootsTech Family Discovery Day in March 2018. President Oaks reported, "A recent study by a university . . . concludes persuasively that if you want a happier family," you should "create, refine, and retell the stories of your ancestors' positive moments," something he had worked hard to do. Sister Oaks affirmed, "Most of us are here today because we heard stories of our ancestors. I know that I would not be sitting on this stage without such stories. The journals we keep and the stories we tell have the capacity to teach the gospel to those who come after us—even if faith may have skipped a generation or if ancestors are not on earth to share their testimonies."[23]

As part of their responsibility for the sealing keys, the new First Presidency began early on to revise the language and procedures of temple ceremonies. President Nelson spoke for the entire First Presidency in announcing these changes during a general conference leadership meeting, reported on the Church's official newsroom. "As leaders in the Lord's Church," he said, "we need to understand the eternal truths taught in the temple. We need to know the importance of and the difference between sacred covenants, ordinances, and procedures." The new adjustments did "not change the sacred nature of the covenants being made" but did "allow for covenants to be planted in the hearts of people living in different times and circumstances."[24]

One of the adjustments made it possible for women to serve as witnesses for baptisms and sealings of both the living and the deceased. This change not only expanded the role of women in the Church but also helped make temple worship a family affair.[25] Another change removed the waiting period between civil and temple marriages.[26] Yet another provided for more refined temple recommend questions. Speaking at the annual seminar in October 2018 for new temple presidents and matrons, President Oaks encouraged improvements in how temples are run.[27]

In addition to changes in temple ordinances and procedures, the First Presidency authorized the construction of scores of new temples to be built throughout the world. They also authorized renovations and upgrades of the Church's pioneer-era temples, including the flagship Salt Lake Temple, that would protect the buildings against seismic damage and allow for better use of the sacred structures. President Nelson launched the Church into one of the most active temple building and renovation periods in its history.[28]

As a member of the First Presidency, President Oaks participated in temple dedications. In December 2018, he traveled to Barranquilla, Colombia, to dedicate the temple there.[29] Then, in March 2019, he joined the other members of the First Presidency and Twelve and their wives in Rome as part of that temple's dedicatory events. It was the first time in Church history that all the members of both quorums had been together outside the United States, and they commemorated the event with photographs at the temple visitors' center in front of statues of the ancient Twelve.[30] "What a trip! A lifetime memory," President Oaks rejoiced in his journal.

"In these houses of the Lord we are taught the most important knowledge we can learn in mortality," he declared at one of the dedicatory sessions. "Temple covenants help us stay worthy of His blessings and help us translate the knowledge we receive in the temple into service to our fellowmen. This knowledge of eternal truths and these covenants are so important and so valuable that they are referred to as an 'endowment' (see D&C 110:9; 124:39), which means a precious gift."

When asked how his service in the First Presidency had affected him, President Oaks offered three thoughts. First, he said, "My understanding of the power of the Atonement of Jesus Christ has increased enormously. As a judge, I applied mortal laws and penalties. In contrast, as I have reviewed the cases of persons who have sinned seriously and now seek renewal in the Church, I have been awed by the love of God and His merciful forgiveness of those who repent and return to Him." Second, he responded, "I have greatly increased in knowledge of and appreciation for the inspired service of the members of the Twelve, the Seventy, the Presiding Bishopric, our General Officers, and our local leaders." Finally, he said, "I have grown in my testimony of the reality of revelation to our living prophet, President Russell M. Nelson."

In the March 2020 *Ensign,* President Oaks published an important article titled "The Lord Leads His Church through Prophets and Apostles." The article established the essential need for prophets and apostles to lead the Lord's Church at a time when "many seem to want spirituality or religion but think they can have it without any religious organization." He declared that "a paramount function" of these leaders is "to hold the keys of the priesthood," which "assure heavenly effect to the authorized actions of priesthood authority on earth." He also confirmed that "doctrine is not canonized until the body of the Church has received it by the law of common consent" and that questions "about doctrine or policy that is not clearly defined in the scriptures or handbooks are to be referred to the First Presidency."

On March 13, he spoke at the annual Church History Symposium in Salt Lake sponsored by the Church History Department and BYU. In his address, he reviewed his Joseph Smith research of over half a century and reaffirmed a key learning from his study: "Past actions should be judged by the laws and culture of their time," not by standards of a different day.

Spring of 2020 marked the bicentennial of Joseph Smith's First Vision. The First Presidency used the anniversary and April general conference to commemorate the Restoration of the gospel and reinforce the correct name of the Church with a new symbol emphasizing the centrality of the Savior.[31] President Oaks spoke twice in the conference, which was unlike any previous one because a pandemic led the First Presidency to restrict in-person attendance. But the conference was broadcast to additional millions worldwide. President Oaks declared: "Even in the midst of unique trials and challenges, we are truly blessed! This general conference has given us an outpouring of the riches and joy of the Restoration of the gospel of Jesus Christ."[32]

As part of the commemoration, the First Presidency and Twelve issued a proclamation.[33] In a conference address, President Oaks quoted the proclamation, affirming that "those who prayerfully study the message of the Restoration and act in faith will be blessed to gain their own witness of its divinity and of its purpose to prepare the world for the promised Second Coming of our Lord and Savior, Jesus Christ."[34]

One of his addresses, given at a special Saturday evening conference session of men and women, reiterated what he had said previously about priesthood in the Church and the family. He emphasized that in the Church, priesthood keys allowed both men and women to exercise priesthood authority in their callings, including in missionary and temple service.[35]

President Oaks's other talk focused on the Father's great plan of happiness. While laying out the plan from the scriptures, he focused on "four great assurances . . . given to us through the Atonement of Jesus Christ, the centerpiece of the plan." The first was that we can be cleansed from repented sins. Second, because the Savior bore "all other mortal infirmities," He can give us "divine help and strength to bear the inevitable burdens of mortality, personal and general, such as war and pestilence"—including the virus that was then plaguing the earth. Third, the Savior's Atonement "revokes the finality of death and gives us the joyful assurance that all of us will be resurrected." Fourth, the Atonement means "that our progress need not conclude with the end of mortality. . . .

"In this year of 2020," President Oaks said, "we have what is popularly called 20/20 vision for the events of the past. As we look to the future, however, our vision is far less sure." But we know "the spirit world now includes many mortally experienced workers to accomplish the preaching that occurs there. We also know that we now have many more temples to perform the ordinances of eternity for those who repent and embrace the Lord's gospel on either side of the veil of death," and that "God's love is so great that, except for the few who deliberately become sons of perdition, He has provided a destiny of glory for all of His children."[36]

Speaking at an October 2018 general conference leadership session, President Oaks quoted an English clergyman who said, "If you have not chosen the kingdom of God first, it will in the end make no difference what you have chosen instead," revising the saying to read, "If you have not chosen Jesus Christ first, it will in the end make no difference what you have chosen instead." With all the other responsibilities he took on as a member of the First Presidency, President Oaks never forgot that he was an Apostle, a special witness of the name of Christ in all the world, and he repeatedly brought people back to the fundamental principle of faith in the Lord Jesus Christ.

With all the thorny issues that modern life threw at him and the Church, President Oaks always fell back on the Savior and His love for humanity. Over and over again, he told listeners, "In my persistent prayerful ponderings, I have never found a better, shorter answer to our many questions than a thorough knowledge and total faith in the love of our Heavenly Father and His plan of salvation for the blessing of all of His children. The central truth of that plan is the Atonement of His Only Begotten Son, our Savior, Jesus Christ. If we trust in the Lord and trust in His plan, we will have the strength to resist persuasive imitations and temptations to abandon our quest for eternal life, which is the greatest of all the gifts of God (see D&C 14:7)."[37]

CHAPTER 30

"DO THINGS RIGHT OR NOT AT ALL"

A Life of Integrity

As a young boy, Dallin H. Oaks lost his father, suffered through his mother's breakdown and absences, endured bullying from classmates, and moved multiple times. He endured these challenges and as a youth gradually grew spiritually, mentally, emotionally, and physically, developing qualities of independence and resourcefulness through hard work at school and on his grandparents' farm. In his grandfather, uncles, bishops, and Scout leaders, he found role models who helped him develop into a man of faith and integrity.[1]

Advancement in the Aaronic Priesthood and through the ranks of Scouting taught him principles of honesty, loyalty, trust, and service. Inspired seminary teachers helped him feel loved and valued as they taught him gospel principles from the scriptures. Schoolwork, Church service, Scouting, extracurricular activities, and labor on the farm taught him firmly the law of the harvest—that if he sowed well, he could reap well. His resourcefulness turned his hobby of radio into a fascinating pastime and a job at the start of the technology age.

His mother's decision to move the family to a larger city temporarily rocked his world. But the ups and downs of life had taught him resilience, and after moving, he set about making a new life for himself in his new environment. Before long as a high schooler, he became a radio engineer and announcer, learning from experience how to think on his feet and handle pressure well. The move, which could have put him in a tailspin, instead lifted him to new heights. When he joined the Utah National Guard during his last year of high school and the Korean War began just after his graduation, he suddenly found himself facing life as an adult.[2]

Ordination to the Melchizedek Priesthood, studying at Brigham Young University, military experience, and marriage to June Dixon helped move him into adulthood. His marriage to June called forth his best school efforts and laid a solid foundation for entering the University of Chicago Law School. Becoming a father also helped give purpose and meaning to his life.[3]

Excelling in law school, followed by clerking for the Chief Justice of the United States Supreme Court, prepared him for a distinguished career in the law. These were also years in which he might have slighted things spiritual but instead chose to maintain a balanced life.[4] The years that followed his experience in Washington, DC, saw him balancing his career as a large-firm lawyer with his responsibilities as a husband, father, and active member of the Church.

The time pressure from the firm was intense, and when he received a call to serve as a stake missionary, he might easily have declined it on the grounds that he lacked the time to fulfill the role well. Instead, he accepted on faith that the Lord wanted him to serve, and his faith was rewarded as he somehow became able to succeed in his Church calling and excel in his profession. His missionary work helped fill the gap created when the Korean War kept him from serving a full-time mission as a young man. His later call to the stake presidency strengthened him spiritually and taught him leadership and other skills he would use for the rest of his life.

He continued to follow spiritual impressions, one of which led from practicing law full-time to accepting a prestigious professorship at his alma mater.[5] Academic life proved rewarding in many ways, while giving him more time to spend with family. It provided opportunities to enhance his reputation as a scholar and public servant and gave him valuable administrative experiences as associate and then acting dean of the law school. His appointment as executive director of the American Bar Foundation enhanced those skills. Concurrent with his professional employment, he fulfilled callings that prepared him for a future of Church service.[6]

Throughout his professional career, he had a premonition that the Lord was preparing him for some kind of special service. That premonition saw partial fulfillment when Church leaders selected him as president of Brigham Young University while he was still in his thirties. As president, he became both the academic and spiritual leader of the university and found himself in many meetings with senior Church officials, who took their measure of the man.[7]

As with previous roles in Dallin Oaks's life, service as university president forced him to balance the spiritual and the secular and make decisions about which to follow when they conflicted. Consistently, he chose to do what he felt was right, what he felt the Lord would have him do, even if it seemed to threaten his reputation from a worldly perspective. Always, he would sacrifice for the right, regardless of the personal consequence.[8]

After being released as BYU president, he followed his spiritual impressions to become a justice on the Utah Supreme Court and to decline other opportunities.[9] His name was advanced for consideration as a justice of the United States Supreme Court, and, for a time, he wondered if the latter part of his life would be occupied by that service. But when an opportunity came to be a judge on the U.S. Court of Appeals for the District of Columbia—a position seen as a stepping-stone to the Supreme Court—he again followed his spiritual impressions and declined, instead helping a former colleague take the role. That colleague later ascended to the Supreme Court.[10]

Dallin Oaks had done all he could to follow the Spirit but wondered what would happen to him after all this preparation. How did the Lord want him to serve in the latter years of his life? That question was answered by a phone call that came to him while he was out of town—a call from President Gordon B. Hinckley, who informed him he had been called as a member of the Quorum of the Twelve Apostles. Brother Oaks's long impression that the Lord had some kind of service for him to perform was fulfilled as he became an Apostle, a special witness of the name of Jesus Christ in all the world.[11]

Neither fame, nor fortune, nor the cravings of the flesh drew him from following the direction the Lord gave him in his life. One small decision after another added up to a lifetime of service for and in behalf of the Savior. When President Hinckley called him to be an Apostle, Dallin H. Oaks replied, "My life is in the hands of the Lord, and my career is in the hands of His servants."[12]

From the day of his ordination to the apostleship onward, he gave all his time, talents, and other resources to the Lord's work. During a moment of introspection before his ordination, he counted the cost of his discipleship. "Throughout the remainder of your life," he asked himself, "will you be a judge and lawyer who has been called to be an Apostle, or will you be an Apostle who used to be a lawyer and a judge?" Human nature, he knew, was to focus on the familiar and slight the unfamiliar and challenging.

"I knew," he realized, "that if I concentrated my time on the things that came naturally and the things that I felt qualified to do, I would never be an Apostle. I would always be a former lawyer and judge." He chose to take the more difficult and honorable path. "I decided," he resolved, "that I would focus my efforts on what I had been called to do, not on what I was qualified to do. I determined that instead of trying to shape my calling to my credentials, I would try to shape myself to my calling."[13]

Over the succeeding years, he did just that, aided first by his wife June, and then by his wife Kristen, who supported and greatly assisted him through the decades following June's death. Kristen McMain Oaks came into his life with the talents, experience, and personality that made her the perfect companion for him in his ministry. "They're very genuine," observed Elder Ronald A. Rasband. "There's no holds barred in their marriage. They're very open. They speak openly, and they support each other." Sister Kristen Oaks was someone who could teach and testify in her own right.

The Oakses always believed strongly in the fundamental role of the family in the Lord's plan. All six of the Oaks children have continued to remain faithful to the parental and grandparental teachings and encouragement that they received.

By November of 2019—more than thirty-five years after his ordination as an Apostle—Dallin H. Oaks was a member of the First Presidency and went to Chicago on assignment. While there, he visited his alma mater, the University of Chicago Law School, where he drove around the campus, conversed with students who belonged to the school's Dallin H. Oaks Law Society, and had a pleasant chat with the current dean and one of his associates. They discussed, as President Oaks recorded in his journal, "some ancient history at the law school and my part in" it. The memories of those days remained, but he had moved far beyond them. As he wrote later of that trip, "Life goes on."

During the general conference in which he was sustained as First Counselor in the First Presidency, President Oaks quoted Brigham Young as saying, "Our lives are made up of little, simple circumstances that amount to a great deal when they are brought together, and sum up the whole life of the man or woman."[14] Margie McKnight, President Oaks's secretary, pointed out that removing the D from Dallin spells "all in." She said she didn't know anyone who was more "all in" than President Oaks.

Elder Ulisses Soares put it a different way. "Everybody talks about his career as a judge . . . and as president of BYU," Elder Soares said. "And we, of course, admire all his experience. We treasure all the stories and experiences that he has had in his life. But for me, his humbleness and consideration to people is what really gives me a great feeling of gratitude to my Heavenly Father—to call men like him to serve and to direct His work."

Dallin H. Oaks's life was built on principled decisions, small and large, made one after another, day after day, year after year, decade after decade. Elder David A. Bednar wrote: "President Oaks comes to his new assignment in the presiding quorum of The Church of Jesus Christ of Latter-day Saints with 'tranquil and steady dedication of a lifetime'—a life devoted to the Savior and His restored Church. President Oaks's personal discipleship, powerful teachings, and the consistency of his righteous example will influence positively people throughout the world and assist them in following the Lord's ways.

"President Oaks," Elder Bednar concluded from years of close observation, "is a man of integrity. His beliefs and behavior are grounded in gospel principles, and he lives what he believes. Expediency is never an option for him because he is determined to do what is right, even if a course of action does not advance his personal reputation or viewpoint. There are no shortcuts in his life—do things right or not at all."[15]

NOTES

For the sake of readers, quotations from the sources below that appear in the text have generally been edited to standardize spelling, punctuation, capitalization, and in some cases grammar, as well as to correct other errors.

Chapter 1: "Faith and Assurance"

1. On Lloyd's medical practice in Provo, see "Explosion May Impair Sight of Student at B.Y.U.," *Salt Lake Tribune,* Apr. 7, 1933, 9.
2. Rell G. Francis, *Cyrus E. Dallin: Let Justice Be Done* (Provo: Springville Museum of Art; Utah American Revolution Bicentennial Commission, 1976).
3. "Pioneer Celebration Ready at Springville; To Unveil Monument," *Sunday Herald* (Provo, UT), July 24, 1932.
4. Two days after Dallin was born, and before Jessie approached Stella, the local newspaper had reported, "Mother and baby are doing nicely." "Congratulations to These Happy Parents," *Sunday Herald,* Aug. 14, 1932, 5.
5. "Babe and Woman Hurt in Crash," *Daily Herald* (Provo, UT), May 29, 1933; "Mrs. Lloyd Oaks and Infant Child Injured in Crash on Saturday," *Vernal Express* (Vernal, UT), June 1, 1933. The latter newspaper account said Stella was the person most seriously injured and did not mention Jessie.
6. "Maeser," *Vernal Express,* Sept. 7, 1928; "Wedding Reception to Dr. Lloyd E. Oaks and Bride Formerly Miss Stella Harris," *Vernal Express,* June 27, 1929.
7. "Maeser," *Vernal Express,* May 18, 1923; "Wedding Reception to Dr. Lloyd E. Oaks and Bride Formerly Miss Stella Harris," *Vernal Express,* June 27,

1929; "Six Internes Begin Duties at Geisinger Memorial Hospital," *Danville Morning News* (Danville, PA), July 5, 1930.

8. "Provo Doctor Moving Away," *Daily Herald* (Provo, UT), Apr. 12, 1934; "Provo Physician to Head Society," *Daily Herald*, May 28, 1935; "Opticians Attend Dinner in Provo," *Daily Herald*, Apr. 21, 1937; "Former Interne Died at Denver," *Danville Morning News*, July 30, 1940. While still in medical school, Lloyd had expressed an interest in developing a specialty. Harrison R. Merrill, "Trailing the 'Y'sers," *Daily Herald*, Mar. 6, 1930.
9. Merrill, "Trailing the 'Y'sers"; "Changes Carried Out at Stake Conference," *Daily Herald*, May 23, 1932; "Lawrence Bees Hosts to Board," *Daily Herald*, Mar. 2, 1933; "Reorganize Utah Stake Presidency," *Daily Herald*, Sept. 5, 1933; "Mutual Messages," *Daily Herald*, Sept. 19, 1933; "Provo Leaders Back Scouting," *Daily Herald*, Mar. 2, 1934; "Dr. L. E. Oaks, Formerly of Provo, Dies," *Daily Herald*, June 10, 1940; "Dr. Lloyd E. Oaks Succumbs at Denver Hospital," *Vernal Express*, June 13, 1940.
10. "Congratulations to These Happy Parents," *Daily Herald*, Jan. 16, 1936.
11. "Dr. L. E. Oaks, Formerly of Provo, Dies"; "Dr. Lloyd E. Oaks Succumbs at Denver Hospital"; "Maeser," *Vernal Express*, June 13, 1940; "Former Interne Died at Denver."
12. "Faith in the Lord Jesus Christ," *Ensign*, May 1994, 100; Dallin H. Oaks, *Life's Lessons Learned: Personal Reflections* (Salt Lake City: Deseret Book, 2011), 8.
13. Oaks, *Life's Lessons Learned*, 10–11.
14. Oaks, *Life's Lessons Learned*, 11.
15. Oaks, *Life's Lessons Learned*, 11–12.
16. Oaks, *Life's Lessons Learned*, 12–13.

Chapter 3: "Life Was Coming into Focus"

1. Robert C. Oaks, Oral History, Dec. 8, 2009, 2, Church History Library, The Church of Jesus Christ of Latter-day Saints, Salt Lake City, Utah; Cathy Allred, "Former four-star general and LDS general authority speaks at local Veterans Day program," *Daily Herald*, Nov. 9, 2014.
2. Dallin's mother copied the verses out of the guest book and later gave them to him.
3. Provo Eighth Ward Births and Blessings, 1953, 608, Church History Library.
4. Don L. Searle, "Elder Dallin H. Oaks," *Ensign*, June 1984, 14.

Chapter 4: "The Capabilities to Be a Leader"

1. James R. Elkins, "Rites de Passage: Law Students 'Telling Their Lives,'" *Journal of Legal Education* 35, no. 1 (March 1985): 27–55.
2. Dallin H. Oaks, *Life's Lessons Learned* (Salt Lake City: Deseret Book, 2011), 23–24.

3. "Dallin Oaks Tops Field at Chicago U.," *Daily Herald*, Feb. 21, 1955.
4. Michael L. Closen and Robert J. Dzielak, "The History and Influence of the Law Review Institution," available at www.uakron.edu.
5. Dallin H. Oaks, "The Single Rental as a Trade or Business under the Internal Revenue Code," *University of Chicago Law Review* 23 (1956): 111.
6. "Dallin Oaks Wins Editorship of Law Publication," *Daily Herald*, June 7, 1956.
7. "Former Resident Appointed Aide to Supreme Court," *Vernal Express*, Apr. 4, 1957; "3 U. of C. Men Named Aids of U.S. Justices," *Chicago Tribune*, Apr. 12, 1957; "Student Wins Scholarship," *Ogden Standard-Examiner*, Apr. 24, 1957.

Chapter 6: "To Equip Me for Some Future Job"

1. *People v. Tranowski*, 20 Ill. 2d 1 (1960).
2. Dallin H. Oaks, "My Most Influential Teacher," *Church News*, Mar. 11, 1978.

Chapter 7: "The Dividends of Academic Life"

1. Sharmon Oaks Ward and Dallin D. Oaks, "June Dixon Oaks," in Marian Wilkinson Jensen, *Women of Commitment: Personal Portraits of Selected BYU Women* (Bountiful, UT: Horizon Publishers, 1997), 27.
2. These included the University of Colorado School of Law (Nov. 1963); Florida State University College of Law (1965); University of New Mexico School of Law (Mar. 1965); Boston University School of Law (May 1966); University of Oregon School of Law (July 1967); University of Oklahoma Law Center (July 1969); University of Buffalo Law School (Dec. 1969).
3. The schools that offered visiting professorships that he declined were Harvard University; Stanford University; the University of California, Berkeley; the University of California, Davis; the University of California, Los Angeles; the University of Ghana; the University of Pennsylvania; the University of South Dakota; and the University of Utah.
4. "Two New Units Created from Original Chicago Stake," *Church News*, Feb. 9, 1963.
5. Dallin H. Oaks, "Antidotes for the School Prayer Cases," *Improvement Era* 66, no. 12 (Dec. 1963): 1048–50, 1134–36.

Chapter 8: "My Work Is Progressing"

1. Dallin H. Oaks and Marvin S. Hill, *Carthage Conspiracy: The Trial of the Accused Assassins of Joseph Smith* (Urbana: University of Illinois Press, 1975).

Chapter 9: "Going All the Time"

1. Elmer Gertz, *For the First Hours of Tomorrow: The New Illinois Bill of Rights* (Urbana: University of Illinois Press, 1972), 35–37.
2. Dallin H. Oaks, "Studying the Exclusionary Rule in Search and Seizure," *University of Chicago Law Review* 37 (1970): 665.
3. Albert Alschuler, "Studying the Exclusionary Rule: An Empirical Classic," *University of Chicago Law Review* 75 (2008): 1365.
4. For more detail on this experience, see Dallin H. Oaks, "Bible Stories and Personal Protection," *Ensign*, Nov. 1992, 39–40.
5. Dallin H. Oaks, "The Beginning and the End of a Lawyer," *Clark Memorandum* (Spring 2005), 10–11; Dallin H. Oaks, "The Beginning and the End of a Lawyer," in Scott W. Cameron, Galen L. Fletcher, and Jane H. Wise, *Life in the Law: Service & Integrity* (Provo, UT: J. Reuben Clark Law Society, Brigham Young University Law School, 2009), 221–22.
6. "Oaks Expected BYU Position," *Deseret News*, Aug. 10, 1971; Roger Aylworth, "Months of searching: Oaks named to post," *Daily Universe*, Nov. 12, 1971.

Chapter 10: "The Lord Marked Him Out"

1. Kevin Mansfield, "Oaks' record shows distinguished service," *Universe,* May 8, 1980, 1.
2. "Chicago Law Professor Named BYU President," *Church News*, May 8, 1971.
3. "New President for University," *Daily Herald*, May 5, 1971.
4. "Chicago Law Professor Named BYU President"; "Brigham Young Fan Becomes Its President," *College and University Business*, July 1971.
5. "Y. Inaugural Rites Install Pres. Oaks," *Church News*, Nov. 13, 1971; "Dr. Oaks Begins Work as President," *BYU Today*, Aug. 1971.
6. "Cheese," *Daily Universe*, Sept. 16, 1971.
7. Giles H. Florence Jr., "Oaks Home Has Informal Atmosphere," *BYU Today*, Feb. 1973, 12.
8. "Oaks meets the press," *Daily Universe*, Sept. 21, 1971.
9. "Inactivity 'unfair, unwise use of university,'" *Daily Universe*, Sept. 24, 1971.
10. "Chicagoan at Head of Mormon School Tells Goals," *Chicago Tribune*, Sept. 30, 1971.
11. "Y. Inaugural Rites Install Pres. Oaks," *Church News*, Nov. 13, 1971.
12. "Prominent citizens at inauguration," *Daily Universe*, Nov. 12, 1971; "Distinguished gathering," *Daily Universe*, Nov. 15, 1971.
13. "Mr. President," *Daily Universe*, Nov. 12, 1971; "Y. Inaugural Rites Install Pres. Oaks."
14. "Inauguration of 'Y' President," *Daily Herald*, Nov. 15, 1971.
15. "Distinguished gathering."

16. "BYU President Is Inaugurated," *Church News*, Nov. 20, 1971.
17. Dallin H. Oaks, "Talk of the Month: Standards of Dress and Grooming," *New Era*, Dec. 1971, 48.
18. "Oaks' First Year Marked by Changes at BYU," *Herald*, Aug. 1, 1972.
19. "Dr. Oaks Begins Work as President," *BYU Today*, Aug. 1971.
20. "Oaks' First Year Marked by Changes at BYU."
21. Carl Stewart, "Oaks—a man who never wastes a minute," *Daily Universe*, Aug. 3, 1972.
22. "Reject the mediocre," *Daily Universe*, Sept. 6, 1972.
23. Florence, "Oaks Home Has Informal Atmosphere," 9, 12.
24. Jack Jarrard, "Rites Dedicate Center at BYU," *Church News*, Feb. 10, 1973.
25. "President injures arm," *Daily Universe*, Mar. 2, 1973; "Pres. Oaks in hospital," *Universe*, Mar. 7, 1973; "Dr. Oaks Okay, Is Released after Surgery," *Herald*, Mar. 14, 1973; "Oaks recuperates," *Universe*, Mar. 20, 1973.
26. Robert McDougall, "Benson Speaks at Ground Rites for BYU Law School Building," *Herald*, May 2, 1973.

Chapter 11: "Absolutely Extraordinary"

1. Deanna Lloyd, "Oaks reflects on Y tenure," *Universe*, July 31, 1980.
2. Robert McDougall, "Benson Speaks at Ground Rites for BYU Law School Building," *Herald*, May 2, 1973; David Clemens, "Two years of change," *Daily Universe*, Aug. 30, 1973; "Three Y buildings dedicated Tuesday," *Daily Universe*, Feb. 20, 1974; "Rites Begin Work on Y. Tower," *Salt Lake Tribune*, Feb. 14, 1975; "Oaks Reveals BYU Plan for New Buildings," *Herald*, Aug. 26, 1976; "Expanded Lee Library Dedicated by Romney," *Daily Herald*, Mar. 15, 1977; "Monte L. Bean Museum Dedicated Today at BYU," *Daily Herald*, Mar. 28, 1978; "30-year Period of Rapid Growth in Construction Ends at BYU," *Herald*, Feb. 24, 1980; Etel Englund, "Oaks responsible for major expansion of Y," *Universe*, July 31, 1980.
3. "$56 million drive launched at BYU–Hawaii Campus," *BYU Today*, Feb. 1978; "Center in Jerusalem to Expand Campus," *Herald*, Feb. 24, 1980.
4. "And parting words of the president," *BYU Today*, Aug. 1980, 7.
5. Chuck Kofoed, "Oaks helped new law school," *Universe*, July 31, 1980.
6. "Local officials praise Warren," *Universe*, July 11, 1974.
7. "New 'Y' Law School Holds Convocation, Dedication," *Herald*, Sept. 5, 1975.
8. "Oaks years called 'extraordinary,'" *Universe*, July 31, 1980; "Oaks' presidency re-emphasizes academics," *Daily Universe*, Oct. 8, 1975; David Clemens, "Two years of change," *Daily Universe*, Aug. 30, 1973.
9. "Oaks Appointed to International Advisory Council for Scholars," *Herald*, Mar. 3, 1974; "27 New Regional Aides," *Church News*, June 15, 1974; "Oaks is teacher at Y law school," *Daily Universe*, Feb. 5, 1975; "Outstanding

Leaders Serve on IHCI Board," *McKay-Dee Hospital Center Scanner*, March-May 1975; "Pres. Oaks will advise U.S. Attorney General," *Universe*, Apr. 10, 1975; "Oaks recounts Carthage trial," *Deseret News*, April 14, 1975; "Association names Oaks," *Deseret News*, Dec. 9, 1975; "Oaks is elected to college board," *Deseret News*, Jan. 17, 1977; "Oaks selected by private colleges," *Universe*, Jan. 18, 1977; "BYU's Dallin Oaks Named To Board of New Association," *Herald*, Jan. 20, 1977; "Oaks elected to TV board," *Deseret News*, Apr. 6, 1977; "Dr. Oaks Elected By Public Network," *Herald*, Apr. 7, 1977; "Oaks Named PBS Official," *Herald*, June 7, 1978; "PBS elects officers," *BYU Today*, May 1977; "Monson Named to Post," *Herald*, May 18, 1977; "Oaks will speak to American Bar," *Deseret News*, June 3, 1977; "Law textbook published, prepared by Pres. Oaks," *Daily Universe*, Nov. 15, 1977; "Trusts Law Text Edition by Dr. Oaks to Be Released," *Provo Herald*, Nov. 15, 1977; "Pres. Oaks appointed to law advisory board," *Daily Universe*, Jan. 5, 1978; "Oaks ends term as AAPICU head," *Universe*, Dec. 6, 1978; "Y president at meetings," *Universe*, Feb. 5, 1979; "Two PBS Committees Named to Structure Reorganization," *CPB Report*, July 23, 1979; "Minow's successor?" *Closed Circuit*, July 1979; "Pres. Oaks to chair new PBS committee," *Today*, Aug. 1979; "Oaks to speak Tuesday," *Universe*, Sept. 10, 1979; "Union Pacific Elects Oaks to Directorship," *Daily Herald*, Sept. 27, 1979; "Oaks on Union Pacific board," *Universe*, Sept. 28, 1979; "BYU's Dallin Oaks Elected a Director of Union Pacific Corp.," *California Intermountain News*, Nov. 29, 1979.

10. "Oaks outlines Y. school year," *Deseret News*, Aug. 28, 1973.
11. It was a theme he sounded throughout his presidency. See, e.g., "Oaks affirms necessity of education for women," *Daily Universe*, Feb. 13, 1974; "Does Mother Need an Education?" *Daily Herald*, Jan. 2, 1975; "Y. Success Formula Still Not Changed," *Salt Lake Tribune*, Sept. 12, 1979; "President's Annual Message," *BYU Today*, Sept. 1979, 31.
12. "Oaks affirms necessity of education for women."
13. "Oaks have new baby: 'It's a girl!'" *Deseret News*, May 28, 1975.
14. Dallin H. Oaks, "The Student Body and the President," *Brigham Young University 1975 Speeches*, 10.
15. "A Proud Father," *Herald*, Apr. 20, 1975.
16. See, e.g., "Football team accepts bid to Tangerine Bowl in Florida," *BYU Today*, Dec. 1976; Dick Harmon, "Tangerine Bowl official watches as Cougars trounce New Mexico," *Universe Monday Magazine*, Oct. 3, 1977; "Trojans Atop Grid Poll; Cougars Ranked 12th," *Daily Herald*, Oct. 4, 1977; "Y ranks 14th in AP poll," *Universe*, Nov. 1, 1977; Dave Heylen, "Y wins WAC crown," *Daily Universe*, Mar. 2, 1979; Marion Dunn, "Gasp! Cats Win Title in 96–95 Thriller," *Herald*, Mar. 2, 1979; Brad Roghaar and

Carl Haupt, "Cougars rip Aztecs for WAC title," *Daily Universe*, Nov. 27, 1979; Lee Benson, "Changing of the guard," *Deseret News*, May 27, 1980.

17. "Oaks urges students to use 'high level' sportsmanship," *Universe*, Nov. 30, 1977.
18. Steve Benson cartoon, *Daily Universe*, Dec. 12, 1977.
19. "WAC Okays Sunday Fiesta Date," *Daily Herald*, Mar. 30, 1977; Marion Dunn, "BYU Won't Be There," *Daily Herald*, Mar. 30, 1977; Lee Benson, "CBS, Fiesta Bowl kayo BYU's postseason bid," *Deseret News*, Mar. 30, 1977; "No Fiesta Bowl for Y," *Daily Universe*, Mar. 30, 1977.
20. "22,000 Hear Rockefeller in Provo Address," *Daily Herald*, Oct. 2, 1974; "Rockefeller pledges openness, lauds BYU," *Deseret News*, October 2, 1974.
21. "Rockefeller's BYU Speech Advocates International Economic Cooperation," *Salt Lake Tribune*, Oct. 3, 1974.
22. Bill Hickman, "Oaks' legal expertise aids Y defense vs. government," *Universe*, July 31, 1980.
23. "Y. President Raps HEW," *Salt Lake Tribune*, March 12, 1977; "Oaks urges colleges to resist regulation," *Deseret News*, June 19, 1976; Hickman, "Oaks' legal expertise aids Y."
24. "College Curbs Opposed," *Herald*, June 26, 1975; "Y challenging 6 HEW sex bias rules," *Daily Universe*, Oct. 17, 1975.
25. "Oaks Reaffirms Title 9 Stand," *Herald*, Jan. 11, 1976; "Y. President Raps HEW"; Kent Rappleye, "Pres. Oaks repeats Title IX stand," *Daily Universe*, Mar. 15, 1977.
26. "U.S. Strangling us, Oaks says," *Deseret News*, May 19, 1976.
27. "Educators aim to stem government regulation," *Deseret News*, Feb. 3, 1978; "Oaks says BYU will fight if given HEW ultimatum," *Daily Universe*, Aug. 31, 1978; David Webb, "BYU—School with Spunk," *Liberty*, Sept.-Oct. 1979.
28. Webb, "BYU—School With Spunk."
29. Webb, "BYU—School With Spunk"; "U.S. threatens to sue 'Y' in Fair Housing Act case," *Universe Monday Magazine*, Mar. 6, 1978; "Oaks seeks clarification of housing suit," *Universe*, Mar. 16, 1978.
30. Webb, "BYU—School With Spunk"; "U.S. Threatening to File Housing Rights Suit Against BYU," *Salt Lake Tribune*, Mar. 4, 1978; "Sen. Hatch introduces bill to keep housing separate," *Universe*, Mar. 16, 1978.
31. "Justice officials meet with Oaks," *Universe*, Apr. 6, 1978; "BYU wins battle on off-campus housing," *Deseret News*, June 8, 1978; Webb, "BYU—School with Spunk."
32. Hickman, "Oaks' legal expertise aids Y"; "New Title IX discrimination ruling handed down," *Y News*, May 9, 1977; "Educators aim to stem government regulation"; "Oaks says BYU will fight if given HEW ultimatum"; Webb, "BYU—School With Spunk."

33. Denise Wadsworth, "Oaks refuses IRS demands," *Daily Universe*, Nov. 9, 1979; "IRS files court petition, seeks Y donors' names," *Daily Universe*, Jan. 8, 1980; "IRS Action Said 'Fishing Expedition' in BYU Filing," *Herald*, Jan. 20, 1980.
34. "IRS Action Said 'Fishing Expedition.'"
35. "Y wins in IRS case," *Universe*, Mar. 12, 1980.
36. "Dallin Oaks Explains BYU Stand on Title IX to HEW," *Herald*, Feb. 11, 1979; David Long, "Oaks defies HEW stand," *Daily Universe*, Feb. 12, 1979; "Fight HEW encroachments," *Deseret News*, Feb. 19, 1979.
37. McKay Johnson, "Oaks discusses duties, rewards of executive job," *Universe*, July 5, 1977.
38. "Stay different, Oaks tells colleges," *Deseret News*, June 22, 1979; "BYU President Talks to Church-Related Universities Meeting," *Herald*, June 22, 1979; "Church-Related Colleges Urged to Resist Secularization, Fight Undue Regulation," *Chronicle of Higher Education*, July 9, 1979.
39. "Rites Begin Work on Y. Tower."
40. "CosmOaks?" *Daily Universe*, Feb. 26, 1979; David Scott Smith, "Oaks avoids stereotype," *Daily Universe*, Mar. 7, 1979.
41. "BYU Establishes Farming Institute," *Church News*, Sept. 27, 1975.
42. See, e.g., Debbie Boothe, "Oaks tells faculty, staff to use gospel insights," *Daily Universe*, Sept. 1, 1977.
43. "Oaks' presidency re-emphasizes academics."
44. "Y. Success Formula Still Not Changed."
45. Jeff Farley, "Pres. Oaks gives formula for reaching success at Y," *Daily Universe*, Sept. 12, 1979.
46. "BYU President 'Greets' Visiting Travelers," *Salt Lake Tribune*, Dec. 1, 1976.
47. "BYU President Is Students' Choice," *Church News*, Feb. 14, 1976.

Chapter 12: "Judicial Experience"

1. "'Provo City Mother' Stella Oaks Dies at 73," *Herald*, Jan. 9, 1980.
2. "PBS appoints Oaks chairman of board," *Daily Universe*, Feb. 11, 1980; "President Oaks adds PBS to his hat rack," *Deseret News*, Feb. 29, 1980.
3. "Dallin Oaks: Utah justice bringing balance to PBS," *Broadcasting*, June 20, 1983, 103.
4. Larry Werner, "Oaks steps down after 9 years," *Universe*, May 8, 1980; Jeff Hurd and Val Hale, "Oaks' release startles faculty," *Universe*, May 8, 1980.
5. "Dallin Oaks will leave BYU helm this summer," *Deseret News*, May 7, 1980; "Oaks: An Impressive Leader," *Daily Herald*, May 9, 1980.
6. "And parting words of the president," *BYU Today*, Aug. 1980, 7.
7. Dallin H. Oaks to Faculty, Staff, and Students of Brigham Young University, in "President tells BYU friends 'Thanks,'" *Y News*, July 28, 1980.

8. Oaks to Faculty, Staff, and Students, in "President tells BYU friends 'Thanks.'"
9. "Dallin Oaks will leave BYU helm this summer"; Rod Collett, "Dallin Oaks to Leave BYU, Board Says," *Daily Herald,* May 7, 1980; "Oaks: An Impressive Leader"; "Author, Oaks to get BYU honors," *Deseret News,* Aug. 8, 1980; Chuck Kofoed, "Oaks helped new law school," *Universe,* July 31, 1980.
10. "Dallin Oaks lauded for BYU service," *Church News,* Aug. 23, 1980; "Y. pays tribute to Dallin Oaks," *Deseret News,* Aug. 16, 1980.
11. Kevin Mansfield, "Oaks' record shows distinguished service," *Universe,* May 8, 1980.
12. Dallin H. Oaks, *Life's Lessons Learned* (Salt Lake City: Deseret Book, 2011), 82–83.
13. "Matheson appoints Oaks to top court," *Deseret News,* Nov. 22, 1980; "Thank you, Dr. Oaks," *Deseret News,* Nov. 24, 1980.
14. Dallin H. Oaks, "The Beginning and the End of a Lawyer," *Clark Memorandum* (Spring 2005): 10–11; Dallin H. Oaks, "The Beginning and the End of a Lawyer," in Scott W. Cameron, Galen L. Fletcher, and Jane H. Wise, *Life in the Law: Service & Integrity* (Provo, UT: J. Reuben Clark Law Society, Brigham Young University Law School, 2009), 221–23.

Chapter 13: "What Will Become of Me?"

1. Dallin H. Oaks, *Life's Lessons Learned* (Salt Lake City: Deseret Book, 2011), 83.

Chapter 14: "A Delicate Transition"

1. Gordon B. Hinckley, "The Sustaining of Church Officers," *Ensign,* May 1984, 5.
2. Dallin H. Oaks, "President Russell M. Nelson: Guided, Prepared, Committed," *Ensign Supplement,* May 2018.
3. Gordon B. Hinckley, "Special Witnesses for Christ," *Ensign,* May 1984, 49.
4. Edward L. Kimball and Andrew E. Kimball Jr., *Spencer W. Kimball: Twelfth President of The Church of Jesus Christ of Latter-day Saints* (Salt Lake City: Bookcraft, 1977), 188–93.
5. Richard E. Turley Jr., "The Calling of the Twelve Apostles and the Seventy in 1835," in *Joseph Smith and the Doctrinal Restoration: The 34th Annual Sidney B. Sperry Symposium* (Provo, UT: Religious Studies Center, Brigham Young University; Salt Lake City: Deseret Book, 2005), 369–80.
6. "Bridges," Brigham Young University, J. Reuben Clark Law School Fireside, Feb. 8, 1987, *Clark Memorandum,* Fall 1988, 10–15, as quoted in *A Collection of Stories, Experiences and Anecdotes from the Teachings of Elder Dallin H.*

Oaks, 49–50. See also Dallin H. Oaks, *The Lord's Way* (Salt Lake City: Deseret Book, 1991), 6–8.

7. Cf. Doctrine and Covenants 112:10.

Chapter 15: "A Witness of the Name of Christ"

1. "Counsel for Students," BYU Devotional, Sept. 18, 1984; *BYU 1984–85 Devotional and Fireside Speeches,* 7–12; as quoted in A *Collection of Stories, Experiences and Anecdotes from the Teachings of Elder Dallin H. Oaks*, 48–49.
2. Dallin H. Oaks, "What Think Ye of Christ?" *Ensign*, Nov. 1988, 65, citing John A. Hardon, *Christianity in the Twentieth Century* (Garden City, NY: Doubleday, 1971), 356, 359.
3. Oaks, "What Think Ye of Christ?" 65, citing "One Clergyman's Views on the 'Death of God,'" *U.S. News & World Report,* Apr. 18, 1966, 57.
4. Oaks, "What Think Ye of Christ?" 65, citing *The Encyclopedia of American Religions: Religious Creeds,* 1st ed., ed. J. Gordon Melton (Detroit: Gale Research Co., 1973), 641.
5. Oaks, "What Think Ye of Christ?" 66, citing John 1:29; Matthew 26:28; see also D&C 20:79.
6. Oaks, "What Think Ye of Christ?" 66.
7. Oaks, "What Think Ye of Christ?" 66, citing *Ensign,* Nov. 1986, 5–6.
8. Oaks, "What Think Ye of Christ?" 66, citing *Ensign,* Nov. 1986, 5.
9. Oaks, "What Think Ye of Christ?" 67, citing 2 Nephi 2:6–7; see also 2 Nephi 9:7; 25:26; Alma 22:14; 34:8–16.
10. Oaks, "What Think Ye of Christ?" 68, citing John Taylor, *The Mediation and Atonement of Our Lord and Savior Jesus Christ* (Salt Lake City: Deseret News Co., 1882), 148–49.
11. Oaks, "What Think Ye of Christ?" 68, see Acts 4:10, 12; 2 Nephi 25:20; Alma 38:9; D&C 18:23.
12. Dallin H. Oaks, "The Great Plan of Happiness," *Ensign*, Nov. 1993, 75, citing Alma 7:11–12.
13. Oaks, "Great Plan of Happiness," 75.
14. Dallin H. Oaks, "Witnesses of Christ," *Ensign*, Nov. 1990, 29.
15. Oaks, "Witnesses of Christ," 30.
16. Elder Oaks thanked Professor McConkie and Professor H. Curtis Wright for their research and insights in the preface to *His Holy Name* (Salt Lake City: Bookcraft, 1998), vii.
17. Oaks, *His Holy Name*, vii-ix.
18. Oaks, *His Holy Name*, 63–72.
19. Dallin H. Oaks, "Teachings of Jesus," *Ensign*, Nov. 2011, 93, citing Matthew 6:33, footnote a, from Joseph Smith Translation, Matthew 6:38.
20. Oaks, "Teachings of Jesus," see Matthew 7:7; John 7:17.

Chapter 16: "Things as They Were"

1. The interest in hearing about his father never left him. On February 3, 1991, while he presided at a stake conference in Twin Falls, Idaho, he enjoyed hearing from "a half dozen senior citizens" about his father.
2. Dallin H. Oaks and Marvin S. Hill, *Carthage Conspiracy: The Trial of the Accused Assassins of Joseph Smith* (Urbana: University of Illinois Press, 1975); Dallin H. Oaks and Joseph I. Bentley, "Joseph Smith and Legal Process: In the Wake of the Steamboat *Nauvoo*," *Brigham Young University Law Review* (1976): 735–82.
3. N. B. Lundwall, comp., *The Fate of the Persecutors of the Prophet Joseph Smith* (Salt Lake City: Bookcraft, 1952).
4. Richard E. Turley Jr., *Victims: The LDS Church and the Mark Hofmann Case* (Urbana: University of Illinois Press, 1992), 149–56.
5. Turley, *Victims*, 79–111, 157–66.
6. Turley, *Victims*, 311–34.
7. Turley, *Victims*, 343–44.
8. Turley, *Victims*, 344. This response reflected a passage in a revelation about the theft of the Book of Lehi manuscript from Martin Harris in 1828, a passage making it clear that although God is omniscient, His servants are not. The Lord told Joseph Smith on that occasion, "You cannot always tell the wicked from the righteous" (D&C 10:37).
9. See Richard E. Turley Jr., "The Mountain Meadows Massacre," *Ensign*, Sept. 2007, 14–21.
10. Davis Bitton, *George Q. Cannon: A Biography* (Salt Lake City: Deseret Book, 1999).

Chapter 17: "Things as They Are"

1. Dallin H. Oaks, "Recent Events Involving Church History and Forged Documents," *Ensign*, Oct. 1987, 63–69.
2. Richard E. Turley Jr., *Victims: The LDS Church and the Mark Hofmann Case* (Urbana: University of Illinois Press, 1992).
3. On his global perspective, see, e.g., Peggy Fletcher Stack, "Expansion Means Growing Pains, Tests Flexibility for LDS Church," *Salt Lake Tribune*, May 22, 1993, in which Elder Oaks explains how during his lifetime the Church has grown from local, to national, to world church.
4. Dallin H. Oaks, "Getting to Know China," BYU Devotional, Mar. 12, 1991.
5. Gordon B. Hinckley, "The Family: A Proclamation to the World," *Ensign*, Nov. 1995, 102.
6. *Obergefell v. Hodges*, 576 U.S. 644 (2015).

Chapter 18: "She Cultivated the Flowers"

1. In an *Ensign* interview when he served on the Utah Supreme Court, he said, "I did not perform at a consistently high level until June came into my life. I owe so much to her" (Lavina Fielding Anderson, "Dallin H. Oaks: The Disciplined Edge," *Ensign*, Apr. 1981, 34).
2. Sharmon Oaks Ward and Dallin D. Oaks, "June Dixon Oaks," in Marian Wilkinson Jensen, *Women of Commitment: Personal Portraits of Selected BYU Women* (Bountiful, UT: Horizon Publishers, 1997), 27.
3. Ward and Oaks, "June Dixon Oaks," 31.
4. Ward and Oaks, "June Dixon Oaks," 29–30.

Chapter 19: "A New Era in My Life"

1. Dallin H. Oaks, *Life's Lessons Learned* (Salt Lake City: Deseret Book, 2011), 144.
2. Oaks, *Life's Lessons Learned*, 144–45.
3. Oaks, *Life's Lessons Learned*, 145.
4. Kristen M. Oaks, *A Single Voice: The Unexpected Life Is No Less a Life* (Salt Lake City: Deseret Book, 2008), 14–16; Oaks, *Life's Lessons Learned*, 143–48; Genelle Pugmire, "Provo native, Dallin H. Oaks now serves as first counselor in the First Presidency," *Daily Herald*, Mar. 28, 2018.
5. Kristen Oaks, *A Single Voice*, 16–17.
6. Kristen Oaks, *A Single Voice*, 18.
7. Kristen Oaks, *A Single Voice*, 18–19.
8. Kristen Oaks, *A Single Voice*, 19.
9. Oaks, *Life's Lessons Learned*, 145–46.
10. Kristen Oaks, *A Single Voice*, 19.
11. Oaks, *Life's Lessons Learned*, 147.
12. Kristen Oaks, *A Single Voice*, 244.
13. Oaks, *Life's Lessons Learned*, 146.
14. Pugmire, "Provo native, Dallin H. Oaks."
15. Oaks, *Life's Lessons Learned*, 146.

Chapter 20: "Eternal Salvation Is a Family Affair"

1. Dallin H. Oaks, "Parental Leadership in the Family," *Ensign*, June 1985, 7.
2. Oaks, "Parental Leadership in the Family," 9.
3. Dallin H. Oaks, "Good, Better, Best," *Ensign*, Nov. 2007, 104–8.
4. Dallin H. Oaks, "Values," BYU Management Society, Dec. 17, 1998.
5. Dallin H. Oaks, "Push Back against the World," CES Fireside for Young Adults, Pocatello Institute of Religion, Nov. 4, 2007, available at https://www.churchofjesuschrist.org/prophets-and-apostles/unto-all-the-world/push-back-against-the-world?lang=eng.

6. See Kristen M. Oaks, *A Single Voice: The Unexpected Life Is No Less a Life* (Salt Lake City: Deseret Book, 2008), 40–41.

Chapter 21: "Accomplished Wonders"

1. Jay M. Todd, "President Gordon B. Hinckley," *Ensign*, Apr. 1995, 6.
2. "New Area Presidency Assignments," *Ensign*, Sept. 2002, 76–77.
3. The "balanced effort" was a term applied to achieving equal emphasis by missionaries and members on baptism and on retention.

Chapter 22: "Go Ye Therefore and Teach All Nations"

1. On Testimony Gloves, see Kristen M. Oaks and JoAnn F. Phillips, *The Testimony Glove* (Salt Lake City: Deseret Book, 2011); "Testimony Glove," *Friend*, Oct. 2008, 24.
2. Scott Taylor, "Family history given to Michelle Obama," *Deseret News*, Mar. 20, 2010.
3. Although confidential at the time, the dedication of Pakistan was public by 2015, when it was mentioned in Jason Swensen, "Promise, potential define LDS Church in India, Pakistan," *Church News*, Dec. 3, 2015.

Chapter 23: "A Mutually Reinforcing Relationship"

1. Dallin H. Oaks, "Priesthood Authority in the Family and the Church," *Ensign*, Nov. 2005, 26.
2. Oaks, "Priesthood Authority in the Family and the Church," 26.
3. Oaks, "Priesthood Authority in the Family and the Church," 27.
4. *The Teachings of Spencer W. Kimball* (Salt Lake City: Bookcraft, 1995), 315–16; Oaks, "Priesthood Authority in the Family and the Church," 26.
5. Oaks, "Priesthood Authority in the Family and the Church," 24.
6. Oaks, "Priesthood Authority in the Family and the Church," 27.
7. Dallin H. Oaks, Priesthood Restoration Broadcast, May 5, 1991.
8. Oaks, "The Keys and Authority of the Priesthood," *Ensign*, May 2014, 50; emphasis added.
9. Oaks, "Priesthood Authority in the Family and the Church," 26.
10. Oaks, "The Keys and Authority of the Priesthood," 50–51.
11. Oaks, "The Keys and Authority of the Priesthood," 52.
12. Oaks, "Priesthood Authority in the Family and the Church," 25.

Chapter 24: "An Apostle, Not a Judge"

1. *Hearings Before the Subcommittee on Civil and Constitutional Rights of the Committee on the Judiciary, House of Representatives, One Hundred Second Congress, Second Session, on H.R. 2797, Religious Freedom Restoration Act*

of 1991, May 13 and 14, 1992, Serial No. 99 (Washington, D.C.: U.S. Government Printing Office, 1993), 23.

2. *Hearings*, 23.
3. *Hearings*, 24.
4. "My Brother's Keeper" (video), *Ethics in America II*, available at http://www.learner.org/series/ethics-in-america-ii/my-brothers-keeper/.
5. "Notre Dame Forum events to explore future of American democracy," *Notre Dame News*, Aug. 23, 2012, available at https://news.nd.edu/news/notre-dame-forum-events-to-explore-future-of-american-democracy/.
6. The Church of Jesus Christ of Latter-day Saints, *General Handbook of Instructions: Book 1, Stake Presidencies and Bishoprics* (Salt Lake City, UT: The Church of Jesus Christ of Latter-day Saints, 1998); The Church of Jesus Christ of Latter-day Saints, *General Handbook of Instructions: Book 2, Priesthood and Auxiliary Leaders* (Salt Lake City, UT: The Church of Jesus Christ of Latter-day Saints, 1989). A revision of *Book 1* was later issued in 2006. The Church of Jesus Christ of Latter-day Saints, *General Handbook of Instructions: Book 1, Stake Presidencies and Bishoprics* (Salt Lake City, UT: The Church of Jesus Christ of Latter-day Saints, 2006).
7. The Church of Jesus Christ of Latter-day Saints, *Handbook 1: Stake Presidencies and Bishoprics, 2010* (Salt Lake City, UT: The Church of Jesus Christ of Latter-day Saints, 2010); The Church of Jesus Christ of Latter-day Saints, *Handbook 2: Administering the Church, 2010* (Salt Lake City, UT: The Church of Jesus Christ of Latter-day Saints, 2010).

Chapter 25: "A Lifelong Interest"

1. Dallin H. Oaks, "The Complementary Functions of Religion and Government in a Global Setting," Rothemere American Institute, St. John's College, University of Oxford, England, June 9, 2016, available at https://newsroom.churchofjesuschrist.org/article/transcript-elder-oaks-university-oxford.
2. Dallin H. Oaks, "The Boundary Between Church and State," Second Annual Sacramento Court-Clergy Conference, Sacramento, CA, Oct. 20, 2015, available at https://newsroom.churchofjesuschrist.org/article/transcript-elder-oaks-court-clergy-conference.
3. Oaks, "Boundary Between Church and State."
4. Dallin H. Oaks, "Challenges to Religious Freedom," Address at the Argentina Council for Foreign Relations (CARI), Apr. 23, 2015, available at https://newsroom.churchofjesuschrist.org/article/challenges-to-religious-freedom.
5. Oaks, "Boundary Between Church and State."
6. See chapter 11.
7. The talk was later published as Dallin H. Oaks, "Separation, Accommodation, and the Future of Church and State," *DePaul Law Review* 35 (1985): 1–22.

8. Dallin H. Oaks, "Hope for the Years Ahead," Constitutional Symposium for Religious Freedom, Center for Constitutional Studies, Utah Valley University, Apr. 16, 2014, available at https://newsroom.churchofjesuschrist.org/article/transcript-elder-dallin-oaks-constitutional-symposium-religious-freedom.
9. Oaks, "Separation, Accommodation, and the Future of Church and State," 21.
10. Oaks, "Hope for the Years Ahead."
11. For a brief summary of Elder Oaks's testimony, along with links to a video recording and a complete transcript, see https://newsroom.churchofjesuschrist.org/article/apostle-senate-finance-committee-preserve-deductions-charitable-giving.
12. Dallin H. Oaks, "Strengthening the Free Exercise of Religion," address at The Becket Fund for Religious Liberty Canterbury Medal Dinner, New York, NY, May 16, 2013, available at https://newsroom.churchofjesuschrist.org/article/transcript-strengthening-free-exercise-of-religion-elder-dallin-h-oaks.
13. Dallin H. Oaks, "Elections, Hope, and Freedom," BYU Devotional, Sept. 13, 2016, available at https://speeches.byu.edu/talks/dallin-h-oaks/elections-hope-freedom/.
14. Dallin H. Oaks, "Religious Freedom in a Pluralistic Society," 2016 Religious Freedom Conference, Religious Freedom in the 21st Century, Claremont Graduate University, Mar. 25, 2016, available at https://newsroom.churchofjesuschrist.org/article/transcript-elder-oaks-claremont-graduate-university-religious-freedom-conference.
15. Oaks, "Hope for the Years Ahead."
16. Oaks, "Religious Freedom in a Pluralistic Society."
17. Oaks, "Challenges to Religious Freedom." See also Oaks, "Boundary Between Church and State"; Oaks, "Complementary Functions of Religion and Government."
18. Oaks, "Complementary Functions of Religion and Government."
19. Oaks, "Challenges to Religious Freedom."
20. Dallin H. Oaks, "Religious Freedom: Essential for a Free and Prosperous Society," Johns Hopkins School of Advanced International Studies, Washington, DC, summarized at https://www.churchofjesuschrist.org/church/news/religious-freedom-essential-for-free-and-prosperous-society-says-elder-oaks?lang=eng.
21. Oaks, "Boundary Between Church and State."
22. Oaks, "Religious Freedom in a Pluralistic Society."
23. Oaks, "Hope for the Years Ahead."
24. Oaks, "Religious Freedom: Essential for a Free and Prosperous Society."
25. Oaks, "Hope for the Years Ahead."

Chapter 26: "Always Look toward the Master"

1. Dallin H. Oaks, "Revelation," BYU Devotional, Sept. 29, 1981.
2. Dallin H. Oaks, "Sin and Suffering," BYU Devotional, Aug. 5, 1990.
3. Dallin H. Oaks, "Our Strengths Can Become Our Downfall," *Brigham Young University Speeches, 1991–1992*, 107–15; Dallin H. Oaks, "Our Strengths Can Become Our Downfall," *Ensign*, Oct. 1994, 11–19.
4. Dallin H. Oaks, "Judge Not and Judging," BYU Fireside Address, Mar. 1, 1998, *Brigham Young University 1997–98 Speeches*, 1–9.
5. Dallin H. Oaks, "Good, Better, Best," *Ensign*, Nov. 2007, 104–5.
6. Dallin H. Oaks, "Desire," *Ensign*, May 2011, 42, 44.
7. Dallin H. Oaks, "Same Gender Attraction," *Ensign*, Oct. 1995, 7–14.
8. See Dallin H. Oaks, "Love and Law," *Ensign*, Nov. 2009, 26–29; "Loving Others and Living with Differences," *Ensign*, Nov. 2014, 25–28; "The Plan and the Proclamation," *Ensign*, Nov. 2017, 28–31; "Two Great Commandments," *Ensign*, Nov. 2019, 73–76.
9. D. Todd Christofferson, "The Joy of the Saints," *Ensign*, Nov. 2019, 15, 17.

Chapter 27: "I Will Undertake to Answer"

1. Heidi S. Swinton, *To the Rescue: The Biography of Thomas S. Monson* (Salt Lake City: Deseret Book, 2010), 141–43; Thomas S. Monson, "The Fatherless and the Widows—Beloved of God," *Ensign*, Nov. 1994, 68–71; Jeffrey R. Holland, "President Thomas S. Monson: Finishing the Course, Keeping the Faith," *Ensign*, Sept. 1994, 13–14.
2. See, e.g., Gordon B. Hinckley, Thomas S. Monson, James E. Faust, Letter to Local Priesthood Leaders, Jan. 27, 2004.
3. Dallin H. Oaks, *The Lord's Way* (Salt Lake City: Deseret Book, 1991), 69.

Chapter 28: "Whom the Lord Had Prepared"

1. "President Thomas S. Monson Dies at Age 90," News Release, The Church of Jesus Christ of Latter-day Saints, Jan. 2, 2018; Madison Park and Keith Allen, "Thomas Monson, Mormon church president, dies at age 90," CNN, Jan. 3, 2018; Robert D. McFadden, "Thomas Monson, President of the Mormon Church, Dies at 90," available at https://www.nytimes.com/2018/01/03/obituaries/thomas-monson-dies.html; Gary E. Stevenson, "A Legacy of Succession," BYU–Idaho Devotional, Jan. 23, 2018, available at https://www.byui.edu/devotionals/elder-gary-e-stevenson.
2. Stevenson, "Legacy of Succession."
3. Russell M. Nelson, in "A Message from the First Presidency," Jan. 16, 2018, available at https://www.churchofjesuschrist.org/bc/content/ldsorg/church/news/2018/01/19/2018-01-1000-a-message-from-the-first-presidency.pdf.
4. Stevenson, "Legacy of Succession."

5. "A Message from the First Presidency" (video), available at https://www.youtube.com/watch?v=yCOrxH3gzRo.
6. "First Presidency News Conference" (video), Jan. 16, 2108, available at https://www.youtube.com/watch?v=C8Cd3vcWYnc.
7. Henry B. Eyring, "Solemn Assembly," *Ensign*, May 2018, 6–8.
8. Dallin H. Oaks, "The Sustaining of Church Officers," *Ensign*, May 2018, 30.
9. Dallin H. Oaks, "The Powers of the Priesthood," *Ensign*, May 2018, 65–67.
10. Oaks, "Powers of the Priesthood," 65–67.
11. Dallin H. Oaks, "Small and Simple Things," *Ensign*, May 2018, 90.

Chapter 29: "A Constant Joy"

1. Dallin H. Oaks, "President Russell M. Nelson: Guided, Prepared, Committed," *Ensign* and *Liahona* Supplement, May 2018.
2. Dallin H. Oaks, "Two Great Commandments," *Ensign*, Nov. 2019, 73–75.
3. The Church of Jesus Christ of Latter-day Saints, *Handbook 2: Administering the Church, 2010* (Salt Lake City, UT: The Church of Jesus Christ of Latter-day Saints, 2010), section 2.2.
4. Valerie Johnson, "2018: The Year in Review," *Church News*, Dec. 28, 2018, available at https://www.churchofjesuschrist.org/church/news/2018-the-year-in-review?lang=eng.
5. Tad Walch, "President Russell M. Nelson tells 65,000 of the faith's 'Arizona battalion' to strengthen themselves and others," *Deseret News*, Feb. 10, 2019.
6. Johnson, "2018: The Year in Review"; Tad Walch, "Keeping up with President Russell M. Nelson: 'It's going to be a busy year,'" *Deseret News*, Apr. 2, 2019; "2019 Year in Review," available at https://newsroom.churchofjesuschrist.org/article/2019; Trent Toone, "The events that shaped the decade for Latter-day Saints," *Deseret News*, Dec. 20, 2019.
7. Dallin H. Oaks, Young Marrieds Devotional, Chicago Area, Feb. 2, 2019, reported at https://www.thechurchnews.com/leaders-and-ministry/2019-02-04/president-oaks-advice-to-young-married-couples-in-chicago-on-how-to-tackle-faith-threatening-questions-5149.
8. Dallin H. Oaks, "Joseph Smith: The Prophet and the Man," 2018 Mission Leadership Seminar, June 25, 2018; Johnson, "2018: The Year in Review"; Toone, "The events that shaped the decade"; Walch, "Keeping up with President Russell M. Nelson."
9. Johnson, "2018: The Year in Review"; Toone, "The events that shaped the decade"; "2019 Year in Review."
10. Dallin H. Oaks, Phoenix Arizona Devotional with President Russell M. Nelson, State Farm Stadium, Feb. 10, 2019; Scott Taylor, "President Nelson

Invites Record Crowd in Arizona to Help Gather Israel," *Church News*, Feb. 11, 2019.

11. Dallin H. Oaks, "Be One," First Presidency Celebration of the 40th Anniversary of the Revelation on the Priesthood, June 1, 2018, available at https://newsroom.churchofjesuschrist.org/article/president-oaks-remarks-worldwide-priesthood-celebration; Johnson, "2018: The Year in Review"; Toone, "The events that shaped the decade."
12. Oaks, "Be One."
13. Dallin H. Oaks, Young Marrieds Devotional (for nine stakes), Los Angeles California Santa Monica Stake Center, Aug. 24, 2018, reported in Sarah Jane Weaver and Meg Zullo, "President Oaks talks Church history, LGBT issues, mental illness," *Church News*, available at https://www.thechurchnews.com/leaders-and-ministry/2018-08-28/president-oaks-talks-church-history-lgbt-issues-mental-illness-at-los-angeles-devotional-9061; Dallin H. Oaks, "The Paradox of Love and Law," BYU–Idaho Devotional, Oct. 30, 2018, reported at https://newsroom.churchofjesuschrist.org/article/president-oaks-paradox-of-love-and-law-byu-idaho; Dallin H. Oaks, Young Marrieds Devotional, Chicago Area; Oaks, "Two Great Commandments," 73–76.
14. Dallin H. Oaks, Eight-Stake Hispanic Devotional, Illinois Chicago Area Coordinating Council, Chicago Wilmette Stake Center, Nov. 23, 2019, reported in Sarah Jane Weaver, "President Oaks addresses issues important to immigrants during Spanish language meeting in Chicago," *Church News*, Dec. 5, 2019, available at https://www.thechurchnews.com/leaders-and-ministry/2019-12-05/president-oaks-addresses-immigrants-spanish-language-chicago-168764; https://www.churchofjesuschrist.org/church/news/president-oaks-addresses-issues-specific-to-immigrants-during-spanish-language-meeting-in-chicago?lang=eng.
15. Johnson, "2018: The Year in Review"; Walch, "Keeping up with President Russell M. Nelson"; Dallin H. Oaks, Message at Oakland Temple Youth Devotional, Interstake Center, Oakland, California, June 15, 2019; "2019 Year in Review"; Toone, "The events that shaped the decade."
16. Dallin H. Oaks, "Joseph Smith: The Prophet and the Man."
17. Dallin H. Oaks, "Counsel for Mission Leaders," 2019 Mission Leadership Seminar, June 24, 2019.
18. Toone, "The events that shaped the decade"; Johnson, "2018: The Year in Review."
19. The Church of Jesus Christ of Latter-day Saints, "Church Statement Supports Deferred Action for Childhood Arrivals (DACA)," available at https://www.churchofjesuschrist.org/church/news/church-statement-supports-deferred-action-for-childhood-arrivals-daca?lang=eng.
20. "First Presidency Releases Statement on Refugees," Dec. 2, 2019,

available at https://newsroom.churchofjesuschrist.org/article/first-presidency-releases-statement-refugees-2019.

21. Jason Swensen, "President Oaks, Elder Bednar visit Florida after Hurricane Michael and answer why bad things happen to good people," *Church News*, Oct. 22, 1018, available at https://www.thechurchnews.com/leaders-and-ministry/2018-10-22/president-oaks-elder-bednar-visit-florida-after-hurricane-michael-and-answer-why-bad-things-happen-to-good-people-7410; https://www.youtube.com/watch?v=NI9gwExt_34; Johnson, "2018: The Year in Review."
22. Oaks, "President Russell M. Nelson: Guided, Prepared, Committed."
23. Dallin H. Oaks and Kristen M. Oaks, Keynote Presentation, RootsTech Family Discovery Day, Mar. 3, 2018.
24. "General Conference Leadership Meetings Begin," Oct. 2, 2019, available at https://newsroom.churchofjesuschrist.org/article/october-2019-general-conference-first-presidency-leadership-session; Walch, "Keeping up with President Russell M. Nelson"; "2019 Year in Review."
25. "General Conference Leadership Meetings Begin"; "2019 Year in Review."
26. "2019 Year in Review."
27. Johnson, "2018: The Year in Review."
28. Walch, "Keeping up with President Russell M. Nelson"; Toone, "The events that shaped the decade"; "2019 Year in Review."
29. Jason Swensen, "A Defining Day," *Church News*, Dec. 16, 2018, 3–4; "'Love and Thanks to Thee As We Dedicate This Temple,'" *Church News*, Dec. 16, 2018, 5; Jason Swensen, "Choosing Faith over 'Futbol,'" *Church News*, Dec. 16, 2018, 6–7.
30. "Rome Italy Temple Dedication," available at https://www.churchofjesuschrist.org/church/events/rome-italy-temple-open-house-and-dedication?lang=eng; "Rome Italy Temple Is Dedicated," Mar. 10, 2019, available at https://newsroom.churchofjesuschrist.org/article/rome-temple-dedication; Tad Walch, "President Nelson refers to apostles Peter, Paul during Rome Temple dedication," *Deseret News*, Mar. 10, 2019, available at https://www.deseret.com/2019/3/10/20668245/president-nelson-refers-to-apostles-peter-paul-during-rome-temple-dedication; Sarah Jane Weaver, "President Nelson dedicates Rome Italy Temple 170 years after Church opened a door which no man can shut," *Church News*, Aug. 9, 2019, https://www.thechurchnews.com/temples/2019-03-10/president-nelson-dedicates-rome-italy-temple-170-years-after-church-opened-a-door-which-no-man-can-shut-156006; Toone, "The events that shaped the decade."
31. "The Church's New Symbol Emphasizes the Centrality of the Savior," available at https://newsroom.churchofjesuschrist.org/article/new-symbol-church-of-jesus-christ.
32. Dallin H. Oaks, "The Great Plan," *Ensign*, May 2020, 93–95.

33. The First Presidency and Quorum of the Twelve Apostles of The Church of Jesus Christ of Latter-day Saints, "The Restoration of the Fulness of the Gospel of Jesus Christ: A Bicentennial Proclamation to the World," in Russell M. Nelson, "Hear Him," *Ensign*, May 2020, 91–92.
34. Dallin H. Oaks, "The Great Plan," *Ensign*, May 2020, 93.
35. Dallin H. Oaks, "The Melchizedek Priesthood and the Keys," *Ensign*, May 2020, 69–72.
36. Oaks, "The Great Plan," 95.
37. Dallin H. Oaks, Eight-Stake Hispanic Devotional, Illinois Chicago Area; Dallin H. Oaks, Phoenix Arizona Devotional with President Russell M. Nelson, State Farm Stadium; Dallin H. Oaks, "Trust in the Lord," *Ensign*, Nov. 2019, 26–29.

Chapter 30: "Do Things Right or Not at All"

1. See chapters 1–2.
2. See chapter 2.
3. See chapter 3.
4. See chapters 4–5.
5. See chapter 6.
6. See chapters 7–9.
7. See chapter 10.
8. See chapter 11.
9. See chapter 12.
10. See chapter 13.
11. See chapter 13.
12. See chapter 13.
13. See chapter 14; "Bridges," Brigham Young University, J. Reuben Clark Law School Fireside, Feb. 8, 1987, *Clark Memorandum*, Fall 1988, 10–15. See also Dallin H. Oaks, *The Lord's Way* (Salt Lake City: Deseret Book, 1991), 6–8.
14. Dallin H. Oaks, "Small and Simple Things," *Ensign*, May 2018, 91.
15. David A. Bednar, "President Dallin H. Oaks: Following the Lord's Ways," *Ensign*, Sept. 2018, 30.

INDEX